Turning Points
in Analytic Therapy

Turning Points in Analytic Therapy

From Winnicott to Kernberg

Gerald Schoenewolf, Ph.D.

JASON ARONSON INC.
Northvale, New Jersey
London

The author gratefully acknowledges permission from Jason Aronson Inc. to quote passages from *Object Relations Theory and Clinical Psychoanalysis* by Otto Kernberg, copyright © 1976, and from *Psychotherapy of Preoedipal Conditions* by Hyman Spotnitz, copyright © 1976.

Library of Congress Cataloging-in-Publication Data

Schoenewolf, Gerald.
    Turning points in analytic therapy: from Winnicott to Kernberg/
Gerald Schoenewolf.
      p.   cm.
    Includes bibliographical references.
    ISBN 0-87668-809-1
    1. Psychoanalysis—Case studies.   2. Psychoanalysis—History.
I. Title.
    [DNLM: 1. Psychoanalysis—history—case studies.
2. Psychoanalytic Therapy—case studies.   WM 40 S365t]
RC509.8.S36   1990
616.89′17′09—dc20
DNLM/DLC
for Library of Congress   89-17949
                     CIP

Manufactured in the United States of America. Jason Aronson Inc. offers books and cassettes. For information and catalog write to Jason Aronson Inc., 230 Livingston Street, Northvale, New Jersey 07647.

To Jay

CONTENTS

PREFACE

The great discoveries of psychoanalysis have usually come from the great cases. *Turning Points in Analytic Therapy: The Classic Cases* charted the discoveries derived from the classic cases of the first half of the twentieth century. This book continues on the same path, exploring the famous cases of the second half of the century. It was a period that saw a "widening scope of psychoanalysis," as various forms of analytic therapy were shown to be effective with all types of patients.

During this period several schools of psychoanalysis blossomed: both D. W. Winnicott, in his work with Philip, and W. R. D. Fairbairn, in his analysis of Harry Guntrip, expanded on object relations theory; Erik H. Erikson, Edith Jacobson, and Otto Kernberg applied ego psychology to their work with Violet, Peggy, and Miss B.; Margaret Mahler, Frieda Fromm-Reichmann, Harold F. Searles, and Robert Lindner, utilizing more or less eclectic analytic approaches, demonstrated new techniques for working with child and adult psychotics; Heinz Kohut, founder of the self psychology school, worked effectively with narcissistic personalities such as Mr. Z.; and Hyman Spotnitz applied what he termed *modern psychoanalysis* to borderline, narcissistic, and schizo-phrenic patients such as Fred and Harry.

As in *Turning Points in Analytic Therapy: The Classic Cases*, this book attempts to look not only at the great cases, but also at the people—both therapists and patients—who made them great. Each chapter is designed to illustrate a particular turning point in the history of analytic therapy, and to review that advance in light of current understanding. The final chapter, "Analytic Therapy," defines analytic therapy, explores the use of case histories in ana-lytic research, and ponders the future of our profession. I hope that this book, together with the earlier one, will provide a useful as well as illuminating and entertaining reference tool for a broad range of social scientists and intelligent laypersons.

Acknowledgment

I would like to thank Jason Aronson, M.D., for his invalua-ble support and assistance in shaping both books; Mary E. Re-mito, M.S.W., for her ongoing encouragement; David Glassman, Ph.D., Gerd Fenchel, Ph.D., and Jacob Kirman, Ph.D., for their support and feedback on this project; and Tess Elliot for helping with the preparation of the manuscript.

1

HATE IN COUNTER-TRANSFERENCE

D. W. Winnicott and the Orphan Boy (1947), and Philip (1953)

One of the most universally beloved of all psychoanalysts, D. W. Winnicott impressed colleagues with both his ideas and his engaging personality. Khan (1958) reports that "Winnicott listened with the whole of his body, and had keen unintrusive eyes that gazed at one with a mixture of unbelief and utter acceptance. A childlike spontaneity imbued his movements. Yet he could be so still, so very inheld and still. I have not met another analyst who was more inevitably himself" (p. xi). Many used the word "pixie" to describe him. He was said to have been so humble that he would often thank his supervisees for helping him, and would frequently rush home after work and exclaim to his wife, Clare, "I have learned so much from my patients today" (Grosskurth 1986, p. 399).

Until the late 1940s Winnicott was known primarily as a pediatrician with a psychoanalytic bent. However, when he presented his paper "Hate in the Countertransference" before the

British Psychoanalytic Society in 1947, he dramatically changed the prevailing view of countertransference and mothering. He went on to become one of the more prolific psychoanalysts since Freud—writing ten books and seventy-six chapters in books and journals. Through "Hate in the Countertransference," with its poignant case history of the orphan boy who lived with him and his wife, and through other brief case histories, he demonstrated his own particular version of object relations theory and therapy, an amalgamation of his work and that of Freud and Klein.

Donald Woods Winnicott was born in 1896 in Plymouth, England. He studied medicine at Cambridge and then, in 1923, was appointed Consultant in Children's Medicine at Paddington Green Children's Hospital, where he remained for forty years. In the same year he began a ten-year analysis with James Strachey, most noted as the translator of the *Standard Edition* of Freud's work, followed by a brief analysis with Joan Riviere, a close collaborator of Melanie Klein. He was in supervision with Klein herself between 1936 and 1940 and analyzed one of her children, Erich. Although in some ways much influenced by Klein, he once sarcastically called her a "Eureka shrieker," alluding to her tendency to regard all her discoveries as ultimate truths (Grosskurth 1986). For twenty-five years he was on the training staff of the British Psychoanalytic Society, serving at various times as president and physician-in-charge of the Child Analysis Department. During the years when the British Psychoanalytic Society was split between those supporting Anna Freud and Glover, and those supporting Melanie Klein, Winnicott stayed out of it, steering an independent course along with Balint and Bowlby.

Winnicott's prose has an elusive quality, since most of his papers and books were originally presented as talks. His arguments are informal, more discursive than tightly reasoned, yet presented with humility and with the use of paradoxes that entice and engage the reader. He was decidedly not a scholar in the psychoanalytic tradition, but was more a doer. Khan (1958) relates that when he recommended a book about Freud to him,

Winnicott hid his face in his hands and replied, "It is no use, Masud, asking me to read anything! If it bores me I will fall asleep in the middle of the first page, and if it interests me I will start re-writing it by the end of that page" (p. xvi). He added that Winnicott was "a joyous and troubled soul; and he exploited both these assets to the maximum in his life and work" (p. xiii).

In "Hate in the Countertransference" (1947), Winnicott asserts that it is crucial to therapeutic success, particularly in working with psychotics and psychopathic patients, for a therapist to be able to hate his patients objectively. "What we as analysts call the countertransference needs to be understood by the psychiatrist too. However much he loves his patients he cannot avoid hating them and fearing them, and the better he knows this the less will hate and fear be the motives determining what he does to his patients" (p. 195). He points out further that it is an error to be loving to a psychotic who expects hate. When such an individual is in a "coincident love–hate" state of being he becomes convinced that the analyst feels the same toward him. "Should the analyst show love, he will surely at the same moment kill the patient" (p. 195). Since the patient will project "crude feelings" onto the analyst, the analyst "is best forewarned and forearmed, for he must tolerate being placed in that position." He must not, Winnicott stresses, deny his hatred of the patient. "Hate *that is justified* in the present setting has to be sorted out and kept in storage and available for eventual interpretation" (p. 196).

To explain his thesis, Winnicott provides a brief case history about a 9-year-old boy whom he treated during World War II. He first attempted to work with the boy while he was living in a hostel for evacuated children, to which he had been sent from London because of a truancy problem. Winnicott felt that he "established contact" with him during one session, in which he played squiggles with the boy. Squiggles was a game he had developed for working with children and adolescents, in which he would make a doodle on a sheet of drawing paper and ask the patient to turn it into something, then have the patient make a doodle so he could turn it into something. During this game he "could see and interpret through a drawing of his that in running away he was unconsciously saving the inside of his home and preserving his mother from assault, as well as trying to get away from his own inner world, which was full of persecutors" (p. 199). However, Winnicott's work with the boy was interrupted when he ran away from the hostel. He had a history of running away from places that had begun at the age of 6 when he first ran away from home.

Winnicott was not surprised when, a short time later, the boy turned up at a police station near his home. It was, he notes, one of the few police stations that did not know him intimately. His wife took the boy into their home for "three months of hell"—and Winnicott attempted to treat him while he stayed there. "He was the most lovable and most maddening of children, often stark staring mad. But fortunately we knew what to expect" (p. 199). He and his wife gave the boy complete freedom and a shilling whenever he went out, and he had only to telephone them and they would fetch him from whatever police station he ended up at. Soon the truancy symptom "turned around", and he started "dramatizing the assault on the inside." Winnicott does not say how the boy dramatized the assaults, only that handling him was a full-time job for him and his wife. The worst episodes happened when he was away from home. Winnicott found himself having to make interpretations at any minute of the day or night and discovered that the boy valued a correct interpretation above everything.

The most significant aspect of the case, according to Winnicott, was the way in which the boy's behavior engendered hate in Winnicott and how he handled it:

> Did I hit him? The answer is no, I never hit. But I should have had to have done so if I had not known all about my hate and if I had not let him know about it too. At crises I would take him by bodily strength, without anger or blame, and put him outside the front door, whatever the weather or the time of day or night. There was a special bell he could ring, and he knew that if he rang it he would be

readmitted and no word said about the past. He used this bell as
soon as he had recovered from his maniacal attack. [p. 200]

Each time he put the boy outside the door, Winnicott told
him, "What has happened has made me hate you." This was easy
for him to say, he explains, because it was true. Saying these words
was important not only for the boy's progress, but also because it
enabled Winnicott to tolerate the treatment situation "without
losing my temper and without every now and again murdering
him" (p. 200).

The boy was eventually sent to an "Approved School," but
his deeply rooted relationship to Winnicott and his wife remained
a stabilizing factor in his life. Winnicott uses the boy's story to
illustrate the thesis that "hate justified in the present" must be
distinguished from "hate that is only justified in another setting"
(p. 200). In other words, there is a difference between hate justified by a patient's hateful behavior toward a therapist and hate
unjustified by a patient's behavior, but related to something unresolved from the therapist's own past. The former hate should be
expressed, the latter should not.

Winnicott goes on to say that not only should analysts learn
to hate their patients objectively, but also mothers should learn to
hate their infants objectively. "I suggest that the mother hates the
baby before the baby hates the mother, and before the baby can
know his mother hates him" (p. 200). He lists many reasons for a
mother to hate her baby, including:

- the baby is a danger to her body during pregnancy and birth
- the baby has been produced to placate her mother, her father, or her
  husband
- the baby hurts her by sucking and chewing on her nipples
- the baby is ruthless, treats her as scum or as a slave
- she has to love him unconditionally, love even his excretions
- his love is "cupboard love," so that having got what he wants he
  discards her

- he has no idea how much she sacrifices for him, and especially cannot "allow for her hate"
- he suspiciously refuses her food, but eats well with his aunt
- after giving her a hard time all morning, he smiles at a stranger on the street, who comments on how sweet he is
- if she fails him she knows she will pay for it later
- he excites her sexually but she cannot act out her feelings

Mothers need to be able to hate without "paying the child out"; perhaps, Winnicott suggests, by singing nursery rhymes which the child cannot understand, rhymes with lyrics such as "Rockabye baby, on the treetop,/When the wind blows the cradle will rock,/When the bough breaks the cradle will fall,/Down will come baby, cradle and all." By singing such words, mothers are able to release pent-up hate without actually hurting the child, and "without sentiment." "It seems to me doubtful whether a human child as he develops," Winnicott remarks, "is capable of tolerating the full extent of his own hate in a sentimental environment. He needs hate to hate" (p. 202).

Winnicott concludes that telling a patient about one's hate is fraught with danger and requires the most careful timing. Yet he asserts that an analysis will remain incomplete unless at some point the analyst lets the patient know how much the patient's behavior aroused his hate in the early stages. "Until this interpretation is made the patient is kept to some extent in the position of infant— one who cannot understand what he owes to his mother" (p. 200).

In this paper and in the one that follows, Winnicott alludes to (without actually mentioning) three ideas for which he is famous: the "holding environment," "good-enough mothering," and the "impingements" which characterize a nonholding environment or mothering which is not good enough. The acknowledgment and expression of objective hate is necessary for the establishment of a holding environment for both infant and patient. Denial of this hate will become an impingement (a lack of ego-support) and will be experienced by infant and patient as a form of deprivation; it will impinge upon their development.

In "Symptom Tolerance in Paediatrics" (1953), Winnicott shows how these concepts applied to the boy who had come to him with a social problem. This paper, presented to the Royal Society of Medicine, was intended to demonstrate to pediatricians the psychoanalytic way of treating cases such as enuresis. Winnicott was critical of enuresis clinics run by pediatricians at that time, the aim of which was to cure the symptom without attempting to understand or resolve the underlying conflict. The symptom, according to Winnicott, is "a little bit of a huge problem of a human being engaged in trying to develop to maturity in spite of handicaps" (p. 103). In other words, a child who wets his bed is a child whose development has been impeded by impingements. To illustrate his way of working with such a symptom, he cites the case of Philip, a boy he treated in 1947, the same year in which he wrote "Hate in the Countertransference."

Philip was brought to Winnicott by his mother when he was 9 years old. She told him that the headmaster of the prep school that Philip and his brother attended had written to his parents to demand that they take Philip home because he had caused an epidemic of stealing. In a long preliminary interview with the mother, Winnicott took a detailed history that, he said, "turned out to be substantially correct, although in one important detail the exact truth did not emerge until I had an interview with the boy" (p. 104).

Philip had not caused any problems until he was 6, according to his mother. His older brother had been breast-fed for five months and had a straightforward personality. Philip's birth had been difficult, and the mother remembered it as a long struggle. "The amniotic fluid broke through ten days before birth, and from the mother's point of view the birth started and stopped twice before the boy was actually born" (p. 105). He was breast-fed for six weeks and weaned. The mother and father had both wanted a baby girl after their first son, and there was some disappointment at Philip's birth, but the mother said that they adapted. When Philip was 2 his father left to serve in World War II and did not return until right before the consultation with Winnicott. Soon after that Philip was put into a nursery and he became "excessively catarrhal," developing a habit of not blowing his nose. "The catarrhal tendency" had continued to the present.

When he was 6 he had a tonsillectomy, but it did not affect the catarrhal problem. That same year his little sister was born. His mother said that he was jealous of the sister at first but then became fond of her. The first incident of stealing involved taking a nurse's watch from the hospital where his sister was born. He stole other watches, money, and various other objects—including a car registration filched from some people with whom his family had been staying during a holiday. Often the object he stole would later be damaged.

Winnicott decided, as he often did, to do his therapy primarily through the mother. He sat down with her and told her that the boy would need her help, as "it was clear that he had missed something at the age of 2 years and he would have to go back and look for it."

"Oh well," the mother replied, "if he has to become an infant, let him come home, and as long as you help me to understand what is happening I can manage" (pp. 107–108).

Winnicott then saw the boy for three sessions, in order to establish a rapport with him, to provide him with some insight for which he was ready, and to find out where he stood in the management of the case. Unlike Freud, Winnicott did not believe that insight was necessary for cure. He met with Philip for these sessions, then instructed his mother over the phone.

He began the first session by playing squiggles with the boy. Winnicott made a squiggle and the boy turned it into what he called a map of England; he made a squiggle and Winnicott delayed turning it into anything, so the boy made it into a "rope going into the air;" he made another squiggle and Winnicott turned it into a face, which the boy called a fish; Winnicott made a squiggle and the boy added a few lines to it and then called it "a mother and baby sea-lion."

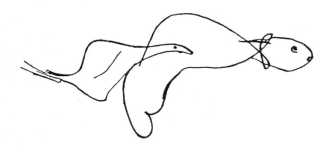

Winnicott saw that the boy had a powerful maternal identification and that the mother–baby relationship was of special importance to him, but he said nothing at that point. They did a few more squiggles, and Winnicott noticed that the boy was in "what could be called a sleepwalking state," which he would understand better later.

Soon Philip began telling Winnicott of a dream. *He was in a car with his mother. The car was going downhill. There was a ditch at the bottom of the hill and the car was going so fast that it could not possibly stop. At the critical moment magic happened, good magic, and the car went over the ditch without falling into it.*

Winnicott interpreted the dream: "You're frightened that in the dream you had to use good magic because this means you have to believe in magic, and if there's good magic there also has to be bad magic. You don't like to use magic but you have to when you are forced to deal with things that happen in your life."

The boy then told Winnicott of a detail of his history that his mother had omitted. He said the saddest time in his life, a time he called "dreary times," had been when his mother had left him. This had happened when he was 6 and his mother had gone away to a nursing home to give birth to his sister. He and his brother had been left to the care of an aunt and uncle. "The awful thing that happened there," the boy said, "was that I would see my mother cooking in her blue dress and I would run up to her but when I got there she would suddenly change and it would be my aunt in a different colored dress" (p. 111). During this period, the boy was constantly hallucinating about his mother, and he was apparently in the dream-walking state which Winnicott had noticed during the game of squiggles. To counter what he thought was laziness, the boy's uncle began ordering the boy around. The uncle seemed harder on Philip than on his older brother. His brother was different from him. "Now my brother, he thinks of nothing but ships and of sailing, and that is quite different. I love beauty and animals and I like drawing," he explained (p. 111).

Winnicott understood that this was the first opportunity Philip had ever had to talk about the problem during that period, "which was to come to terms with the mother's capacity to have a baby, which made him acutely jealous of her" (p. 112). The squiggle of the mother and baby sea lion showed how much he had idealized and become fixated on the mother–infant relationship.

In another squiggle, the boy had drawn a wizard. Winnicott asked him about this wizard and he turned out to have the overcoat of his uncle, the man who had dominated his life and saved him from his depression. Philip told Winnicott that the wizard had a voice just like his uncle's, and that at school this voice continued to dominate him, telling him to steal. If he hesitated, the voice would say, "Don't be a coward; remember your name. In our family there are no cowards" (p. 112). He then told Winnicott about the main incident for which he was expelled: On a dare, he had stolen dangerous drugs from the matron's cupboard.

By the end of the session Winnicott was exhausted, but the boy sat down to do one last drawing. The picture showed his father in a boat and an eagle flying above him carrying a baby rabbit. Winnicott observed that Philip was drawing not only to "seal off" the interview but also to report progress. He told Philip that the eagle stealing the baby rabbit represented his own wish to steal the baby sister from his mother. He was jealous of the mother for being able to have a baby by his father, and also of the baby, since he had an acute need to be a baby himself.

After he had presented Philip with this interpretation, the boy replied, "And there's father, all unconcerned" (p. 113). Winnicott realized that the son needed his father, who had been away in the armed forces during this period, for masculine support; if it had not been for his uncle and his older brother, "he would have been sunk when his relation to his mother was interrupted by the separation and by his jealousy of her."

Winnicott saw him about a week later. Philip had already undergone an important change in his relationship with his analyst, which was demonstrated by the drawing he did at the beginning of this session. He drew the wizard's house. Winnicott was in the house with a gun, the wizard was retreating from the house, his wife was in the kitchen cooking, and Winnicott went in to take the magic from her. "The wizard and his voice have disappeared since our first session," the boy told him (p. 114). Winnicott noted that the boy's need to find his mother cooking represented the substitute for finding the witch at her cauldron conjuring her bad magic, which is such a terrible fear for young children. Winnicott was also alluding to the process of splitting, which Klein, his mentor, had written about. Winnicott understood that Philip now regarded him as somebody he could trust.

Two more drawings of the wizard show him walking down a school corridor with a candle, and being laughed at. Winnicott notes that the wizard's candle was associated with genital erection and with ideas of fellatio and burning hair. The second drawing indicated to Winnicott that the child had now stopped making fun of himself, as he had been in the habit of doing, and was making fun of the wizard instead; that is, he had begun to externalize rather than internalize his conflicts. Since this was not to be a regular analysis, Winnicott held on to these interpretations. He had given him just enough interpretations to establish a rapport. "I was simply a person who fits in and understands, and verbalizes the material of play. In verbalizing I talk to a conscious self and acknowledge the PLACE WHERE FROM in his total personality, the central spot of his ENTITY, without which there is no HE" (p. 115). This explanation is an allusion to another of Winnicott's often-used concepts, that of the "true" and the "false" self. During his interviews with Philip he wanted to reach his true self, the "central spot of his ENTITY."

The third hour began with another drawing, in which Philip's enemy dropped a knife on his favorite dog, a greyhound. The enemy turned out to be his cousin, the son of the uncle who became the wizard. After discussing this drawing for a few minutes, the session turned into an "ordinary play–hour," and Winnicott just sat and watched Philip play with his train sets. (Subsequently, when the boy paid follow-up visits, he would just play with the trains.)

Winnicott describes how he managed the case from then on:

> I now come to the illness that the boy had to have during which the parents provided him with asylum. . . .
> Philip was accepted at home as a special case, an ill child needing to be allowed to become more ill. By this I mean that there had been a controlled illness and this was to be allowed to come to full development. He was to receive that which is the right of every infant at the start, a period in which it is natural for the environment to make active adaptation to his needs. [p. 115]

Although during his three sessions with Winnicott, Philip had mainly spoken about the abandonment that had occurred when he was 6, Winnicott knew that it was the first abandonment, when Philip's father left his 2-year-old son to join the army, that represented his primary fixation. Perhaps there was a fixation even further back. His mother had wanted a baby girl and had stopped breast-feeding him after six weeks. His jealousy of his sister revived unresolved feelings from his own infancy, when he had not received good-enough mothering, when his environment had been less than holding, when there had been impingements to his development.

During the three months following his visits to Winnicott, Philip gradually became withdrawn. His mother said he seemed to live in a fairy world; he did not so much get up in the morning as change from being in bed to being out of bed—and that only if she dressed him. He did not care how he looked or how he ate, becoming less and less able "to live in his body or interested in his appearance" (p. 116). He began to walk in a strange way—hopping and skipping and waving his arms like a windmill. He made noises which his brother described as "elephant noises." No remark was ever made about his eccentricities by his family, who had been instructed by Winnicott not to. Once, at a local dance, his "queer attitude to girls came to the fore. He danced a little, but only with a very odd and fat creature known as 'the galleon', assumed in the locality to be mentally defective" (p. 116). His life revolved around a radio thriller that he listened to each day and caring for his greyhound. When his aggression reached its lowest point he began to wet his bed. He had gotten to a point, in fact, where he did not want to get out of bed at all. During this bed-wetting stage, his mother got him up between 3 and 4 A.M. each night, but he was usually already wet. "I dream so vividly that I have got to the pot," the boy would say. At the same time, he became "addicted" to water. "It's such fun, it's delicious," he would say. "It's good to drink" (p. 116).

Then one morning he wanted to get up again. This signaled the beginning of his recovery. His symptoms disappeared one by one, and by the fall he was able to return to school. Winnicott maintained contact with his mother until Philip was 14. By then he was 5 feet 5 inches tall, had a broad physique, liked to be out doors, and was good at the usual boys' games. His mother reported him to be one year ahead of his age group scholastically.

Winnicott wrote a lengthy case history of his work with an adult patient who had a psychotic breakdown with acute depression—*Holding and Interpretation: Fragment of an Analysis* (1986), which, like Klein's *Narrative of a Child Analysis*, was published posthumously. Also like Klein's case history, Winnicott's longer effort does not have the depth, wit, or excitement of his earlier, shorter pieces, nor was his work with adults as incisive as his work with children and their families.

Winnicott married his second wife, Clare Britton, in 1951. She was also a psychoanalyst—a strong-willed woman who did her training analysis with Klein right before the latter's death. Winnicott remained devoted to Clare until his death in 1971 at the age of 75. He had no children of his own.

Interpretation

In the years since his death, Winnicott's work has enjoyed increasing popularity and influence among psychoanalysts and other mental health professionals. Some people are attracted to the theoretician who spoke and wrote in such an idiosyncratic manner, others to his "Peter Pan" personality, and still others to his highly original manner of doing therapy.

Khan, his closest disciple, attributes Winnicott's success to the fact that he was an authentic person: What you saw was what you got. There was no difference between Winnicott the living person and Winnicott the clinician, nor between his psyche and his soma. "Winnicott the man and Winnicott the therapist were mutual to each other and of a piece" (Khan 1975, p. xi). And, perhaps because of the authenticity of his personality, he had a militant incapacity to accept dogma. Nor, Khan believes, is there any rhetoric or intimidating jargon in his writing. "He wrote as he spoke: simply and to relate. Not to incite conviction or indoctrinate" (1975, p. xii). His idiom was that of ordinary cultured and common usage; everyone, therapist and layperson alike, could at least feel he understood Winnicott.

Khan also praises Winnicott for his understanding of resistance, which he sometimes refers to as "the antisocial tendency," viewing it in positive rather than negative terms—not as something to be resolved or got rid of, but as something to be used for the good of the therapy, just as countertransference feelings are used. The antisocial tendencies of both the orphan boy and Philip, manifested by truancy and stealing, were seen by Winnicott as attempts to find something that had been lost earlier in their lives; they were attempts at self-cure. Winnicott in this sense echoes Binswanger, Ferenczi, and still earlier Breuer, all of whom came to believe that patients knew what they needed in order to be cured; it was the therapist's job to facilitate their patient's inner journey back to the points in their past when they had "lost something." Khan contends Winnicott's concept of the antisocial tendency helped frame the therapeutic encounter in a more constructive way. "It has helped me to change my whole style of relating to my patients in the analytic setting and has enabled me to re-evaluate what looks like resistance or negative therapeutic reaction in a positive light" (1975, p. xxxiii). Winnicott's researches, Khan concludes, intensified and extended the "awesome therapeutic task" of creating an ambiance in which the patient can gradually test and experience that which has been muted and find that which has been lost, "the true capacity to be trusting of others and personalised in themselves, without the threat of either annihilation or that collusive compliance which is the ultimate *dissociation from the True Self*" (1975, p. xxxiii).

Davis and Wallbridge (1981), like Khan, comment on Winnicott's authenticity, and on his artistry as a clinician. Acknowledging that he is sometimes difficult to understand, they explain that he believed a writer on human nature should stay away from psychological jargon, feeling that it was impossible to talk about human nature without the intrusion of his own life experience and that of the reader. Hence, they contend he is an artist and a scientist at the same time. His writing is imbued with both human experience and an underlying theoretical structure. "His words have a double depth and significance, and the reader can go back to his books year after year with pleasure, finding in them each time some new approach to a truth and some new stimulus to reflection" (Davis and Wallbridge 1981, p. x).

Another of the hallmarks of his greatness, according to Davis and Wallbridge, was the lack of sentimentality with which he viewed and treated children. Though one might find Words-worthian overtones in his writings, it was apparent from cases such as the one described in "Hate in the Countertransference" that he was in no way "starry-eyed about children" (p. 8). They point out that although Winnicott had no children of his own, he knew what a burden they could be. His work with the orphan boy typifies his unsentimental, pragmatic understanding of the realities of caring for a child.

Epstein and Feiner (1979) claim that Winnicott's paper "Hate in the Countertransference" went far beyond the traditional view of countertransference as hindrance. It showed how counter-transference could be useful as a source of information about the patient and the ongoing process of analysis; how the analyst's objective and timely expression of intense countertransference feelings might be necessary for the patient's maturational needs; and how the analyst could detoxify intense countertransference feelings so as to continue functioning constructively with a pa-tient. They call this paper a "pithy" treatment of the core issues surrounding countertransference.

Sandler and colleagues (1979) also hail Winnicott's argument on the benefits of acknowledging such objective countertransfer-ence feelings as hate. They note that there are times when the patient unconsciously forces a role on the analyst, and the analyst then has the opportunity to provide a deeper insight through mirroring. They also point out that "It is of some interest that this extension of the concept of the countertransference is similar to Freud's change in his view of the function of transference, first regarded only as a hindrance but later seen as an asset to therapy" (p. 66). Spotnitz (1985) also applauds Winnicott's extension of the meaning and use of countertransference, calling "Hate in the Countertransference" a "highly influential paper." He especially agrees with Winnicott's emphasis on the importance of objectively hating a patient, an aspect of therapeutic technique that Spotnitz later developed into a methodological approach in working with schizophrenics.

On the other hand, critics of Winnicott find him overly gratifying, romantic, and confusing. Dare (1976), for instance, accuses Winnicott of being too much of a maverick and both too difficult to understand and too simple in his view of complex psychodynamics. His exposition of developmental theory is characterized by Dare as a "poetic evocation of child development" and of motherhood, written in a highly individual language that is difficult to link up with other approaches.

Balint (1968) chastises Winnicott for the "exalted sincerity" of papers such as "Hate in the Countertransference." He sees in this an apparent need by the analyst to be always "apologetic, continuously confessing to mistakes and blunders, failures and shortcomings" (p. 116), as though through this approach one might better manage regression by being more human. Although Balint believes that regression is necessary in therapy, he steers a middle course between classical analysts, who regard repression as a form of psychopathology and tend to be too depriving, and active analysts, who tend to regard repression as the be-all and end-all of therapy, and who are so gratifying that they allow the patient to pull them into an endless cycle of demands, as was the case with Breuer and Anna O. Balint lumps Winnicott into the latter category, viewing his attempts to provide a facilitating environment for patients such as the orphan boy and Philip as overgratifying. Such an approach may lead to a situation in which the patient expects all demands to be instantly met; "in that world, which I call primary love, there must not, and cannot, be any clash of interests between subject and environment" (p. 112). Any such clash, which is inevitable, leads to a repeat of the traumatic situation that originally caused the fixation at that point in development, and hence to eventual therapeutic failure. Balint believes neither in frustrating nor encouraging regression, but simply in accepting it when it comes and providing an empathic environment in which it can happen, such as empathic silence.

Balint also criticizes Winnicott for using a variety of terms to say the same things and for borrowing terms from others without giving proper credit. For example, at one point Winnicott uses the term "good enough mother"; then he speaks of a "good enough environment"; then he refers to the "medium" in which the patient can revolve like an engine in oil; then he talks about an "ordinary devoted mother"; then he writes about the "primary maternal occupation" of a good enough mother; then he describes the "holding function" of the mother; and finally, borrowing from American literature, he talks about the "facilitating environment." All of these terms are correct, Balint contends, but to use so many terms to say basically the same thing is confusing and unnecessary.

Greenberg and Mitchell (1983) argue that Winnicott misinterpreted Freud and misrepresented himself as somebody who was adding to Freud's theories. For example, they cite Winnicott's contention that his concepts of the true and false selves was an outgrowth of Freud's division of the self into the ego and the id. Greenberg and Mitchell call this "an extremely misleading parallel." While Winnicott's distinction between a true and false self contrasts authentic living with the adaptation to a self-destructive environment, Freud's distinction between id and ego contrasts asocial, undirected impulses with the necessary and realistic demands of the external world. "Freud's distinction does not address itself to the issue of inauthenticity, which is at the center of Winnicott's concern" (p. 207).

Greenberg and Mitchell further criticize Winnicott for going too far in his emphasis on good-enough mothering and a holding environment. They suggest that, in an effort to compensate for Klein's overemphasizing of the child's innate aggression while neglecting the mother's role, Winnicott put too much stress on environmental factors. They contend that studies of babies and mothers have shown that what causes failure in early childhood is a bad fit between the particular mother and the particular infant. "Each baby brings to encounters with caretakers his own particular rhythm of engagement, level of activity, distinct affective and behavioral displays. Each caretaker brings to his encounter with the baby his own style and intensity of responsiveness, attention span, level of interest, anxieties, and so on" (1983, p. 228). The greatest area of relative omission by object relationists such as Winnicott, they say, has been in the consideration of temperamental differences among babies.

I believe that some of the criticism leveled against Winnicott is not valid. When Greenberg and Mitchell argue that Winnicott and other object relationists do not adequately consider the temperamental differences among babies, and that the responsibility for failure in mothering lies in the bad match between mother and baby, they are missing the point. Whether or not there is a bad match, and no matter what kind of temperament her baby has, it is the mother's responsibility to adapt to the needs of the baby, not the reverse. A baby does not have the maturity to make such an adaptation; presumably the mother does. If not, she should seek help. To attribute failure to a bad fit is to absolve mothers of responsibility and blame. In doing this Greenberg and Mitchell are bowing to a feminist trend of the 1970s and 1980s, a trend that, in my opinion, has been quite destructive to childrearing.

Balint's charge that Winnicott was too gratifying or too honest is not well taken. Winnicott's self-revelations, as exemplified by his work with the orphan boy, were never done sentimentally or to exalt sincerity in some narcissistic manner. His management of regression, as in Philip's case, was likewise done without sentimentality or overt gratification. He simply provided a space and then encouraged Philip's family to provide a space in which Philip could regress, go back to infancy, and have a second chance. Winnicott himself played no role in this regression, except for that of trusted listener. Unlike Ferenczi and others, he did not attempt to play the role of mother, father, brother, or other transferred figures. Playing such a role is one of the factors Balint believes brings about therapeutic failure during periods of regression.

Theoretically Winnicott may have had his shortcomings, but these shortcomings can in no way diminish what he accomplished and what he represented. Through his writings and through the example he set as a clinician and human being, Winnicott demonstrated the value of authenticity in therapy. It is not a rigid blank screen that fosters growth, but the timely expression of the real feelings engendered by the patient in the therapeutic setting. The blank screen has its place with some patients all of the time and with all patients some of the time but not with all patients all of the time (to paraphrase Abraham Lincoln).

Winnicott was the first psychoanalyst to formally dispense with the notion that insight is necessary for cure, anticipating the arrival of behavioral therapies. He also understood the therapy process a bit differently than did others. Summing it up in "Hate in the Countertransference," he says, "An analyst has to display all the patience and tolerance and reliability of a mother devoted to her infant" (p. 202). Winnicott succeeded in doing just that.

2

THE IDENTITY CRISIS

Erik Erikson and the Marine (1950), and Mary (1950)

While working at the Mt. Zion Veterans Rehabilitation Clinic in San Francisco during World War II, Erik Homburger Erikson treated a marine suffering from what was then called "battle neurosis." As Erikson studied him and the others like him, he noticed that the young man's ego had lost its shock-absorbing capacity, and he coined the term "identity crisis" to describe what the marine was going through. He later used this case for the introductory chapter of the classic work, *Childhood and Society* (1950). This book is the only work by a psychoanalyst to win both the Pulitzer Prize and the National Book Award.

As a young man, Erikson went through his own identity crisis, which he wrote about in an autobiographical essay (1975). He was born out of wedlock in 1902 in Germany. His real father, whom he never knew, was a Danish Protestant. His mother and stepfather were German Jews. Some time after the age of 3, Erikson explains, he developed the beginnings of an identity crisis. Because his mother and stepfather were Jewish, his Scandinavian heritage of blue eyes, blond hair, and "flagrant tallness" made him feel that he did not belong. (They did not tell him until much later that he was an illegitimate child.) His identity crisis was further intensified when his schoolmates referred to him as a Jew, while at his stepfather's synagogue he was called "goy." After graduating from high school, Erikson studied art and wandered around living a bohemian life—in defiance of his stepfather's expectation that he become a physician. Erikson says that for a time during his adolescence his identity crisis bordered on an "adolescent psychosis" (1975, p. 25). With the help of a friend, Peter Blos, Erikson found work in Vienna as a teacher in an elementary school run by Dorothy Burlingham, a colleague of Anna Freud's. Soon Erikson was accepted into psychoanalytic circles, went into analysis with Anna Freud, and trained to become a child analyst, even though he had no education beyond high school. Thus, he was able to resolve his identity crisis by becoming a psychoanalyst, establishing himself in a field which was "an outsider" like himself, but was at the same time a helping profession, a concession to his stepfather's expectations that he become a doctor. Later he would add the name Erikson after Homburger, his stepfather's name. (He says he chose it in honor of the Norwegian discoverer of America, Leif Eriksson.)

In addition to focusing on identity, Erikson, unlike most other psychoanalysts, looked at the overall social environment and its impact on the individual. Also unlike most other analysts, he studied normal rather than abnormal behavior. He always looked at the broader picture, and one of his primary contributions to psychoanalytic theory was his eight stages of development. These stages incorporated Freud's psychosexual stages and included five others that embraced the entire life span of human beings; each stage was marked by a conflict that needed to be resolved in order for the individual to mature. Thus, the conflict in the oral stage was "trust versus mistrust" of the maternal caretaker; in the anal stage, "autonomy versus shame"; in the phallic stage, "initiative versus guilt"; in the latency stage, "industry versus inferiority"; in the adolescent (early genital) stage, "identity versus role confusion"; in the young adult (genital) stage, "intimacy versus isolation"; in the middle years, "generativity versus stagnation"; and during old age, "ego integrity versus despair."

As a clinician Erikson is classified as an ego psychologist, but his stress was not only on the individual's unconscious psychopathy, but on conscious adjustments to social influences and on healthy maturation. His work with the young marine at Mt. Zion typifies his clinical approach. In a few sessions, Erikson helped him to understand and adjust to the trauma of war. When the marine came to see Erikson, he was in his early thirties. He said he had been discharged during World War II as a "psychoneurotic casualty" and ever since the discharge he had had an "incapacitating headache" that had followed him into a peacetime job as a teacher. When Erikson asked him how the headache had started, he recalled an incident during the war.

The marine had entered the service as a medic, priding himself as someone who could take anything. He was a clean-cut young man who never drank, smoked, or swore, and who claimed to have no hate for anyone. Before the war he had worked with kids. He said he was especially good with "tough kids," but he had not been a tough kid himself. While serving in the marines, he always felt superior to the other men, as though he were again an adult working with tough kids. His position as medical officer, a noncombat role, reinforced his sense of being apart from and superior to the others.

One night he and a group of marines, just ashore, lay in the pitch darkness of a Pacific beachhead within close range of enemy fire. They lay on the beach all night, waiting for supporting fire from the navy. They had been assured by the top brass that this support would come; it never did. As they lay on the beach waiting, they began griping that the brass had let them down. An intense rage, resentment, disgust, and fear filled the group, but Erikson's patient said he felt he was above this rising wave of rage and panic; that is, he denied that he was feeling what the rest of the men were feeling.

In relating the incident to Erikson, he could not remember what happened during most of this night. It was like a bad dream.

He recalled only isolated memories: that the medical corps was required to unload ammunition instead of setting up a hospital tent; that his medical officer at some point broke down and had a temper tantrum during which he swore profusely; and that at another point somebody put a submachine gun into his hands. He woke up the following morning in an improvised hospital, suffering from a severe "intestinal fever." When he was evacuated from the beach the next day, he began to have "raging headaches."

In analyzing this last symptom, Erikson points out that "from the physiological viewpoint the fever and the toxic state had justified his first headache, but only the first one" (Erikson 1950, p. 40). He links the headache to the young marine's chronic aversion to the expression of anger, asking something seemingly far removed from headaches: Why was this man such a good man? "For even now, though practically surrounded with annoying postwar circumstances, he seemed unable to verbalize and give vent to anger. In fact, he thought that his medical officer's angry swearing that night had, by disillusioning him, exposed him to anxiety" (p. 40). Why was he so good? Why was he so shocked by swearing?

In order to help the patient overcome his aversion to anger and to better understand him, Erikson asked him what had irritated him, however slightly, during the past few days. "Give me a list of annoyances," he told the marine (p. 40).

The patient, sitting facing Erikson, thought for a moment, then began to speak. He talked about the vibration of buses, of high-pitched voices, of squeaking tires, of the memory of foxholes full of ants and lizards, of the bad food in the navy, of the last bomb that had exploded close to him, of distrustful people, of thieving people, of high-hat and conceited people, and of the memory of his mother.

Erikson quickly focused on the last and most important irritant—the marine's mother. What about his mother made him angry? The patient said that he had not seen his mother since he was 14, when he had left home abruptly after his mother, in a drunken rage, had pointed a gun at him. He had grabbed the gun, broken it, and thrown it out the window. He had then moved in with the principal of his school, who had become a father-figure and mentor to him. In exchange for this principal's protection, he had promised never to drink, swear, indulge himself sexually, or touch a gun.

Erikson compares the marine's plight with that of others suffering from war neuroses. "What was sick in these men," he asserts, "was their screening system, that ability *not* to pay attention to a thousand stimuli which we perceive at any given moment but which we are able to ignore for the sake of whatever we are concentrating on" (p. 41). Such men could not sleep deeply or dream well. Their nights were interrupted by anxiety dreams, and their days full of failures of concentration. "They could not rely on the characteristic processes of the functioning ego by which time and space are organized and truth is tested" (p. 41). These symptoms, he concludes, were in part the symptoms of physically shaken and somatically damaged nerves. But Erikson also saw something else in them:

> What impressed me most was the loss in these men of a sense of identity. They knew who they were; they had a personal identity. But it was as if, subjectively, their lives no longer hung together— and never would again. There was a central disturbance of what I then started to call ego identity. At this point it is enough to say that this sense of identity provides the ability to experience one's self as something that has continuity and sameness, and to act accordingly. [p. 42]

In the marine's case, his ego identity had been shattered by his superior's sudden fit of temper and swearing, and by the submachine gun that was suddenly put into his hands, which, to him, was a symbol of evil and represented the antithesis of the principles by which he had attempted to safeguard his personal integrity and social status until then. Erikson points to three "contemporaneous processes" that jointly contributed to the marine's problems: (1) *group panic*—the group of marines had wanted to keep the situation under control, but instead they were placed in an untenable position in which they felt betrayed by their leaders; (2) *physical breakdown of the organism*—the marine tried to "maintain homeostasis" against the impact of the panic and the acute infection, but he was sabotaged by severe fever; (3) *breakdown of ego identity*—the patient's ego collapsed when it was upset by the loss of an external support for an internal ideal. "The very superiors on whom he had relied ordered him (or so he thought) to break a symbolic vow on which his self-esteem was so precariously based" (p. 42). This last phenomenon had "opened the floodgate of infantile urges" that up until then he had held rigidly in check. When he was evacuated from the beach, the headaches began. The marine felt "unconsciously obligated" to continue to suffer somatically in order to justify abandoning his fellow marines. There was a lasting conflict between two inner voices: one said, "Let them take you home, don't be a sucker," while the other grumbled, "Don't let the others down; if they can take it, you can" (p. 42).

Erikson notes that, in order to understand any given case of psychopathology, one must always study the somatic changes, personality transformations, and social upheavals involved, as he did in this case. He refers to this clinical approach as "triple bookkeeping." One may start with any of the three areas, but "wherever you begin, you will have to begin twice over again" (p. 45). If one begins with the organism, it will later also be necessary to reconstruct the variations of ego processes and the family history. And the same applies whether one is treating an adult like the marine, or a child.

Mary, a child of 3, was brought to see Erikson by her mother upon the recommendation of a pediatrician. She was said to have frequent nightmares and to suffer from violent anxiety attacks in the playgroup she had recently joined. Her teachers said Mary had "a queer way of lifting things," a rigid posture, and became tense whenever she was told to rest or to go to the toilet. "She is a somewhat pale brunette," Erikson writes, "but looks (and is) intelligent, pretty, and quite feminine. When disturbed, however, she is said to be stubborn, babyish, and shut-in" (Erikson 1950, p. 224).

Erikson used play therapy in her treatment. However, his model of play therapy differed from that of Melanie Klein (1932), as he did not interpret the meaning of the play to the child (unless the child was older) but saw the play as therapeutic in and of itself. Modern play therapy, he notes, is based on the observation that children become insecure because of a secret hate against or fear of their caretakers, and they are able to use the protective sanction of an understanding adult to regain some "play peace." He points out that grandmothers or favorite aunts might have served that role before the advent of child therapists. The presence of a benign adult witnessing the child's play, Erikson explains, allows the child to play out his play intentions without interruption, parental nagging, or sibling rivalry. This playing out, he contends, is the most natural self-healing measure a child can have, comparable to the "talking out" of adults. In this respect Erikson's philosophy is closely aligned with Winnicott's.

Erikson's office was in a hospital, but he tried to furnish it in a way that showed that he was not a medical doctor, nor a doctor at all. In his initial interview with Mary, he was careful to explain to her that he was not a doctor and said that he was going to play with her in order to get acquainted with her. As Erikson talked, she held tightly to her mother's hand, eventually offering Erikson her other hand; it was "both rigid and cold." She gave him a brief smile, then put her arms around her mother and buried her head in her mother's skirt. Erikson interpreted silently that her brief smile seemed to convey a curiosity: "She wanted to see whether or not the new adult was going to understand fun" (p. 225). Her mother tried to get her to play with the toys in Erikson's office, but the child clung to her mother, exclaiming, "Mommy, mommy, mommy!" (p. 225).

Finally she pointed to a doll and demanded that her mother take off the doll's shoes. Her mother told her to take off the shoes herself. Mary's voice became high-pitched and anxious, and she seemed on the verge of tears. The mother asked if it was time for her to leave the room to wait outside.

"Mary, can we let your mommy go now?" Erikson asked her.

She made no objection.

The mother placed the doll in Mary's hand and left.

"Do you know what the doll's name is?" Erikson asked.

Mary did not answer. Instead, she grasped the doll around the legs and, smiling mischievously, began to push the doll's head against various objects in the room. A toy fell from a shelf and she looked at Erikson apprehensively. He smiled permissively, and she continued to knock toys off the shelf and push them on the floor with the doll's head. She was especially gleeful when she poked at a toy train. She pushed each car over, one by one, displaying a growing evidence of "a somehow too exciting kind of fun." After overturning the engine, she stopped suddenly and became pale. She leaned against the sofa, held the doll vertically over her lower abdominal region, and then let it drop to the floor. She picked it up and dropped it again several times. Then she yelled, "Mommy, Mommy, Mommy." Her mother returned to fetch her.

After the session Erikson analyzed Mary's behavior, and decided that the child had conveyed "by counterphobic activity" what her danger was. He saw the mother's anxious interruption as being as significant as the child's play disruption. He asks, "But what had she [Mary] communicated with this emotional somersault, this sudden hilarity and flushed aggressiveness, and this equally sudden inhibition and pale anxiety?" (p. 227). Her "discernible mode content" was that of pushing things with the doll, and then dropping the doll from the genital region. Erikson interpreted that the doll was a phallus, and pushing things with the doll was a dramatization of her vision of the penis as a weapon of power. Dropping the doll from her abdominal or genital region represented the loss from that region of an aggressive tool, a "pushing instrument." He saw her repetition of this scene as an acting out of the trauma of having her penis robbed from her. The mother had told Erikson that Mary had recently gone to a nursery school, had seen a boy's penis for the first time, and had been curious about penises ever since.

While he thought of these things, Mary's mother returned to Erikson's office for a moment to give him another piece of information: Mary had been born with a sixth finger on one hand. The finger had been removed by surgery when she was about 6 months old, and the surgery had left a scar. Just before her recent anxiety attacks in the playgroup, Mary had repeatedly asked her mother what the scar on her hand was, and her mother had said that it was "just a mosquito bite." The mother added that Mary had also been "equally insistent in her sexual curiosity" (p. 228).

Erikson theorizes that in her mind Mary equated the loss of a finger and the scar on her hand with the "scar" in her genital region from the loss of her penis. Such an association, he believed, would also link the observation of sex differences in the play school to the threatening operation. Finally, before Mary's second visit, her mother added two more pieces of information. Mary's sexual curiosity about her father had recently been severely rebuffed. Her father, irritable because of problems on his job, had been impatient with Mary during her usual morning visit to him in the bathroom. He had shoved her out of the room, angrily repeating the words, "You stay out of here!" (p. 228). She had been expressing curiosity about his penis. Also, because of Mary's disturbed sleep and her "foul breath," her pediatrician had recently suggested a tonsillectomy—in Mary's presence. "*Operation* and *separation* are seen to be the common denominators," Erikson points out. "The actual operation on the finger, the anticipated operation of the tonsils, and the mythical operation by which boys become girls; the separation from her mother during play school hours, and the estrangement from her father" (p. 229).

A few days later Mary came in for her second visit. While her first session had been marked by play interruption, the second session contained a dramatic example of play satiation. "The antithesis of play disruption is play satiation," Erikson observes, defining the latter as "play from which a child emerges refreshed as a sleeper from dreams which 'worked'" (p. 229). Almost as soon as Mary entered Erikson's office, she let go of her mother's hand and sat down to play. Erikson quietly gestured for the mother to sit down and closed the door. Mary took a pile of blocks from the middle of the room, carried them to a corner, and knelt down to build a small house for a toy cow. She worked for about fifteen minutes, starting with a rectangular house around the cow, then adding five blocks to one long side and a sixth block to the short side. While she played, Erikson discerned that the "dominant emotional note" was that of peaceful play that had a quality of maternal care and order. When play ended on "a note of satiation," she stood up with a radiant smile. Erikson observed that the final product resembled a hand, with six fingers clasping a cow. Hence, the configuration performed two restorations in one, putting the finger back on her hand and, at the same time, expressing the "inclusive mode"—female–protectiveness—the hand giving comfort or birth to the cow.

At that point Mary suddenly looked mischievously at Erikson and pulled her mother out of the room. When Erikson attempted to come out to the waiting room, Mary yelled at him to "Thtay in there!" and closed the door with a bang. Erikson played along with her, opening the door several more times to be met with the same response. He interpreted to himself that Mary was now acting out a father transference, reversing the actual situation in which her father had thrown her out of the bathroom and told her to "Stay out there!"

This episode, Erikson asserts, illustrated the self-curative trend in spontaneous play. In some cases, spontaneous play is all that is needed. In others, the parents must be advised how to change their relationship to the child. In still others, child psychoanalysis is required, and with advancing age conversation substitutes for play. Erikson decided that in Mary's case her spontaneous play and a little advice to her parents were enough.

Erikson recommended to the parents that they be truthful to Mary about her questions concerning the scar on her hand, her operation, and her genitals. He suggested that they have little boys visit her at home for play. He advised them not to wake her up when she had a nightmare, but to allow her to "fight her dreams out," then hold her lightly and comfort her when she awoke. Finally, he advised them to provide much opportunity for playful activity, particularly instruction in "rhythmic motion that might relax some of the rigidity in her extremities" that had been aggravated by "fearful anticipation since hearing for the first time about the mysterious amputation of her finger" (p. 233).

When Mary visited Erikson a few weeks later for a follow-up session, she was "entirely at home" and asked about the color of the train he had taken on his vacation. He remembered that she had overturned a toy engine during the first session, and upon questioning her found that her father had made the most of her sudden interest in locomotives by taking her for regular walks to the railroad yards, where together they watched the mighty engines. At the time when Mary pushed over the toy engine, her play activity with her father had been interrupted, Erikson explains, and the engine had come to represent "phallic-locomotor anxiety." Since the second session there had been a revived play relationship with her father, her nightmares had ceased, a tonsillectomy had proven unnecessary, and she was making good use of the new play companions in her neighborhood.

It was primarily the father's rejection that had brought about Mary's symptoms. Because he was threatened with the loss of his job, he became irritated and rejecting toward Mary at a time when she had just discovered the differences in the anatomy of the sexes and was most vulnerable to such rejection. The trauma of rejection, of play interruption, then appeared in her play in a condensed form, while she attempted to work her way back to "playful mutuality." She reflected in her own life the historical and economic crises of her parents. Erikson explains that the moment Mary's father recognized the impact of his anxieties on his daughter's development, he realized that her anxieties mattered much more than the threatened change of his work status. "Thus at the end, in any therapeutic encounter with a child, the parent must sustain what the adult patient must gain for himself: a realignment with the images and the forces governing the cultural development of his day, and from it an increased promise of a sense of identity" (p. 234).

The most important gift parents can make their children, according to Erikson, is the strength—through their example—to face realities such as the loss of a job or death without the disintegrating effects of fear and rage. "Healthy children will not fear life," Erikson notes, "if their elders have integrity enough not to fear death" (p. 269). Adults who can face death, Erikson theorizes, are wise enough to view their limited lives as a totality that transcends petty concerns about getting older.

Erikson had a long and distinguished career, lasting almost fifty years. He and his wife, Joan, an American whom he had met while studying at the Vienna Psychoanalytic Institute, came to the United States in 1934, at which time he was recommended by Anna Freud as a training analyst. He settled in Boston, where he worked in Henry Murray's psychological clinic at Harvard (Roazen 1984). Later he participated in research at the Yale Institute of Human Relations, the Institute of Child Welfare at the University of California, and the Western Psychiatric Institute in Pittsburgh, and served as professor of human development and lecturer on psychiatry at Harvard—pretty good for somebody who held only a high school degree. Through his writing he gained one of the widest audiences of any psychoanalyst ever, finding acceptance even among those who were normally hostile to analysis.

His psychosocial approach was useful not only in clinical work, but also as a tool for the analysis of lives of significant historical figures. In *Young Man Luther* (1958) and *Gandhi's Truth* (1969) he pioneered the new literary form which later became known as "psychohistory," seeking in these works to identify the historical, social, and psychological forces that combined with accidental circumstances to produce these highly influential human personalities, and looking in particular at the process of identity formation. Erikson believed that while motives might originate in unconscious or repressed id impulses, still these motives might become free of their id origins as the individual lives out his particular social and historical role.

Interpretation

Although Erikson's work as a clinician was not as well known as his theoretical contributions to psychoanalysis, he nevertheless quietly but firmly made lasting inroads in the treatment of both adults and children. In the case of the marine, he added new dimensions—particularly the dimension of identity confusion—to the understanding of the psychological causes of "shell shock." In the case of Mary, he demonstrated the therapeutic value of play.

It was not until World War I that the psychological factors associated with combat neuroses were recognized. Before that, doctors were prone to attribute them to shell shock—or brain damage caused by the nearby explosion of a shell. Symptoms of shell shock included paralysis, gross tremors, mutism, blindness, headaches, backaches, and intense anxiety. Until the psychological factors of shell shock were recognized, doctors usually prescribed long hospitalization for such patients. However, it was soon discovered that prolonged hospitalization merely fostered and reinforced many symptoms.

A recent textbook of psychiatry (Kolb 1977) backs up Erikson's main findings. Kolb notes that "extreme and repeated battle fear, with a constant threat of death plus intense fatigue" are the precipitating factors. This correlates with Erikson's contention that the marine's actual physical breakdown had come about because of the prolonged feelings of powerlessness and rage he experienced while he and his group were being bombarded. Kolb also agrees with Erikson's theory that the marine's inability to deal with his own anger contributed to his breakdown. "It is not always the unstable and neurotic man who, as might be supposed, lacks resistance to the terror that accompanies long and intense combat," he states. "In general, it is the timid and passive person who cannot mobilize and externalize his anger and react aggressively toward the enemy and thus discharge his tension, who is prone to develop a combat neurosis" (p. 536). Kolb also confirms Erikson's belief that the marine's bad relationship with his mother was associated with his later breakdown. "An unduly large number of combat neuroses occurred in individuals from broken or distorted homes," he writes, "unfavorable for the development of a well-integrated and mature personality" (p. 537). Finally, Kolb's findings validate Erikson's notion that the marine's disillusionment with his leaders helped to bring on his anxiety; he observes that soldiers must have confidence in their units and in the character, capability, and bravery of their leaders. The formation of a deep emotional relationship with their leaders and "buddies" helps them to feel secure. When group morale is threatened by the collapse of leadership, each individual in the group suffers.

From Erikson's account, we do not get a detailed picture of how he worked with the marine or how long the treatment lasted. It would seem to have been a brief therapy rather than a lengthy psychoanalytic treatment, with the emphasis on getting the marine in touch with his anger and helping him to adjust to civilian life. The one intervention highlighted in Erikson's account—his asking the marine to list recent irritations—showed how he utilized active therapy techniques similar to those experimented with by Ferenczi (1919).

Through Erikson's treatment of Mary, we get a more detailed picture of his approach. We see how quickly he develops a therapeutic rapport with her, making her feel comfortable enough so that by the second session she is able to achieve "play satiation." We see him participating in the play, as when he opens and closes the door of his office several times in order to allow Mary to act out her anger at her father. Indeed, when he pushes open the door, he pokes the toy cow through the crack and makes it squeak, much to Mary's delight. But what does this toy cow symbolize? Erikson does not say. In interpreting the child's block construction, in which she enclosed the cow in blocks in the shape of a hand with six fingers, Erikson notes that the construction restored her missing finger and affirmed her femininity. I would add that perhaps this construction also served to both imprison and comfort her father, for whom the cow was symbolic, and toward whom she had ambivalent feelings. On one hand, she wanted to comfort her father so that he would be less irritated with her; on the other hand she wanted to imprison him, possess him, and perhaps have ready access to his penis. (The toy cow pictured in the book had horns.) Erikson does not pursue this line of thinking, but by pushing the cow out the door when he played the game with Mary, he seemed unconsciously to make this connection. At any rate, his work with Mary offers a portrait of a skillfully handled, successful case.

A question that might be asked, however, is whether or not Mary's symptoms would have resolved themselves spontaneously without Erikson's intervention. Since her symptoms were directly related to her father's job stress, would it not follow that when his job situation cleared up he would be able to resume a healthy relationship with Mary, which would in turn have enabled her to "outgrow" her symptoms? Such things often happen with children.

Erikson comes across in his clinical examples, as well as in his writing in general, as a gentle, polite, insightful man. Somehow, when he writes about controversial subjects such as penis envy, he does not spark the hostile reactions that Freud and other psychoanalysts do. Consequently, his work has found a wide acceptance, and concepts of identity, identity crisis, life cycle, ego-strength, and psychosocial development, all pioneered by him, have seeped into areas where psychoanalysis itself would normally be repudiated. At the same time, as Roazen (1984) points out, he has "moved about as far 'left' in the movement as it is possible to go and still be respectfully listened to and influential among analysts" (p. 517). Yankelovich and Barrett (1970), explaining Erikson's curious ability to appeal to analysts and nonanalysts alike, note that he "suggests, he hints, he insinuates. Unfailingly polite and tactful, his most telling criticisms are gently whispered." They assert that unlike other analysts who rebelled against Freud, Erikson "blurred the extent of his divergence from the psychoanalytic movement" (p. 151).

Most criticisms of Erikson focus on his divergences, such as the theory of eight stages of development and the concept of ego identity. Roazen notes that some analysts have seen in Erikson's model of personality development "a conformist image of man, to the extent that he thinks it is necessary for everyone to live through these stages in the order he outlines" (p. 517). Jacobson (1964) cannot accept Erikson's broad use of the term "ego identity," nor what she sees as his de-emphasis of infantile stages of identity formation. She can accept his concept of "identity formation" provided it includes processes of organization with all structures of the psychic apparatus. Blum (1953) observes that Erikson's concept of "ego identity" is quite similar to the orthodox psychoanalytic concept of "self-esteem," and wonders whether it was necessary to come up with a new concept. Erikson defends the use of a new term by stating that self-esteem is conscious, whereas ego identity is something both conscious and unconscious. "The proportion of conscious and unconscious elements in the concept of self-esteem or narcissism is a moot point, as it is in the case of ego identity," Blum asserts. "So we must accept on faith Erikson's statement that his own concept connotes more of the unconscious" (p. 189).

Kernberg (1980) differs with Erikson with respect to the term "identity diffusion." Erikson contends that identity diffusion—a profound disturbance of one's sense of self in the context of the social environment—originates in early childhood and is resolved during adolescence. However, Kernberg found in his work with adolescents that most of them did not present a syndrome of identity diffusion; only those with borderline personalities did. "In fact, a surprising finding has been how very normal adolescents without borderline personality organization are, and how strikingly different their developmental crises are from the chronic chaos and confusion that reflects the syndrome of identity diffusion" (p. 10).

Concerning Erikson's therapeutic approach, Eissler (1971) suggests that he was not an analyst but a psychotherapist. He alludes to the kind of short-term, nonanalytic, active therapy techniques Erikson demonstrated in cases such as the two described here, as well as to the fact that, rather than using the couch, Erikson saw patients face to face and did not require them to attend five times a week. Among orthodox analysts like Eissler, to say that somebody is a psychotherapist is akin to saying that he is not really a bonafide psychoanalyst—not really up there with the "big guys." Such criticisms would seem to smack of a kind of snobbery, having nothing to do with the validity of Erikson's way of working.

Erikson answers critics of his psychosocial scheme of the life cycle, with its accent on identity, by pointing to the link between an individual's life and the life of society. His work, he writes, tends "toward the formulations of the complementary interplay of life history and history. Correspondingly, acute clinical observations and formulations can always be seen to be guided concomitantly by a number of discernable historical processes." He observes that while it may be true, as some critics have said, that his emphasis on identity is a reflection of his own personal history, "at the same time, however, the *therapeutic* and *theoretical* course of my field . . . strongly pointed to the need for an identity concept" (1959, p. 13).

Whether one agrees or disagrees with Erikson's concepts, and whether one calls him a psychoanalyst, social psychologist, or psychotherapist, one cannot deny the far-reaching influence his work has had on all the social sciences since the appearance of *Childhood and Society*. The concepts he originated have now become part of the popular vocabulary, and his name has become a household word. Although he added some ideas to the psychoanalytic lexicon, he did not repudiate existing theory as did other deviants from classic analysis, and he was careful not to attack Freud. Pondering the reasons for the respectability of Erikson's concepts even among critics who are normally hostile to psychoanalysis, Monte notes that Erikson possessed a "unique combination of . . . personal, social, and historical presence" (1977, p. 376). He gave off an appearance of inner calm, gentility, and wisdom that made him stand out in a nonthreatening way.

Psychoanalysis, to Erikson, is simply another name for a process that is as ancient as man himself, a modern contribution to his age-old attempts to systematic introspection. It began as a method of psychotherapy and ended up as a psychological theory. Erikson's aim was to explore "possible implications of both theory and practice for a more judicious orientation in the unlimited prospects and dangers of our technological future" (1950, p. 424).

3

JOINING A PATIENT'S DELUSION

Robert Lindner and Charles (1955), and Kirk Allen (1955)

Before his untimely death of a heart attack in 1957 at the age of 43, Robert Mitchell Lindner had been one of the most promising psychoanalytic writers of his generation. His first book, *Rebel without a Cause* (1944), written when he was only 29 years old, broke new ground in the understanding of criminal psychopaths. It became a psychoanalytic best seller and its title was used for a movie about a disturbed teenager. Utilizing hypnosis and analysis, Lindner was one of the first to successfully treat personalities regarded by analysts such as Freud to be untreatable. In two subsequent books, *Stone Walls and Men* (1946) and *Prescription for a Rebellion* (1952), he launched crusades against the inhumane treatment of prisoners and against what he saw as the mental health field's tendency to impose its value system on patients by pressuring them to adjust and conform to the demands of a "sick" society.

The Fifty-Minute Hour (1955), published two years before his death, established him not only as an astute psychoanalyst, but also as a promising American writer in the mold of Ernest Hemingway or F. Scott Fitzgerald. This classic collection of five case histories created a new literary genre, exploring the human condition in a way no case history had ever done before. The book became one of the best-selling works of all time by a psychoanalyst, having sold more than two million copies by the date of this writing.

Lindner was born in New Jersey in 1914. He received his B.A. degree from Bucknell and his M.A. and Ph.D. degrees from Cornell. After he had completed his doctorate, he became a professor of criminology at Tufts University and served as a prison psychologist at federal prisons in Pennsylvania and Maryland. In 1950, when the National Psychological Association for Psychoanalysis was formed in New York, he became one of its first members.

NPAP was founded by Theodor Reik. A Jewish refugee who had fled Germany and Austria before World War II, Reik had hoped to join the American Psychoanalytic Association, but was barred from doing so, for he did not hold a medical degree. Hence, he formed his own professional association for psychologists, with its own training institute. NPAP has since become one of the leading psychoanalytic institutes in America.

Lindner trained with Theodor Reik during the early 1950s while serving as chief psychologist at a federal prison and conducting a private practice in Baltimore. It was during this period that he met the patients who became the subjects of *The Fifty-Minute Hour*.

The first case history, "Songs My Mother Taught Me," is about a young murderer and rapist named Charles. Charles was assigned to Lindner's prison after having been convicted of a vicious murder. His case had made the newspaper headlines for many days, and Lindner knew a good deal about him before meeting him. He describes Charles as scarcely 21 and with the face of a choirboy. "His eyes were blue and innocent, and he seemed to look at you with a perpetual questioning, as if to ask why a fence of steel must always stand between him and the trees he could see through the bars of his cell window" (Lindner 1955, p. 1).

According to newspaper accounts, one day a young woman had buzzed all the apartments of a building in a big city, trying to sell religious books and records. Charles, who was staying with his mother at the time, let the young woman in and met her on the stairs. She asked if his mother was at home, and he answered that she was inside the apartment. She walked ahead of him down the hallway, and as they passed through the kitchen he grabbed an ice pick and a hammer. "The youth struck her on the head with the hammer. Then he stabbed her sixty-nine times with an ice pick. Then he flung himself on the corpse and raped it" (p. 2).

A preliminary report on Charles diagnosed him as a paranoid schizophrenic with homicidal trends. "The subject is cooperative, although somewhat tense, during the interview," stated the report. "He answers all questions readily but sometimes reveals a rather silly grin, not appropriate to the content of thought" (p. 3). In order to get a deeper understanding, Lindner interviewed Charles after administering sodium pentothal. During the interview Charles said a voice had told him to kill the girl, but he did not know to whom the voice belonged. At one point he said that he had stabbed her breasts because they "make milk." At another point he began to sob when he spoke about attempting to rape her. It turned out he had not been able to rape her because he could not get his penis inside of her. In anger, he had torn her vagina with his fingers.

Lindner began seeing Charles one hour daily in his office. In the first interview Charles expressed the hope that he could find out why he had murdered and raped, so that he would not do it again. Lindner asked if he thought that he might do it again. Charles guessed that he might. Lindner then attempted to forge a therapeutic alliance with him:

> "Suppose you and I study this together," I proposed.
> "That would be fine." He paused, then regarded me with his innocent eyes. "Would that keep me from doing it again?"

"It might," I said.
"I'd like that."
"It takes time," I said.
"I've got lots of that," he said. [p. 10]

Lindner was soon able to put together the basic facts about Charles's background. Even before he was born, the marriage between his parents was falling apart. After a stormy three years, they got a religious dispensation and were allowed by the church to separate. The father disappeared from their lives. Charles and his older brother lived with their mother for a few months and then were both placed in an orphanage. For the next fifteen years Charles lived in foster homes and institutions.

From the outside, Lindner says, the places where Charles spent most of his life seemed pleasant. But in actuality, children consigned to such places suffered from emotional impoverishment. "They grow as weeds in a desert, stretching this way and that for sustenance, twisting themselves out of their natural design, mocking Nature's blueprint. They are exposed . . . to the vagaries of the human elements, now stifled in the heat of emotional suns, now frozen under loveless snows, now drowned, now parched" (p. 11). Charles was severely brutalized in his first home, beginning when he was 4, beaten unmercifully for the smallest infractions and made to do excessive penances for simply doing what small boys do. Later, in a school for boys, he was sexually and physically assaulted and made "the butt of sadisms that make a small boy's life hell" (p. 12). Gradually he was forced to accept the idea that what was happening to him was his fault, and he donned the only defensive posture available to him: he identified with his tormentors. He in turn became a tormentor of other children. By the age of 10, Lindner says, he had already developed the soul of a murderer.

During these years his mother visited him once or twice a year, usually on his birthday or on Christmas, laden with gifts, making a "small excited flurry" in his daily routine. Charles told Lindner she was like a fairy princess who always smelled so good, but her exits always left him feeling undone. He looked forward to her visits and dreamed about her when she was gone, but he also hated her for having placed him in the "purgatory" of his drab existence. Each time she visited he wanted to ask her to take him with her, but feared to do so, knowing she would refuse. Each of her visits was followed by a display of aggression against another boy. On special occasions he was allowed to visit his mother's home. These visits were even more destructive and confusing to him, giving him a taste of what he might have had.

At 11 he ran away from the home in which he then lived and wandered to the outskirts of the city, where three hoboes fed him, got him drunk, and then "used and abused him." Next morning somebody found him—his body bruised from repeated blows, his cavities torn—and took him to the hospital. When he arrived back at the home, he was disciplined even more severely. "Charles emerged from the chrysalis of childhood an antagonist of all values" (p. 13).

After a while he became so unmanageable that the director of the home wrote his mother, saying that he was a bad influence on other children and would have to be reassigned. He was sent to a farm where he became virtually a slave to a childless couple, who treated him like one of the animals on their farm. At the age of 16 he ran away from the farm and showed up at his mother's apartment. She was irritated by his presence and said that her apartment was too small, she could not take care of him, and she did not want him in her hair. After a few weeks she arranged to have him sent to an "industrial school," which was in reality a haven for criminals and criminals-in-the-making. He established himself as the toughest boy in the school. At 17, he ran away from this school and turned up on his mother's doorstep again. This time his mother could not make him leave; he was too old. A few months later, after he was fired from his job as a Western Union messenger, the young woman rang his mother's apartment and came up the stairs toward him.

In the beginning of his therapy, Lindner tried to use standard analytic procedure with Charles, but to no avail. Charles simply rattled off reports about his daily life in the prison, and had almost no memory of his past. Then one day, while making rounds of the hospital, he found Charles on the floor playing with some chess and checker pieces. Lindner immediately bought a bag of toys and began using play-therapy techniques during his sessions. Now Charles began to remember past events as he played with the toys, molded things out of clay, drew on a pad. His therapy progressed and he developed a mother-transference toward Lindner. "Christ Almighty!" he yelled at Lindner one day, when Lindner asked him to clean up a spot of glue he had spilled on his desk. "You make me sick—just like my mother" (p. 28).

Lindner took the statement literally, and asked him if his mother had really made him sick. He recalled feeling sick to his stomach whenever he saw her. "Maybe it was the way she smelled" (p. 28).

As the days passed he remembered more and more about his relationship with his mother. She had been seductive and rejecting toward him, and he had developed a sexual obsession for her. One day, while looking through her trunk, he found her wedding ring. He kept it with him from that time on. When, at the age of 16, he picked up his first prostitute, while living with his mother, he was only able to become aroused after the prostitute, at his suggestion, put on his mother's wedding ring. Lindner concludes that the murder victim was "but the substitute, the unfortunate innocent bystander in a drama of incest and matricide whose origins were removed almost two decades from the time the last scene was played" (p. 44).

After several months of treatment, things seemed to be going well. Charles was getting in touch with his feelings of rage for his mother and beginning to understand how he had displaced this rage onto the murder victim. Then he went through a period in which he was "somewhat apathetic about things." Lindner interpreted this as an expected lull. "A period of quiescence and recovery necessarily follows each high point in therapy" (p. 45). Then one evening he was told that Charles had asked for him and was looking distraught. Lindner rushed to his office to find him sitting on a cot in a highly disturbed state. His hands were gripping the black leather mattress as if holding on for dear life, his eyes were closed tightly, his mouth was clenched, and he was moaning.

The phone rang, and when Lindner rose to answer it, Charles leaped up and began to strangle him, shrieking, "Kill!—Kill!—Kill!" Lindner was saved at the last minute by guards.

Charles was reassigned to another prison. Before he left, Lindner asked him why he had done it. Charles replied that he had felt completely cut off from the world that day, and the voice had begun to command him just as it had done on the day of the murder. "I think my hand touched your shoulder," Charles said. "It felt like a woman's breast. I got excited. Then the voice took over. All I wanted to do was get my hands around a throat. I couldn't hold it back . . ." (p. 48). There was no follow-up on Charles after he left that prison.

The most famous case history in the book is "The Jet-Propelled Couch," about a schizophrenic research physicist. Kirk Allen was referred to Lindner by a physician at a government installation. "The fellow I'm calling you about," he said, "is a man in his thirties, a research physicist with us out here. As far as I can tell, he's perfectly normal in every way except for a lot of crazy ideas about living part of the time in another world—on another planet" (p. 156). Because he was "gone" so much of the time, Allen's work had begun to deteriorate. The reports he was supposed to write were turned in late, and they were often covered by a strange kind of doodling. When Allen's supervisor complained about his work performance, Allen apologized and explained that he had been away a lot. The supervisor finally sent him to the physician. "Seems that all he could get out of the boy was a lot of regretful apologies," the physician told Lindner. "Then Allen made this crazy statement about spending more time on this planet" (p. 157).

Allen arrived in Baltimore three days later and began analytic treatment. Lindner describes him as a vigorous-looking man of average height, with clear eyes and blond hair, who looked like a junior executive. His manner was charming and he spoke with "just enough diffidence" to let Lindner know the situation he now found himself in was slightly embarrassing. He had a slight accent with a musical lilt.

"You were not born in the United States, were you, Mr. Allen?" Lindner asked during the first interview.

"No," he answered. "My first language was a Polynesian dialect, but I thought it was pretty well hidden. Does it annoy you?" (p. 159).

Allen was an only child. His father was already an old man when his son was born, a commander of fighting vessels at sea, a man who was "proud, taciturn, stern, and kept his more tender emotions rigorously in check" (p. 160). He exacted absolute obedience from everybody on the island where Allen grew up, and was seldom out of his uniform. The only contact with him that Allen could remember was that the old man sometimes tousled his hair if he did something right. His mother was thirty-five years younger than his father. She married the commodore, Allen thought, to get out of the possessive clutches of her own mother.

During the first few years of their marriage before Allen was born, the commodore and his wife were the toast of Honolulu, and their home was Honolulu's social center. The commodore indulged his beautiful young wife and was rejuvenated by her youthful zest. From the time of his birth in 1918, Allen was assigned to the care of nannies and governesses.

Immediately after Allen's birth, the family moved to Paris for a year, where his father was assigned to duty at the peace negotiations. Then the commodore was reassigned to Hawaii—only this time as commissioner of a remote, mandated island. The commodore and his wife thought that this assignment would only last a year, but at the end of a year his request for reassignment to Honolulu was denied. His wife begged him to resign from the service, but he refused. At the collapse of her hopes for returning to the life she had loved, Allen's mother "lost her sparkle, became lethargic and melancholy, and went into a decline of spirits from which she did not recover for ten years or more" (p. 161)—until after the commodore's death. Whereas she had until then taken a supervisory interest in Allen, as he approached his third year she abandoned him completely to the care of Myrna, his nanny. Her relations with the commodore became formal. She would come out of her room for dinner and return to it right after the meal. What she did during the long days, Allen did not know. She became a shadowy figure in his life.

Until his 6th year, Myrna was Allen's constant companion. "During the day she was hardly separated from him for a moment, and at night her warm nakedness engulfed him" (p. 162). His first language was her language—a Hawaiian dialect. In addition, he was the only white child on the island, so until he was 14 Allen did not see another boy or girl like himself. While outwardly this situation seemed to have no significance, Lindner notes, it led to the formation of an identity crisis later on. Allen felt excluded by his parents and the white world, and equally excluded by the native Hawaiians. This led to a split in his personality: on one hand, he felt inferior, defective in some way, because he could not be totally accepted in either world; on the other, he felt superior because of the deference accorded him as a white boy and son of the commissioner.

At the age of 6 he lost Myrna, who suddenly died. Once more he felt abandoned. He was cared for until he was 9 by a succession of native women, but none loved him as Myrna had, and he did not become attached to them. At 9 began "the parade of governesses," two of whom remained vividly in Allen's memory. One he called "Sterile Sally" because of her compulsive cleanliness. She considered the native children "filthy niggers," and Allen was forbidden even to converse with his friends. After she left Allen could never again feel comfortable with the native children. The second governess was the one who introduced him to sex. Her name was Miss Lilian, and Allen was 11 when she first came to live with his family.

Although Allen had grown accustomed to sexual play with other children on the island—such play being a naturally accepted way of life there—he was somewhat taken aback by Miss Lilian's Western attitude and aggressive approach toward sex. After she had introduced him to intercourse, he became a "sort of a sex toy" for her; she would engage him in sexual activity two or three times a night and occasionally during the day. He grew fatigued from so much sex and so little sleep. When Allen was unable to respond, Miss Lilian would become furious, beating him, scratching him, and demanding that he use a hairbrush or some other implement to satisfy her. She also became very possessive and jealous of him, further separating him from others on the island. When she ran away with the schoolteacher's husband, Allen was left feeling horrified by his actions. He had broken a cultural taboo by having sex with a white woman (in his soul he was a native), and he had made love with a mother figure, which was tantamount to incest. "So, feeling that he had 'sinned,' Kirk, like any islander, was covered with guilt, which he chose to expiate by separation from society in the same manner as a native might by disappearing into the jungle" (p. 170).

Allen had always retreated to his world of fantasy. Now he did so with even more intensity. He read voraciously, and his books became his only friends. One day he came across a novel whose main character bore his name—Kirk Allen. Several days later he came across another novel with a fictional character bearing his name. Then another and another. Soon he became convinced that these stories were true, and that they were really about himself. As he grew from adolescence to adulthood, attending an Eastern university to study science, he continued to read novels about Kirk Allen. Soon he began to collect facts and fill in gaps in the story himself. Then he began making maps of the planets he had explored. One day, as he was working on a map of a planet, he found himself unable to remember certain details of the terrain, and he wished he were there. Suddenly, just as he thought it, he was standing on the planet. One moment he was just a scientist on X Reservation bending over a drawing board in the middle of an American desert; the next moment he was Kirk Allen, lord of a planet in an interplanetary empire in a distant universe, wearing the robes of his office. It was over in a matter of minutes, and he was again at the drawing board.

Allen's life history took many days to obtain. As Lindner learned more, he pondered how to treat him. It was obvious that Allen was absolutely convinced that he traveled to other planets, and he saw nothing odd about it. He regarded himself as completely normal and was thoroughly convinced that everything he experienced was real and true. He never for a moment doubted his sanity. At the same time, Lindner understood the "life-sustaining necessity" of Allen's delusional system. "What could I or anyone offer him in exchange for this elaborate edifice of imagination that, stone by stone, he had reared over the long years? I knew, in short, that without the fantasy Kirk could not *be*—that he *was* only in his dramatic imaginative life" (p. 179). As Lindner pored over a 2,000-page biography of Kirk Allen, a 100-page glossary, 82 color maps, 161 architectural drawings, 12 genealogical tables, and 44 folders containing writings on such subjects as "The Fauna of Srom Olma I" and "The Transportation System of Seraneb," he formulated a treatment plan. Noting that Allen was so sure of his sanity that he regarded the therapy as a joke, Lindner decided to engage him on a scientific level. Instead of trying to prove to Allen that he was insane, he pretended to take a scientific interest in his patient's findings, and enlisted his aid in verifying the documents he had shown him. On the pretext of discovering just how he did all the remarkable things he reported and why he was given his special gifts, Lindner enlisted his active participation in the treatment.

For a year they worked on this joint venture, and Lindner was able to formulate the underlying psychic factors accounting for Kirk's psychosis. His abandonment by his mother, then by his nanny; his estrangement from his father and from the natives on the island; his sexual abuse by his governess, had all taken their toll on him. "Frustrated in all his affectional aspirations, isolated and turned in upon himself, Kirk began to nourish intense feelings of hatred, which rapidly declared themselves in destructive fantasies" (p. 184). Each traumatic event in Kirk's life corresponded to a further retreat from reality. Thus, after Myrna's death he had fantasies of heroism; after his relationship with the "nymphomaniacal governess" had ended he became convinced that he was the fictional character he was reading about; and after he had been sexually assaulted by a woman scientist on Reservation X, who had been relentlessly pursuing him for some time and would not be denied, he rushed to his room frightened and, for the first time, "traveled" to another planet. "What is of great interest to the psychoanalyst," Lindner observes, "is the fact that this solution of total flight into fantasy occurred to Kirk while he was consciously engaged in the preparation of a map," explaining that maps, charts, architectural plans, and other similar material "often have the unconscious symbolic significance of the human form, especially of curiosity or perplexity regarding sexual details" (p. 187).

After the end of the first year the analysis reached an impasse. Lindner decided to utilize a technique used by John Rosen and Milton Wexler—joining the patient's delusional system. He began to take a personal interest in Allen's "weird yet magnificent fantasy," steeping himself in the "records." For "days on end" Lindner used all his spare moments to study the mass of material Allen had given him, until he knew it so well that the most trivial details were etched in his memory. He found more and more errors in Allen's calculations.

One morning Allen arrived and sat down at the table where Lindner was studying astronomical charts (they no longer used the couch). Lindner was so lost in his thoughts that he did not look up or speak for many minutes. Finally Allen asked what was wrong.

"Plenty," Lindner replied. "These distances are all fouled up. Either your astronomical projection from Srom Norbra X is wrong or the star maps are way off. They just don't make sense. Look here . . ." (p. 190). They went over the calculations for a while, and Lindner observed that Allen was growing increasingly tense. "Maybe you made your mistake in translating from Olmayan measurements to miles," Lindner suggested (p. 190).

Allen tossed the pencil down with a grunt. Lindner tried to comfort him by remarking that the error was not that serious.

"Not serious!" Allen exploded. Anger flashed in his eyes for the first time, and his hands began to tremble. Now he understood, he told Lindner, why he had lost so many ships.

Lindner felt a "thrill of triumph" as he realized that this episode had produced "the first small aperture in the fantasy." As he arose to signal the hour's end, Allen gave him a "long, slow, quizzical gaze."

Explaining how the technique of joining the delusion works, Lindner notes that a delusion such as Allen's had room in it only for one person at a time, and that such psychotic structures were generally rigidly circumscribed as to 'living space.' "When, as in this case, another person invades the delusion, the original occupant finds himself literally forced to give way" (pp. 193–194). By engaging in the same behavior as the patient, the therapist becomes a mirror of the patient's insanity. The patient is thus forced, so to speak, into developing an observing ego.

Unfortunately the technique has its hazards, as Lindner soon discovered. After many episodes such as the one just described, Lindner found himself becoming more and more obsessed with the delusion. Due to a combination of circumstances—his identification with the patient (he, too, had been a lonely child, prone to heroic fantasies); unresolved conflicts in his personal life; psychoanalytic restlessness; and a lifelong interest in science fiction—he began to "enter part way into the incredible universe of Kirk's design" (p. 198). Whereas in the beginning he had preoccupied himself with errors in Allen's calculations in order to advance the therapy, now he was spending all his spare time working out these calculations "in the service of the fantasy." He began to order Allen to go on excursions to planets and to eagerly await his return with the information, relishing his role as the power behind the throne. He became more and more anxious about their joint venture and began to realize that he himself was in trouble. "There arrived a moment when I could not ignore the tell-tale signs of obsession, a moment when the ego realized the threat and allied itself with the forces of light" (p. 202). His increasing obsession did not go unnoticed by Allen.

One day Allen came to his session with a look of concern on his face. When Lindner asked him what was wrong, he hesitated for a while, then finally said he had a confession to make. "I've been lying to you."

"Lying to me?" Lindner replied. "About what?"

"It's all a lie," he said, picking up the papers on the table. "I've been making it up . . . inventing all that—that—nonsense!" (p. 205).

Allen acknowledged that for several weeks he had known he had been crazy and that the whole fantasy was a delusion, but he had been reluctant to tell Lindner because he was afraid of hurting Lindner's feelings. He had noticed how avidly Lindner had taken to the fantasy, and he did not want to shatter Lindner's delusion!

Lindner does not say what happened to Allen after the treatment was terminated. He himself did not do well, for he succumbed to a heart attack three years after the treatment. An informed source has described him as a "driven personality" and suggested that his death may have been partly due to overwork. In "The Jet-Propelled Couch," Lindner writes that during the last stages of his work with Allen he was "in a period of emotional satiation" and felt bored with his work, which offered fewer and fewer satisfactions. "I had not then the wit to comprehend that my boredom was a defense against unresolved personal conflicts, that I was drawing a defensive cloak about myself. . . ." (p. 196). One can only conjecture how much his work with Allen drained him and perhaps contributed to the decline of his health. He was survived by a wife and daughter, age 5.

Interpretation

Lindner's work has not been taken seriously by many analysts. There are several reasons for this. His best work, *The Fifty-*

Minute Hour, was not written for a professional audience, but rather for the general public. Like Winnicott, Lindner eschewed psychoanalytic terminology, so that even when he wrote for professionals, it sounded as if he were addressing the general public. In addition, his work has become quite popular, and the paperback version of *The Fifty-Minute Hour* has been advertised in a sensational way. (It has an illustration of a nude on the cover.)

Many psychotherapists look down on a member of their profession who writes for the general public, refuses to use professional terminology (considered a form of reverse snobbery), becomes too popular, or allows his work to be marketed in a sensational way. (Of course, Lindner had nothing to do with how *The Fifty-Minute Hour* was marketed, and the racy cover was created after his death.) However, there is a double standard with respect to his work, for while many mental health practitioners will privately acknowledge how much they enjoyed reading it and how much they benefited, both personally and professionally, from the insights gleaned from it, they will rarely do so in writing. There is a definite hierarchy in psychoanalysis, as Balint (1968) has pointed out. At the top of this hierarchy are the classical analysts, who, since Freud's time, continue to think of themselves as the only "correct" practitioners of therapy; they have usually graduated from the most prestigious training institutes. Those whose writings are most obscure and replete with psychoanalytic terminology are also accorded much respect, and those who publish frequently in the "correct" journals are next in the hierarchy. In this scheme of things, Lindner's writings do not rank very high.

To judge Lindner from this standard is to misunderstand him. His aim was different from those professionals who write for other professionals. The latter want to persuade their colleagues of the validity of their ideas and hence influence the shape of psychoanalytic theory or technique. Lindner wanted to persuade the general public of the benefits of psychoanalysis and to influence society as a whole. Through the use of metaphor, he hoped to reach not just the intellect but also the unconscious of his public and to allay their resistance to therapy. He was able to convey the intricacies of psychoanalysis with both clarity and art because he was both an artist and a scientist, and he chose to use both skills in his writing. Those who criticize him for being popular miss the point. Who is to say that a psychoanalyst who writes in jargon for other psychoanalysts and creates elaborate theories is more important to science or to society than a psychoanalyst who writes for analyst and public alike in an attempt to have the greatest and most immediate impact on society? Both have an equal value for society. And should one's intellectual stature be judged by the obscurity of one's language or one's facility with jargon? By one's capacity to invent new concepts? Or by one's skill at translating complicated concepts into simple language? Who is to say which is the more important?

Lindner's understanding of both the criminal and the schizophrenic personality—as exemplified by the cases of Charles and Kirk Allen—is profound while at the same time simply and beautifully written. Is there a more poignant illustration of how childhood neglect, abuse, seduction, and rejection can lead to the formation of a homicidal personality? Is there a more finely etched description of the etiology of schizophrenia?

Fromm-Reichmann (1959), writing about the effects of isolation and loneliness on individual development, alludes to the case of Kirk Allen. "The infant thrives on living in intimate and tender closeness with the person who tends and mothers him," she notes (p. 326), and points to experiments with animals raised in isolation that become paranoid and antagonistic toward the other animals of their own species during their adulthood. Children who are neglected by their families and deprived of emotional and physical contact, she adds, also become antagonistic and paranoid, developing substitute satisfactions in fantasy. "Robert Lindner has presented an impressive example of the fatal results of such faulty developments in his treatment history of Kirk Allen, the hero of 'The Jet-Propelled Couch,' a 'true psychoanalytic tale,'" she concludes (p. 327).

Lindner's capacity to be human, to come from behind the blank screen when he felt it was necessary, has also been lauded. Greenwald (1959) observes that Lindner was one of the few analysts who had "the courage to be a participant" in therapy. He was willing to take risks other analysts would never take, and could skillfully demonstrate a wide array of techniques. He was one of the first psychoanalytic eclectics. This naiveté, however, had a negative as well as a positive aspect.

Szasz (1970) observes that Lindner was one of the first psychoanalysts to defend the rights of the mentally ill and to argue against the use of psychiatric labels. In particular, Lindner questioned the psychiatric and psychoanalytic practice of designating homosexuals as "sick" or "maladjusted." Emphasizing that psychiatrists should not have the power to impose on clients their definition of homosexuality as a disease (this, of course, was before recent changes in DSM-III), Szasz confesses that this position is not "held by me alone," but also by "Robert Lindner, a well-known nonmedical psychoanalyst" (p. 176).

In both the cases described in this chapter, Lindner's analytic derring-do got him into trouble. Perhaps due to his naiveté, a lack of adequate training, and a degree of grandiosity, he acted out countertransference feelings and took risks that he should not have taken. In working with Charles, he did not fully recognize the dangers of the patient's strong negative transference, and the murderous rage beneath it. As the patient grew more antagonistic and abusive toward Lindner, Lindner attempted to be all the more tolerant and permissive, allowing Charles to destroy objects in his office and to misbehave in other ways. "If I showed the slightest trace of annoyance or impatience, he was quick to seize on it, to castigate me for it, to accuse me of unfairness, lack of understanding, and a dozen other 'crimes' of feeling against him" (Lindner 1950, p. 32). This allowed Charles to step up his destructive behavior until he eventually attempted to strangle Linder. Lindner might have benefited from Winnicott's advice about being able to objectively hate patients. His mistake with Charles was that he did not interpret the negative transference or feed back to his patient the hatred that was being unleashed at him. Perhaps Lindner was denying the strength of the hatred being aroused in him, because he had a resistance to acknowledging to himself or to the patient that he felt such hatred. Such is the case with many analysts, as Ferenczi (1933) and Reich (1933) had previously noted.

Allen's delusional system offered another pitfall for Lindner. Because of his countertransference, he became more involved in Allen's case than he should have. He describes himself as spending "days on end" working on Allen's projects, until he became anxious and obsessed with the most trivial details. "During this brief but acute period," he writes, "I skirted the edges of the abyss. Although aware of the dangerous game I was playing, I seem to have been willing to play it to the limit for stakes of then unknown neurotic satisfaction" (Lindner 1950, p. 202). While appreciating Lindner's dedication, one must question the amount of self-sacrifice involved. The intervention was quite successful, but at what cost? Would it have worked without his going that far? Psychoanalysts such as Spotnitz (1985), who have perfected the use of paradoxical interventions with schizophrenics, probably would have achieved a similar success, using similar joining techniques, but more judiciously (see Chapter 10). Lindner's authentic involvement in the delusion may have hastened therapeutic progress, but at the sacrifice of his own health.

On the other hand, Lindner's willingness to reveal himself, not only to his patients but also to his readers, is commendable. Like Freud, who admitted his mistakes in working with Dora (1905b), Lindner showed himself at his best and at his worst. In part this willingness to reveal himself may have been in the service of achieving dramatic effects, but in part it was also an act by somebody whose ego was strong enough to allow him to display weakness. As such, he provided a metaphorical framework from which others could benefit: the therapists who followed him could learn by the mistakes he made.

In his introduction to *The Fifty-Minute Hour*, political analyst and literary critic Max Lerner expresses his appreciation of this emerging form of literature, which he views as part documentary and part interpretation within the mold of an art form. "One of the difficulties about this new literary genre is the scarcity of men who are technically able to deal with the fragile web that the sick mind presents, and who can at the same time see the human and dramatic values of their art and communicate them to the nontechnical reader. Dr. Lindner is one of this rare company of men" (p. vii).

He applauds Lindner's honesty, noting that he has not tried to improve on his authentic documentary material and observing that Lindner's self-honesty allows the reader to thoroughly identify with both therapist and patient. "For in a very real sense," Lerner explains, "as the analyst helps the patient to strip away layer after layer of accretion that has hidden his personality, both the analyst and the reader find some of their own skin being stripped away as well" (p. viii). He also praises Lindner's audacity with regard to confronting the "perils of the analytic couch." "Perhaps the greatest peril of all," he concludes, "as shown in the delicious story of Kirk, the young physicist, is that the analyst will become entangled in his own plot. . . . the 'Jet-Propelled Couch' . . . is certain to become one of the classic tales of its kind" (p. xi).

In the years since the publication of "Jet-Propelled Couch," Lerner's prophecy has proven to be correct.

4

CURING
SCHIZOPHRENIA

Frieda Fromm-Reichmann
and Joanne Greenberg (1964)

"One exuberant young patient," Frieda Fromm-Reichmann wrote in her posthumously published book, *Psychoanalysis and Psychotherapy*, "the daughter of indiscriminately 'encouraging' parents, was warned against expecting life to become a garden of roses after her recovery . . ." (1959, p. 204). The young woman to whom Fromm-Reichmann refers went on to become one of the most famous patients in psychoanalytic history. Fromm-Reichmann's warning became the title of a novel, *I Never Promised You a Rose Garden* (1964), in which Joanne Greenberg created a touching depiction of her schizophrenia and her therapy with Fromm-Reichmann. This work represents one of the best examples of a growing body of literature—case histories written by patients themselves.

Indeed, much of what we know of this case was provided by the patient in her popular novel (it was also made into a movie). However, there are also veiled but unmistakable vignettes from the case in three of the papers Fromm-Reichmann wrote during the 1950s, while she was analyzing Greenberg. There is also an overview of the entire case history, based on documents from the archives of Chestnut Lodge, by McGlashan and Keats (1989). Together, these sources provide a well-rounded picture of the case.

At 4 feet 10 inches tall, Fromm-Reichmann often had to stand on a stool or bend the microphones down toward her when she spoke from a podium; however, the power of her personality transcended her size. According to Dexter Bullard, founder of Chestnut Lodge, she would captivate audiences with her charming mixture of smiles, frowns, mimicry, and seriousness. Her presence during the 1940s and 1950s, along with that of Harry Stack Sullivan, Harold Searles, and other notables, made Chestnut Lodge one of the best known and progressive institutions of its kind.

Frieda Fromm-Reichmann was born in 1890 in Koenigsberg, East Prussia, one of several daughters of a kind and understanding father—a banker—and a mother who encouraged her to pursue a career in medicine. She graduated from medical school in 1914 and became interested in psychoanalysis after reading the work of Freud. She underwent psychoanalytic training and established a private psychoanalytic sanatorium in Heidelberg. She and her husband, Erich Fromm, also founded the Psycho-analytic Training Institute of Southwest Germany. Later she and Fromm fled Nazi Germany and immigrated to the United States. Eventually they divorced and she landed at Chestnut Lodge, where she served as supervisor of psychotherapy for twenty-two years. By the time Greenberg entered treatment, Fromm-Reichmann had already written her first book, *The Principles of Intensive Psychotherapy* (1950), and had achieved a measure of fame.

In contrast to Fromm-Reichmann's tiny size, Greenberg was tall and overweight—she weighed about 200 pounds when admitted to Chestnut Lodge—with "long, straggly blonde hair, bitten-off fingernails and unbrushed teeth" (McGlashan and Keats 1989). She could not allow people to walk behind her on the street, and was given to burning herself with cigarettes and peeling off her skin, particularly from her heels. Like Kirk Allen, she had a delusional world that she called her kingdom, where people spoke a special language she had made up and wrote in symbols resembling Chinese.

The initial interview is recorded both in her novel and in one of Fromm-Reichmann's papers. According to Greenberg's version of this initial interview, Fromm-Reichmann first asked if she had anything to tell her. Greenberg (1964) was angered by this question and stood up.

> "All right—you'll ask me questions and I'll answer them—you'll clear up my 'symptoms' and send me home . . . *and what will I have then?*"
>
> The doctor said quietly, "If you did not really want to give them up, you wouldn't tell me." A rope of fear pulled its noose about Deborah [Joanne]. "Come, sit down. You will not have to give up anything until you are ready, and then there will be something to take its place." [p. 23]

Fromm-Reichmann's version (1959), written in order to illustrate her handling of patients' anxieties and defenses, was more clinical:

> A patient shouted at the psychiatrist during their first visit, "I know what you will do now! You'll take my gut-pains, and my trance, and my withdrawal states away from me! And where will I be then?" The psychiatrist first asked for a description of the three pathological states, the loss of which the patient allegedly feared. The patient's answer made it possible for the psychiatrist to demonstrate to her the attempt at escaping anxiety, which three of the states had in common. [p. 191]

In Fromm-Reichmann's version, she then reassured Greenberg that her symptoms would not be taken away, but, on the contrary, she herself would wish to dispose of them when she learned to understand enough about her anxiety to make it decrease. Omitted from Greenberg's version was Fromm-Reichmann's important initial interpretation about the meaning of her symptoms as defenses against anxiety.

Greenberg was the first child of a well-to-do Jewish immigrant family. Her father was a lobbyist and her mother a professional artist. Her father was prone to frightening fits of temper; her mother had a saccharine demeanor and a history of depression. He was always looking for evil, while she tended to deny reality. They were said to be extremely intrusive, particularly her father. During Greenberg's infancy her father's intrusiveness centered on her evacuations. He frequently administered enemas to her, which she experienced as rapes, and constantly reprimanded her for bedwetting, a habit which continued until her 5th year, when it was discovered that she had an abnormal urethral opening and had developed tumors in her urethra. It is not known whether the tumors were congenital or whether they had developed as the result of familial stress. "We have no use for a pantswetting stinker in this house," the father would tell her (McGlashan and Keats 1989, p. 41).

When Greenberg was 3, her mother gave birth to a stillborn son. Her parents went away for two weeks so that the mother could recover, and Joanne was left in the care of a nurse. During this time she "lay in her crib, paralyzed with apathy, and took little food," and when her mother returned she "greeted her with a tremendous shriek" (McGlashan and Keats 1989, p. 42). At around the same time, her father left for six months to settle the estate of a deceased relative, and her fear of abandonment was reinforced. Greenberg also felt that her father was angry at her for not being a son.

When she was 5 her sister was born. Feeling abandoned once again by her mother, she picked up her baby sister one day with the intention of throwing her out the window. Her parents were horrified and punitive, showing no understanding of her feelings. When the problems with her urethra were discovered, Greenberg had to undergo a cystoscopy and two operations. "We're taking your doll to the hospital so it can be operated on," her parents told her (p. 41). This act of deception shattered her trust in her parents and made her feel abandoned once again. As an adult, she developed an olfactory hallucination: when things in her life went bad she smelled ether.

Her childhood and adolescence up to the time she entered treatment with Fromm-Reichmann continued to be a saga of controlling and intrusive parents who never seemed to realize what she was feeling. They sent her to summer camps that were very anti-Semitic. Whenever she complained about that or anything, they would say it was her fault. At about the age of 10 she began to put on weight. Her mother had always been overly preoccupied with Greenberg's food intake because she herself had a weight problem. The child also began developing other symptoms: "she bit her nails, sucked her thumb, picked her nose, ground her teeth, and complained of her eyes going out of focus" (McGlashan and Keats 1989, p. 43).

Although Greenberg had an IQ of about 130, she did poorly in school. After psychological testing, the school recommended that her parents take her to a therapist. She went into therapy, but six months later her mother ended the treatment, not wanting the girl to feel that something was wrong with her. At 12 she withdrew more and more, and her father became more intrusive. He was obsessed with rape and constantly lectured her about it. He was always watching over her, keeping her under surveillance. To stop him from reading her poetry, she invented a language she called "Irian." She also developed her own religion, which featured gods, goddesses, and seven worlds. She began sitting in the dark in the living room gorging herself with sweets. She complained of constant abdominal pain and put herself into trances during which nobody could talk to her. Finally her parents could not ignore what was happening, and a psychiatrist referred them to Chestnut Lodge.

The treatment by Fromm-Reichmann lasted four and a half years. Greenberg saw Fromm-Reichmann four times a week during the three years she was at Chestnut Lodge, and once or twice a week for another year and a half as a private patient. In the beginning Greenberg came to the sessions slouching around and smoking a pipe. Soon the pipe-smoking was dispensed with and she began lying on the couch. Fromm-Reichmann's goal during the beginning phase was to "relieve Joanne of early wariness while at the same time allowing suspicion to be expressed: and to demonstrate that the therapist was not god-like, but instead fallible, human, liable to err, and open to correction" (McGlashan and Keats 1989, p. 49). She stressed from the outset that therapy would be a collaborative effort, and she was quite open about expressing her feelings.

Fromm-Reichmann utilized many of the same techniques as innovators like Ferenczi and Lindner. However, she used these techniques a bit differently, never losing sight of her own objectivity. For example, she actively supported Greenberg's resentment about the deception practiced on her at the time of her surgery, when she was told a doll would be operated on, only to find herself going under the knife. In her book Greenberg describes how afterwards, in the ride home from the hospital, her parents were strangely joyous. They had driven home from the hospital through a light rain and Joanne had stood up in the back of the car and looked out at the gray skies, thinking, "Reality was not inside the car with her singing mother and cheerful father, but toward the murky sky finishing with its rain, exhausted and dark. It occurred to her that this darkness was now, and was forever going to be, the color of her life" (Greenberg, pp. 60–61). When Greenberg spoke of this memory, Fromm-Reichmann would express her own anger at her parents. "Will parents ever learn not to lie to children?" (Greenberg 1964, p. 62). On other occasions she expressed similar sympathy with respect to Greenberg's murderous impulses toward her younger sister and toward the anti-Semitic children at the summer camp she had attended.

When Greenberg talked about her intrusive and tyrannical father, Fromm-Reichmann play-acted the father. She would get up from her chair and prance about the room, pretending to hunt about for Joanne, calling in a gruff voice. "Get me my slippers, damn-it! Get me my newspaper! Get me a beer from the ice-box! Now!" (McGlashan and Keats 1989, p. 50). When Greenberg said that she felt confused, Fromm-Reichmann joined her delusional world, knowing that this world was used not only as a defense but also as an indirect way of expressing her thinking about current, everyday issues. "Would you ask Antilobia [the chief Irian god] if he will permit letting me in on the secret of the confusion?" she asked Greenberg.

Taken aback, Greenberg replied, "Nobody ever told me such a thing. I will try, but it will take a lot of concentration" (McGlashan and Keats 1989, p. 50). She did make contact with Antilobia, and Antilobia told her that even though Fromm-Reichmann seemed all right and was from the 'sixth world' Greenberg could not share the secret with her because nobody can share anybody else's experiences.

"Of course not," Fromm-Reichmann replied. "I think he's quite right, or you who talk to him are quite right. But I want to intensely participate in the experience while I am observing it and come as near it as I can, so I can help you understand it" (McGlashan and Keats 1989, p. 50).

Fromm-Reichmann not only entered the fantasies for her own understanding, but also to impart that understanding to Greenberg. When Greenberg kept expressing fears of being raped, Fromm-Reichmann told her that her fears had been caused by her father's paranoia about rape. Rape did occur, Fromm-Reichmann said, but only about one millionth as frequently as her father would have her believe. This combination of active therapy, deep empathy, understanding, and interpretation characterized the treatment from beginning to end. At its core was Fromm-Reichmann's realness and genuine respect and affection for Greenberg, an authenticity that was appreciated and, in time, returned.

Toward the end of the first year of treatment Fromm-Reichmann began to encourage the establishment of an observing ego in Greenberg. She had noticed that whenever she announced that she had to cancel an appointment or go away for a vacation, Greenberg would always act out immediately after the announcement. When Greenberg tried to explain why she acted out, Fromm-Reichmann interspersed, "I don't think you know why. You told me before about an 'it' inside you that makes you do things. I think this time the 'it' made you do it, and you should not believe that you yourself did it" (McGlashan and Keats 1989, p. 52).

One of Greenberg's most destructive forms of acting out was burning herself with cigarettes. Greenberg describes one such occasion when Fromm-Reichmann went away for a vacation and Greenberg assumed that her therapist was dead. She went into a trance, all her own senses went dead, and the inside of her felt as though it were a volcano about to explode:

> [Joanne] perceived that by burning she could set a backfire that would assuage the burning kiln of the volcano, all the doors and vents of which were closed and barricaded. And by this same burning she could prove to herself finally whether or not she was truly made of human substance. Her senses offered no proof; vision was a gray blur; hearing merely muffled roars and groans, meaningless half the time; feeling was blunted, too. [Greenberg 1964, p. 161]

Fromm-Reichmann returned to find Greenberg in a wet pack, strapped to her bed. (Thirty years later, in a follow-up interview, Greenberg claimed she found this wet pack a relief, like a strong, wet hug that prevented her from destroying herself.) Fromm-Reichmann exclaimed her surprise and shock.

Greenberg said, "I thought you were dead!" (Greenberg 1964, p. 169).

Fromm-Reichmann told Greenberg that she had gotten herself in such bad shape, as a way of telling her how angry she was with her. Greenberg reacted by thrashing around, and Fromm-Reichmann encouraged her to express her anger and hate.

After some difficulty, Greenberg for the first time verbalized some of her feelings about how she was poisonous and hated it, how she was going to be destroyed in shame and degradation and hated it, how she hated herself and the deceivers. "I hate my life and my death. . . . God curse me! God curse me!" She began to cry and then stopped herself.

"Maybe when I leave," Fromm-Reichmann said, "you can learn to cry. For now, let me say this: measure the hate you feel now, and the shame. That quality is your capacity also to love and to feel joy and to have compassion. Also, I'll see you tomorrow" (Greenberg 1964, pp. 169–170).

Writing about her attempt to understand Greenberg's often cryptic communication, Fromm-Reichmann explains that it was truly a collaborative effort. No psychiatrist can understand a schizophrenic patient's communication without the patient's help, she asserts, just as one cannot understand a dream without the dreamer's associations. To illustrate, she cites two pieces from Greenberg's history which at first defied understanding. Greenberg had been a bed- and pants-wetter as a child, and she came from a family in which the women were disposed to become overweight, and so the avoidance of becoming fat was made into a religion. Fromm-Reichmann suspected that these two factors were somehow connected, but did not realize how until one day Greenberg told her, "Pants-wetting and overweight belong together, and not only because both are connected with defiance and resentment against my parents and with the anxiety connected with these feelings" (Fromm-Reichmann 1959, p. 182). The patient remembered being at a camp during her childhood and, being unable to make it to the toilet in her cabin in time, she had wet the Turkish towel she was wearing. At that moment she heard her roommate's footsteps and tried to wring out the towel; but she was only a little girl and the towel was too heavy to wring out. "It was the *weight* of the *wet* towel which made it so hard," she stated. "There you are, 'weight and wet.' 'Wet' has to do with my resentment against my father, 'weight' with my defiance against mother. . . . 'Wet' and 'weight' are father and mother, and the camp stands for both of them" (p. 183).

At times Fromm-Reichmann would have Greenberg show her a poem, sing a song, or play the piano, and afterwards she would say, "Now we both know what it (the poetry, singing, etc.) is like. Even though I enjoy it, we can't spend too much time on it, and I am sure the artistic quality won't be lost" (McGlashan and

Keats 1989, p. 55). At other times she would concentrate her efforts on interpreting to Greenberg her imaginary world of "Iria." She told Greenberg that Iria did not exist but that Greenberg made use of it to indirectly express forbidden thoughts and feelings, such as murderous rages. She also hammered away at the point that believing in Iria increased rather than diminished her unhappiness. Gradually Greenberg began to see how the Irian gods encouraged her self-destructive tendencies, pushing her, for example, into penances, during which she was not allowed to eat. However, each time she resolved and gave up a symptom, she became upset, burned herself, and was sent to the disturbed ward.

As the months and years passed, Greenberg slowly developed the capacity to verbalize rather than act out her feelings. Shortly before relinquishing Iria for good, Greenberg burned herself one more time. Fromm-Reichmann asked her why she did it, and Greenberg was now able to say, "I am so ugly, fat, and mean that I might just as well make myself more ugly, fat, and mean. . . . I don't know where to go with my intense feelings of anxiety and need for action and so I turn it against myself. . . . I have so much passion and I can't have men" (McGlashan and Keats 1989, p. 58).

Fromm-Reichmann seems to have used whatever intervention she thought would work at a particular time. On one occasion, after a particularly good session, she broke off a flower growing in a pot in her cottage and handed it to Greenberg, saying that she did not usually give gifts to patients but thought Greenberg had worked hard that day (Greenberg 1964, p. 151). On another occasion she used suggestion to help Greenberg get rid of the last character from the world of Iria—Gloria. "One of these days I suppose you will throw Gloria out the window and see that she can go through the window without the window being opened and that there is no spot on the ground where she lands and then you will realize she was your creation" (McGlashan and Keats 1989, p. 58). Three days later Greenberg reported that Gloria was gone.

Once she had given up her delusional world, Greenberg began to lose weight. Within several weeks she had dropped down to her normal weight, and then began talking about not having a boyfriend, and other common adolescent problems. By the middle of the second year she went back to school and sang in several church choirs. She made advances and had setbacks in connection with these new activities. Each setback was analyzed and the feelings were resolved.

She began to relate to her parents in a different way. She was less frightened of her father's tyranny and more able to see both her father's and her mother's shortcomings. The hardest part was separating from her mother. Her mother had repeatedly told her that she was very understanding, full of love, and only wanted to do what was right by Joanne. Joanne knew that her mother could also be very contrary, especially if her vanity had been pricked, but for a long time she needed to protect her mother and maintain the idealization.

Soon Greenberg was in college and she began to see Fromm-Reichmann as an outpatient. A college professor liked her poetry so much that he told her that she was the best student he had had in his creative writing class in twenty years. She was well-groomed, had boyfriends, kept her own apartment, and gave dinner parties for professors and fellow students. When Fromm-Reichmann brought up the subject of termination, however, there was an immediate flare-up of Joanne's symptoms. Dr. Fromm-Reichmann interpreted them as an expression of her dependency needs. For a period of time one symptom after another returned: the overeating, the peeling of skin from her heels, and the burnings with cigarettes. Each was once again analyzed and resolved.

After four and a half years the treatment began to wind down. At that point, they saw each other every six months. Fromm-Reichmann told Greenberg, "Your activities in life will begin to be more important than our meetings. Soon you're just not going to want to fit them in" (McGlashan and Keats 1989, p. 64). That is exactly what happened.

At one of their last sessions, Greenberg told Fromm-Reich-mann about a recent visit to her parents. She had described to her parents the success she had been having in her creative writing class, and her father immediately asked her to write a poem. She did so regretfully, and later complained to Fromm-Reichmann about her compliance. She felt she should have asked her father if he would tell a real poet to go in the next room and do a poem. Then she reminded Fromm-Reichmann of a story she had once related about a father who called his grown son "my darling goldfish" and kissed and hugged him, and had to be told that that would in no way help bring about a real, mutual, adult relationship with him. Greenberg and Fromm-Reichmann shared a good laugh.

When her professor offered to get her poems published in a poetry magazine, Greenberg told him that she definitely did not want this to happen. Later she confided to Fromm-Reichmann that she did not want to be known as 'that girl whose poetry is published.' She was afraid boys would be scared of her and she would get no dates. She was confident in her poetry but felt that she had missed out on normal teenage experiences. Fromm-Reich-mann saw Greenberg's concern with her attractiveness to boys as a sign of normal adolescent growth that had been impeded by her illness.

Throughout the treatment, up until its final phase, Fromm-Reichmann held monthly case conferences in which she discussed her treatment of Greenberg with others on the Chestnut Lodge staff. (It is from the notes of these staff meetings that the McGla-shan and Keats study is based.) Fromm-Reichmann used these conferences to keep herself objective and free of countertransfer-ence interference. She had written in her first book (1950) that when a therapist is unable to establish a workable relationship with a schizophrenic patient, it is invariably due to the therapist's personality difficulties, not to the patient's psychopathology, and she was always careful to make sure her own "personality difficul-ties" did not get in the way of her treatment with Greenberg.

The last conversation, according to Greenberg's novel, took them full circle, focusing once again on her fear of letting go of her symptoms, which Fromm-Reichmann referred to as "garbage." "I love you, too," Greenberg exclaimed in parting, "but I haven't forgotten your power, you old mental garbage-collector!" She cried and asked, "Does it all have to go? Do we pile it up and throw it *all* out?"

"It cannot be a decent bargain now—don't you see," Fromm-Reichmann answered. "You have to take the world first, to take it on faith as a complete commitment . . . on my word, if no one else's. Then, on what you yourself build of this commitment, you can decide whether it's a decent bargain or not" (Greenberg 1964, p. 248).

Fromm-Reichmann felt that her treatment of Greenberg had been quite unusual. Never in her previous experience had she had such a quick success or seen such a complete recovery. And this recovery was borne out by a follow-up interview some thirty years after the treatment had been terminated. During these years Greenberg had written eight books and become a famous author. She married a psychotherapist and settled down in Colorado, where she had two sons.

McGlashan telephoned her and she told him that she had not had a relapse since termination, although in the first few years of her marriage, when she had lived in a cabin in the woods, she had had bouts of "cabin fever." For a few minutes at a time she would think she was going crazy again, but then she was able to understand the difference between the past circumstances and the present ones and she would come out of it.

She said that it had taken ten years for her to be able to write about her experience at Chestnut Lodge. First she wrote the book under a pseudonym, Hannah Green, but later the secret got out and she used her real name. Then she was invited to talk at various places, and she used this as a chance to integrate the past with the present. But, she reported, "It got kind of old, being a professional ex-nut. I only do it now when they let me talk about the deaf"

(McGlashan and Keats 1989, p. 67). She explained that since she herself had become deaf in one ear, she has developed an interest in the problems of the deaf.

Asked to review her work with Fromm-Reichmann, she said what she appreciated most in her former therapist was a kind of matter-of-factness and ordinariness, and the fact that Fromm-Reichmann treated her like an equal. She cited what she thought were the most valuable aspects of Fromm-Reichmann's treatment: her interpretation of Greenberg's burning herself as an inverted expression of anger at Fromm-Reichmann, which made her realize how important her therapist was to her; her genuine concern about the burnings—telling her repeatedly, "You are an attractive young girl and if you get well and your arms are full of scars, that will be too bad!"; her insistence that the therapy was a collaborative venture; and, finally, her remark that, even if Greenberg recovered, life would not be a rose garden. This last intervention made Greenberg feel that her therapist really took her seriously and was willing to talk practically with her, woman to woman.

In addition to writing, Greenberg taught a class in English etymology and tutored several other students in Hebrew. She also served on the fire and rescue squads and belonged to the League of Women Voters and the National Association for the Deaf. A striking feature of the follow-up, according to McGlashan, was the ease with which Greenberg spoke. He describes her as engaging and charming, and it was evident to him that she had advanced well beyond other patients he followed up on.

Asked if she were having fun, she answered, "I go skiing. I talk with friends. That's play. On the other hand, skiing is not play. It's a form of prayer. It's what God does on Saturday afternoons. I know, because I saw him on the slopes" (McGlashan and Keats 1989, p. 70).

As for Fromm-Reichmann, she died soon after the treatment was terminated. On April 28, 1957, at the age of 67, she suffered a fatal acute coronary thrombosis. She had no children, but she was mourned and missed by those who knew her and had grown to love her at the Lodge.

Interpretation

Fromm-Reichmann is reported to have said that a patient will forgive mistakes of the head, but not of the heart (see Searles 1965, p. 17). Perhaps for that reason she and others who worked at Chestnut Lodge dispensed with the classical analytic stance, particularly the use of a blank screen. She tried to reach patients on a human-to-human level, while at the same time adhering to certain rules she had discovered were necessary in working with schizophrenics.

Epstein and Feiner (1979) point out that Fromm-Reichmann "humanized" the therapist, maintaining that the analyst must be a real object, not a blank screen, because it was impossible for the analyst to really hide her humanness, especially with schizophrenics, who are keenly aware of any falseness. Indeed, the awareness and confrontation of the myth of the analyst's anonymity actually furthered the work. In this respect Fromm-Reichmann echoed the words of Ferenczi (1933) and Winnicott (1947), who also dispensed with the blank screen, expressed real feelings, and admitted their errors to their patients.

However, Fromm-Reichmann eschewed an overpermissive therapeutic attitude. In a paper written at the time she was working with Greenberg, she cautions therapists to listen to verbal hostile outbursts with an eye to investigating, not indulging, them. "Retrospectively, schizophrenic patients loathe themselves for their hostile outbursts, and do not respect the therapist who lets them get away with it" (1959, p. 180). She recommends addressing the adult part, rather than the child part, of the patient's personality (encouraging an observing ego), and discourages the therapist from offering closeness, friendship, or love. "The psychoanalyst who feels tempted to do so should ask himself whether he may not be motivated by his own anxiety rather than by an alleged concern for the patient's welfare" (p. 187). She also maintains that schizophrenics are afraid of any offer of closeness, seeing it as false, fearing rejection. Her approach, then, was to humanize the therapist while assuming strict boundaries of professionalism.

Searles (1955) agrees with Fromm-Reichmann's view about overindulging schizophrenics, stressing that, since it is related to the patient's fears of dependency, it can destroy the therapeutic relationship. However, there is a tendency for therapists to develop countertransference anxiety in response to the patient's hostility and to act it out by indulging the patient. "The therapist who is afraid of the patient's hostility, and of his own counterhostility, is likely to function in an overindulgent, smothering manner which is repetitive of the schizophrenic's pathogenic early experience with the original mother person" (p. 148).

Spotnitz (1985) gives credit to Fromm-Reichmann for being one of the therapists who, from the 1950s onward, identified countertransference as the crucial factor for success in working with schizophrenics such as Greenberg. He reiterates her assertion that any problems in the therapist–patient relationship were the result of countertransference, and adds: "In the treatment of the schizophrenic patient, the need for an exquisite balancing of evenly hovering attention with emotional sensibility gives rise to special problems" (p. 222).

McGlashan and Keats (1989), in reviewing the case history, note that from the outset Fromm-Reichmann had achieved a good "treatment alliance" with Greenberg. Each adapted to and accepted her respective role with the aim of advancing treatment. "From the beginning, their alliance was largely analytic rather than supportive in nature. One of the most striking things about Joanne was her love of truth" (p. 168). Reichmann's plain-spokenness and Greenberg's love of the truth combined to forge the alliance that was necessary for success. In this sense, Fromm-Reichmann became an antidote to the deceptive behavior of Greenberg's parents, modeling an authority figure who always behaved and spoke truthfully, fulfilling Greenberg's frustrated craving for sincerity.

Of equal importance, according to McGlashan and Keats, was Fromm-Reichmann's ability to understand Greenberg's language and religion, which helped her to achieve "linguistic consensual validation." She did not use force in developing communication, but rather deciphered Greenberg's narrative by being intensely interested and creative, as when she asked Greenberg's chief Irian god for permission to understand her confusion, played the role of her father, or assigned responsibility for Greenberg's acting out to an "it."

Fromm-Reichmann also functioned as an advisor and consultant, particularly toward the end of the treatment, again breaking away from classical psychoanalytic technique. She actively supported Greenberg's pursuit of educational, social, and recreational activities, and helped her solve problems that came up along the way. For example, McGlashan and Keats (1989) point out that when Greenberg complained that her mother had typed up her poems rather poorly, Fromm-Reichmann advised her to send them back and insisted, over Greenberg's objections, that "she had to let people know when she was displeased" (p. 169).

Finally, they point out that Fromm-Reichmann actively encouraged Greenberg's natural desire for independence. As the treatment progressed, Greenberg began more and more to analyze herself. Just before giving up Iria for good, she burned herself. In the next session, she initiated associations that went from burning to anxiety to her frustrated passion for men. She had so internalized Dr. Fromm-Reichmann by then that she initiated and carried on the work by herself. The process of internalization was natural, automatic, and largely silent.

There is not much, if anything, to criticize about Fromm-Reichmann's work in this case. Both therapist and patient agreed that it was an extraordinarily successful treatment, and we have the follow-up study by McGlashan and Keats, done thirty years later, to further validate the results. Fromm-Reichmann was not known for building theory or inventing new techniques, as were many of her predecessors in this work; rather she was gifted at understanding which theories or techniques worked and which did not, and making excellent use of those she decided were workable. In addition, she had the humility to truly listen to her patient, and if one technique did not achieve a positive response, she would discard it and try another.

As in the case of the "Wolf Man," we have here the advantage of the patient's input as to what helped her the most. For example, Greenberg validated Fromm-Reichmann's technique of making the treatment a collaborative venture, saying that it was quite helpful to her progress. This collaboration, she said, was most significant in understanding and resolving her longest-lasting symptom, that of pulling skin from her heels. Even after she had lived on her own and started college, she would still come home at night and peel off skin. In discussing the matter with Fromm-Reichmann, it finally occurred to her that she was still feeling terribly frightened, and the fear had to do with the notion that she was pretending to be a normal college girl when she was really a crazy nut from a mental institution. Upon analyzing this in Fromm-Reichmann's presence, she realized that peeling off skin safeguarded her against the dangers of change and gave her a sense of continuity. Once she understood that, this last symptom disappeared. The fact that both therapist and patient have emphasized the importance of their teamwork gives this aspect of the treatment more meaning. Similarly, Greenberg's recognition of the value of Fromm-Reichmann's matter-of-factness, her occasional toughness and her occasional permissiveness, and some of her interpretations, also adds weight to the importance of those interventions. "Our collaboration was the model for how I now live," Greenberg said in the follow-up interview. "I don't have much trouble with authority because I see things basically as collaborative. This began with my collaboration with Dr. Fromm-Reichmann, with whom I worked against the illness" (McGlashan and Keats 1989, p. 68).

Summing up the essence of Fromm-Reichmann's therapeutic technique, Weigert (1959) observes that although Fromm-Reichmann called her therapy with psychotic patients "psychoanalytically oriented psychotherapy," she did not feel her modifications of classical technique were that great. The main difference, according to Weigert, was that her technique was not so much interpretation as it was communication of understanding. "She worked, in particular, to elucidate all those defenses that had delayed and distorted [the patient's] ego development" (p. vii). She adds that Fromm-Reichmann's success was based "not only on her knowledge and experience but also on the exceptional character qualities which she brought to her challenging experiments. . . . She did not flinch. She was all there with the patient" (p. viii).

Francis, in the foreword to the McGlashan and Keats account of the case (1989) applauds "the remarkable encounter between a great therapist, Frieda Fromm-Reichmann, and a great patient, Joanne Greenberg," observing that Fromm-Reichmann was "extraordinary in her sensitivity, simplicity, and great common sense," and Greenberg was equally extraordinary "for her creative, but uncontrolled, immersion in fantasy, and also for her insight, honesty, and personal charm." He appreciates the special chemistry that took place between this therapist and this patient, asserting that "together they make a grand treatment team and provide a wonderful example of that special magic that can occur in interpersonal relationships, including therapeutic ones" (p. xiii). Francis underscores an important point: the success of a therapy relationship, like any other relationship, depends upon whether or not the participants are a good match. Fromm-Reichmann herself acknowledged that she was surprised at how fast Greenberg recovered; she was undoubtedly not as effective with other patients, with whom she was not as well matched.

There is an anecdote about Fromm-Reichmann told by her younger sister. During their early childhood, Fromm-Reichmann threw herself between her sister and a barking dog with the words, "You don't need to be afraid." This protective attitude toward her younger sister became the chief characteristic of her relationships with her patients: she became their protector until they could stand on their own feet.

5

CHILDHOOD PSYCHOSIS

Margaret Mahler and Violet (1968)

Many consider Margaret Schoenberger Mahler's delineation of infantile stages of development the most comprehensive modification of psychoanalytic developmental theory since Freud (1905a) formulated his psychosexual stages. Lost in the hubbub about Mahler the theory builder, however, has been Mahler the psychoanalyst who understood and treated a childhood malady that nobody had treated successfully before—infantile psychosis. Likewise, her case history about Violet, who was brought to her mute and wan at the age of 2½, also received less notice than other genres of her writing, yet it remains an excellent example of her pioneering treatment of psychotic children.

Mahler was born in 1897 in Hungary, almost nine months after her parents were married. In her *Memoirs* (1989), she notes that she was unwanted while her sister, four years later, was wanted, and from early on she saw how uncaringly—even sadistically—her mother related to her while flaunting her love for her younger daughter. "I do not think it an exaggeration," she writes, "to say that my own mother and sister represented the first mother–child pair that I investigated." She adds that during her first year, when she could not sleep at night, her father would instruct her nurse to put her down in her crib, and the nurse would ask him how she could do that while the baby stared at her like a lynx. "This visual overvigilance may initially have been a response engendered by the uncaring mother who, so I thought, wanted me dead" (p. 5). She turned to her father for support and followed his footsteps into medicine, eventually obtaining a medical degree in pediatrics from the University of Vienna.

After practicing pediatrics for a while, she became interested in psychoanalysis. At the recommendation of a fellow Hungarian, Ferenczi, who had taken a liking to her, she entered a training analysis with Helene Deutsch. However, Deutsch dismissed her after about a year saying that she was unanalyzable because she was too paranoid. As a result, the Vienna Psychoanalytic Institute refused to admit her as a candidate for training. She was then rescued by August Aichhorn who, like many men in those days, had taken a fancy to her (she had grown to be a beautiful woman with dark, sensitive, intelligent eyes). He accepted her as an analysand with the avowed purpose of reinstating her at the Vienna Psychoanalytic Institute. She entered analysis with Aichhorn and then went on to attend and graduate from the institute and to have an affair with Aichhorn. After the affair had gone on for a while, however, he referred her to another analyst, Willi Hoffer, with whom she completed her training analysis.

She married Paul Mahler, a chemist and businessman, at the age of 39, and they came to the United States a few years later, part of the wave of Jewish refugees from World War II Europe. It was after coming to the United States that she began to blossom as a psychoanalyst, particularly during the 1950s, when she and Manuel Furer began their historic study of infantile psychosis at the Masters Children's Center in New York. Sponsored by the National Institute for Mental Health, they designed a special nursery where they could observe and treat psychotic children and their mothers. This intensive study continued into the 1960s, when Mahler was joined by Fred Pine and Anni Bergman, and eventually also encompassed the observation of normal mothers and infants. The study resulted in two books—one by Mahler (in collaboration with Furer) (1968), and another by Mahler and colleagues (1975)—and in the development of the theories for which Mahler became famous.

Mahler observed three stages of infantile development. The first stage, the *normal autistic* stage, comprises the first three or four weeks of life. During this stage the infant is totally uncathected to the environment and spends most of its time sleeping. For the next four or five months, the infant goes through the *normal symbiotic stage*, during which it lives in a symbiotic fusion with mother, behaving as if they were a unitary, omnipotent system. Both of these stages fall within what Freud called the period of primary narcissism (Freud 1911). The infant emerges at about the fifth or sixth month into the final stage, the stage of *separation-individuation*. This major stage is divided into four subphases. The *differentiation subphase*, characterized by exploration of the mother's body, continues until about 10 months. The *practicing subphase*, from approximately the tenth to the fifteenth month, begins when the infant learns to walk and is characterized by the child practicing walking away and separating from mother. Then the child must traverse the *rapprochement subphase*, from about the fifteenth month to the third year. During this phase the child undergoes toilet training and discovers the anatomical differences between the sexes, both of which bring about a rapprochement with mother. The final subphase, the *phase of libidinal object constancy*, is an open-ended phase beginning in the third year, roughly equivalent to Freud's oedipal stage, during which the child develops concepts of the self and of primary objects. The successful completion of this stage marks the firm establishment of stable self–other relationships.

Mahler links the development of neurosis to this last subphase, while she traces the beginnings of borderline psychopathology to the rapprochement subphase. She distinguishes between two types of psychosis, autistic and symbiotic, the first linked to a failure of the infant to emerge from the autistic stage due to a constitutionally defective "ego anlage," and the second resulting from maternal deprivation during the symbiotic stage. Violet suffered from the second.

When Violet first came to the Masters Children's Center at 2 years and 7 months of age, "she had an absolutely blank and unanimated facial expression, and she focused on nothing and nobody. She had no verbal language" (Mahler 1968, p. 152). A pretty little girl with long, stringy blond hair, she was well coordinated and moved with an "elflike grace that some psychotic girl patients display," but while her features were pixielike, they were at the same time congealed into a "flat and spiritless expression." During the intake, her mother complained that Violet was destructive and unmanageable, that she would not go to sleep, would not eat, was not toilet trained, did not speak, and threw frequent temper tantrums during which she would tear books, chew phonograph records, and strew them around the room.

Mahler describes the mother as a tense, slender woman in her early twenties, "who smiled a sphinx-like, enigmatic smile" (p. 153). She was easily irritated by the child and tentative in her contacts with her. Mahler observed that she would frequently offer some half hearted guidance to the child, but at the first sign of withdrawal on the child's part, the mother would also withdraw. There were sessions when the mother did not utter a single word to the daughter. The only way the child communicated with the parents, who were both musicians, was through the medium of sound. The child displayed an unusual ear for music and would smile when her mother played the piano. But if her mother or father failed to play a piece precisely as Violet had heard it on a record, she would have a temper tantrum. "In Violet's case," Mahler concluded, "we have a schizoid mother who is warding off her own murderous impulses by detachment and isolation" (p. 154).

Violet's parents had been rather young and infantile when they had her. Her mother had grown up "friendless and alone" in the house of a "brutally sadistic grandmother" and a crippled uncle. She had felt deeply abandoned by both her parents. When the uncle died suddenly, she had nightmares about him in which he came to her room and folded himself up like a fetus. She decided that a baby might bring her out of her misery so she had Violet. Seven weeks after Violet's birth, her own father died, and she sank back into a depression. From that time on, her relationship with the child changed.

The mother reported that her care of Violet was limited to breast-feeding her. In between she was never played with, talked to, or smiled at. "There was thus an alternation of extremes—on the one hand, the very intense relationship of the breast-feeding; on the other, the mother's complete withdrawal between feedings" (p. 151).

During the first nine months, the infant cried a lot. The mother frequently responded to this with rage and with physically aggressive acts. At 8 or 9 months, Violet attempted to smear her feces. When her mother discovered this, she flew into a violent rage and beat the infant. Violet never smeared again. The mother had been unable to gratify Violet's symbiotic needs. "Not even a fully structuralized ego—let alone the rudimentary ego of an infant—could possibly have synthesized and integrated such a compartmentalized pattern with its sharply contrasting feeling tones" (p. 151). By the age of 15 months, the child no longer tried to engage the mother or anybody else with her eyes, and all signs of social contact-seeking had stopped.

The description of Violet's daytime routine, provided by her parents at the intake interview, indicated the kind of deprivation the child had been subjected to all along. For many hours each day the parents would "lock out" the child—that is, lock her in her room—while they practiced their instruments. Violet would bang her head on the floor and thrash her arms and legs about to no avail. The mother explained that she was determined that the child would not get anywhere with her tantrums.

Mahler and her assistants (including Anni Bergman and Miriam Ben-Aaron) employed a treatment technique for Violet

which was composed of two stages: an introductory stage and a
stage of treatment proper. The treatment process involved mother,
child, and therapist. The therapist's first task was to establish some
form of contact with Violet, who was unable to establish or
experience any direct relationship to another person and had, in
fact, regressed to "secondary autism." "The therapist's task can be
conceived as being that of somehow making her presence felt,
allowing the child to experience it as something positive without
any need to acknowledge the existence of the therapist as a person" (p. 195). In the beginning the first therapist, Miriam Ben-
Aaron, never approached Violet from within her visual field, but
from behind. Sometimes she would allow Violet to rest against
her, use her body as a cushion, or use her arms as extensions of her
own. She did not talk much at first, and when she did it was in a
neutral, singsong way, devoid of any emotional appeal "so as not
to intrude upon the child by seeming to demand a response"
(p. 197). After a time, Violet would lean on the therapist more
obviously. Then she allowed the therapist to feed her.

It was observed that at first, when the therapist fed only the
child, the mother took food from Violet's plate while the therapist
was not looking. Only during later periods of treatment, after the
mother had been offered a meal along with her child, and after
other symbolic forms of love had been supplied to both mother
and child, could the mother herself be giving to the child.

The first physical contact between therapist and child that
was acknowledged by Violet was made through a transitional
object—a soap bubble. While they were playing together in water,
Violet lifted her skirt and allowed the therapist to blow a soap
bubble onto her naked stomach. Violet derived great pleasure
from the sensation. Soon the beginning structure of a language
was established—a language of music. Knowing that Violet was
interested in music, the therapist began singing simple, familiar
tunes as she accompanied the child while she played with toys.
There was a song for playing with trains, one for playing with
pegs, and one for playing together.

During this beginning stage of treatment, Mahler asserts, the psychotic child experiences the therapist as a "mothering principle." "The place of the 'mothering principle' in the child with a predominantly autistic defense organization may perhaps be comparable with that stage of the normal symbiotic phase at which the baby dimly recognizes that ministrations that re-establish homeostasis are coming from a good outside environmental source" (p. 198). Gradually Violet came to take for granted the soothing atmosphere emanating from the mothering principle, to seek it out, and to recognize it as coming from the therapist, who, however, was not yet perceived as a whole separate human object.

When Violet had tantrums, the therapist would maintain contact with her through a singsong commentary in a low and soothing voice, which seemed to lessen the intensity of the self-destructiveness. This commentary, like a Greek chorus, interpreted the child's feelings and emphasized the presence of the therapist and mother. "Oh, it hurts!" the therapist would sing. "Don't hurt Violet. She's a nice girl. You are angry with Violet, but we don't want you to hurt yourself because we love you" (p. 199).

After the therapist had established contact with Violet and Violet had begun to accept her as a mothering principle, the therapist led the mother into the same kind of relationship with her child. (The ultimate aim was to reestablish a symbiotic tie to the original object—the mother.) In the beginning Violet's mother was almost as unresponsive as Violet herself. She would sit in rigid silence, and would interpret Violet's unresponsiveness to the therapist and to her as rejection of herself, to which she could only retaliate in kind. To draw the mother into a tripartite relationship with the therapist and the child, the therapist and the therapeutic institution itself had to become a mothering principle to the mother, who had suffered from emotional deprivation in her own childhood. When she was angry, she was fed; when she was tired, she was given a place to nap; when she was talked to by the therapist, it was in a soft voice, and the therapist was always careful to shelter her from criticism. Gradually the mother was able to identify with the therapist and at times even to be more gratifying to Violet.

The therapist succeeded finally in making contact with both mother and child. Her next step was to ask the mother to talk about their life at home, in order to draw her more actively into the treatment process. It took a while, but once the mother began to talk about it, she and her daughter began to grow closer. Music was, in the beginning, the primary mode of communication. One day when the mother spoke of how Violet had been upset that morning, Violet started to play a Mozart sonata on the piano. The mother explained, "This morning Violet's father played a record of this sonata, to quiet Violet when she was upset" (p. 201). On another day, when the mother was very angry with Violet and had relapsed into her old hostile silence, Violet played a tune on the xylophone, and the mother ruefully explained, "That is a song I sing to Violet at night. The words to it are 'I love you, my dear'" (p. 201). As the treatment progressed, Violet showed an "astonishing capacity" to bring about a reconciliation with the mother at times when the mother was retreating into a sullen rage.

The second phase of treatment was concerned with helping the child in "reliving and understanding of the traumatic experiences" that had hampered her development. "The therapist here forms the bridge between the psychotic preoccupations and the reinvestment of the mother" (p. 204). To reestablish a stable investment of the mother by the child, Violet's therapist and her mother had to understand the meaning of her psychotic fetish—the piano.

Violet's relationship with the piano had begun in earliest infancy, when her cradle had been placed near the piano during her parents' practice sessions. At first the piano had been her friend; later it became her rival. When her parents practiced, she would show her anger by biting and scratching the piano and by tearing up the parents' music sheets. Later, when Violet was locked in her room, she would have horrific temper tantrums. The piano was both loved and hated, producing a "lifeline of sound" between her isolated world and her parents' world. Once during the therapy

Violet explored the inside of the piano in a way that made the therapist feel that the piano represented her mother's body, as though she were exploring her mother's face and differentiating it from her own.

During the second phase of treatment, from about the middle to the end of the first year of therapy, Violet communicated almost exclusively through the piano, using it to express more and more complex intrapsychic conflicts. One day, before a Christmas vacation, she chose to play a Clementi sonata on the piano. She took all the repeats over and over and thus avoided ending the piece. "You don't want the piece to end," the therapist interpreted, "just as you don't want your time with me to end" (p. 205). Violet had a crying tantrum, indicating that the interpretation was correct. Then she leaned lovingly against her therapist and played her favorite Christmas song, "Jingle Bells," transposed to a minor key: this expressed, according to Mahler, "her libidinal longing and tender parting feelings" (p. 205). Later on she began playing duets with both her therapist and her mother.

After a year of therapy Violet's first therapist had to leave. She gave Violet a good-bye present, a stuffed dog that she called "Happy Dog." Violet spoke the words "Happy Dog," and for a while these were two of the few words in her vocabulary. This first therapist had also called her "Happy Girl," and Violet often used that phrase when she was either happy or unhappy.

During the second year of therapy, now with a new therapist (presumably Mahler herself), object relations between therapist, mother, and child were further stabilized. At a certain point Violet's mother gave her another stuffed animal, a cat, which she called "Kitty Cat"—words that also remained in Violet's vocabulary. However, at the end of the second year, when Violet's new therapist went on vacation, Violet and the mother regressed almost to the level they had started therapy with, and during that summer Violet managed to lose both Happy Dog and Kitty Cat, her two most cherished possessions.

In the third year of therapy, Violet reexperienced and reenacted traumatic incidents from the past via the piano. For a time she tried to reverse the situation in which she had been locked out while her parents practiced the piano; she now "imperiously demanded" that the therapist sit in the corner of the room while she practiced. Later she worked through the feelings connected with the incident in which, at 9 months, she had smeared her feces on her crib and her mother had beaten her. After this incident, Violet had never again looked at her bowel movement and refused to have one unless she wore either a diaper or panties. The therapist began to create an awareness in Violet of both her need to defecate and of her bowel movement after she had defecated. She then stopped hiding in a corner and had her movements near the piano. She also began to have them on cue—when her mother played a descending major third on the piano. Soon she played it herself when she wanted to have a movement, and the therapist interpreted to Violet that she was playing that piece because she wanted to go to the potty.

As Violet began reliving these past traumas, her relationship with her mother grew worse. The mother stopped coming to sessions for a while and Violet was brought by a succession of baby-sitters. Violet began to have temper tantrums again. If the therapist tried to play something on the recorder, Violet would interrupt her by banging on the piano. The therapist made this into a game: she would begin to play something on the recorder and Violet would interrupt by banging and the therapist would stop playing and say something to Violet like, "Bad things can happen, but we have become friends and our friendship can never be broken" (p. 207). Then the therapist would resume playing and Violet, instead of interrupting, would accompany her on the piano.

Later that third year Violet tried to destroy the piano—a reenactment of early experiences, when she had attacked her parents' piano, their sheet music, or their records. There were two pianos in the therapy room, one old and one new. One day Violet began methodically to take out the insides of the old piano. She was doing to the piano what she wanted to do to her mother's piano, the therapist interpreted. In fact she was doing to the piano what she had once wanted to do to her mother. She would have liked to tear her mother apart. The therapist spoke to Violet about her repeated disappointments by her mother and father as Violet continued her destruction.

During the period she was destroying the piano, she showed a growing ability to handle her mother's wrath. Once, when her mother yelled at her, she went to the door as though to leave and then turned and stood on the threshold. She gazed at her mother with sad, dark eyes.

"You're acting more maturely than I am" (p. 209), the mother remarked, and became aware of how destructively she had been behaving. From then on the mother was able to take up a more positive attitude toward the child.

The summer after the third year it was decided that it was not safe for the mother and daughter to be together without the presence of a therapist, and so Violet was sent to a camp for disturbed children. Several events took place that summer. Violet stopped playing the piano, even though one was available to her at the camp; nor did she play for several months the following year. She also gave up her bottle—something her mother had been trying to get her to do since infancy. And, watching the other children at the camp, she became toilet trained. Finally, she stopped talking. By summer's end she was once again mute, withdrawn, and unable to relate.

It took a few months before the therapist was able to reestablish a bond with Violet. At first she ignored the therapist and would dash here and there, going from one activity to another. Both she and her mother were intolerant about any interpretations about the summer. The mother would only say, again and again, that she should have left Violet at the camp, for she seemed happier there. Violet said nothing. She did not seem to notice her mother's existence. Meanwhile Violet, having turned 6, had begun to attend school and to have her therapy sessions in the afternoon. Once, when her mother was late to pick her up after her therapy session, the therapist interpreted, "This is how you must have felt at camp when it was dark and your mother didn't return" (p. 211).

Slowly a new "symbioticlike" tie was established between the therapist and Violet, and then between Violet and her mother. Violet also began to play with dolls. She made the doll have temper tantrums and be sent out of the room, and worked through separation anxiety by throwing the doll out the window and then retrieving it. Soon she was playing with many dolls, one of which always represented her and was given more food than the others. She also began to draw, and to use drawings to console herself over unavoidable frustrations. Once she had wanted her mother to get gasoline out of a red pump, but her mother had taken gas out of a green one instead. As soon as Violet entered the therapy room, she took out her drawing paper, drew a red pump and a green pump, added a hose from the red pump to the car, and then from the green one to the car. The therapist interpreted that she wanted to tell her mother that if she allowed Violet to have her way, her mother could have her own way as well.

She also began to talk more, and to explore her therapist's and mother's faces, and then her own. Mahler explains that during the second part of the treatment phase there is more differentiation between self and object, more awareness of the environment, and more investment in the objects that form the most important part of the environment. There is also an improvement in secondary process thinking and speech. "These changes lead to the ability to differentiate between the thing, such as the toy or fetish, and the word symbol" (p. 209).

Violet had first become aware of sexual differences at the age of 4½, after meeting a little boy at a friend's house. Afterwards, Violet's mother observed her in the bathtub putting bubbles between her legs. About a year later she became interested in her father's body, wanting to touch and grab his penis. At the same time she became upset if her mother wanted to undress or take a bath—which Mahler interpreted as an effort to deny the fact that her mother and she did not possess penises. During this period she would often dress her doll and then put sand in its pants, the sand representing a penis or a bowel movement. Once her mother caught her trying to urinate through a pipe. In her drawings she drew figures with "many protrusions and penises," and during one session she produced a series of drawings of a little girl with a penis, a little girl wearing patterned stockings like those the therapist wore, and then the little girl wearing a hat with a long tassel. Afterwards she insisted on wearing her hair in a ponytail.

During the following summer, when Violet was once again sent to camp, she was able to handle it much better. She did not regress upon her return at the end of the summer. Instead, she began to speak more and more, using new words like "no" and "Mommy" and "Violet" and "Daddy," and then whole phrases and sentences. Other signs of growth included an ability to play with dolls in a new way, assigning roles to them and taking roles herself.

By the age of 7, after about five years of therapy, Violet had established a functional relationship with her mother. When the mother became enraged and withdrew, Violet was able to "show her mother that her feelings had been hurt, to be sensitive, to cry, and even to approach the mother in a spontaneous demonstration of affection, hugging and kissing her" (p. 214).

To my knowledge, no follow-up studies have been done on Violet. Presumably, she and her mother continued to progress after the termination of therapy. As for Mahler, she became a grande dame of psychoanalysis, her theories revered and generally accepted both by psychoanalysts and by professionals in other fields. Like Klein, she was the leader of a new school of psychoanalysis—combining ego psychology and object relations—with a following of admirers and many detractors as well. Also like Klein, she developed a reputation for being a "difficult woman."

Mahler lived until the age of 88, nursed and attended by an array of psychoanalytic colleagues up to her last hours. She died in 1985 in New York.

Interpretation

Freud referred to his theoretical constructs as "metapsychology," partly because they did not stem from empirical research in the strictest sense, but were based instead on adult patients' reports of their lives and their childhoods. Mahler was one of the first psychoanalysts to base her theories on empirical research, and by doing so she gave to psychoanalysis a legitimacy it did not have before. Her study of normal development, contrasted with the development of infantile psychosis, provided a firm framework for the understanding of the mother-child dyad, of childhood psychopathology, and of its treatment. She also made one of the first attempts to merge drive theory with object relations theory. "My concepts of the normal autistic, the normal symbiotic, and the separation-individuation phases of personality development are genetic constructions," she writes, "which refer primarily to the development of object relationships. They are complementary to the concepts of the oral, anal, and phallic phases, constructions referring to the genetic theory of drive development . . ." (Mahler 1968, p. 219).

Critics of Mahler such as Stern (1977) who, like Mahler, has conducted extensive observations of mother–infant interactions (he diplomatically calls them caregiver–infant interactions), disagree with her about the existence of both the normal autistic and the symbiotic stages. According to Stern, the infant is capable of reaching out to and discerning the difference between himself and his caregiver from the first days after birth. This difference of opinion about the early stages of development, however, may simply be the usual splitting of hairs that goes on in all scientific circles. Mahler did not intend for her depictions of infantile stages to be seen as absolutes; in writing of the normal autistic stage, for example, she postulated that there was "a *relative* absence of cathexis of external (especially distance-perceptual) stimuli" (Mahler et al. 1975, p. 41, italics added). The terms *autism* and *symbiosis* were for her relative ones; she was open to the possibility of cathexis of near-perceptual stimuli.

Tanguay (1977) disputes Mahler's methodology, claiming that it lacks a clear-cut view of what really happens between a mother and a child. He notes that the pilot phase of the project at the Masters

Children's Center allowed her and her investigators to delineate a number of hypotheses about development, but these were not all validated through subsequent testing. Therefore he considers the project's results questionable. Mahler's ideas are useful only as a loose framework, he contends, not as proven theorems.

Proponents of Mahler's work, such as Harrison and McDermott (1980), point out that her data and formulations have implications for many pertinent issues. With regard to the mother–infant interaction, Mahler's views abut the normal autistic stage that ends in the "cracking of the autistic shell" correlate with Benjamin's (1961) observation of a neuro-maturational crisis at around 3 or 4 weeks of age. Both Benjamin and Mahler link their notions to Freud's (1920) concept of an infantile stimulus barrier. They see the mature central nervous system as equipped with a "protective shield" which serves as an inhibitory barrier to stimulation, giving way at about 3 or 4 weeks to a need for symbiotic bonding. Benedek (1949) addressed the same phenomenon from the mother's side, and Kennell and colleagues (1980) have postulated a critical period for maternal bonding at this stage.

Harrison and McDermott also note that Mahler's concept of separation–individuation has been a major influence in many fields. Symbiosis, for example, has been useful in understanding childhood psychosis; the "practicing subphase," when the toddler learns to walk (which Mahler refers to as the child's psychological birth), has illuminated the relationship between biological and psychological development; and the understanding of the psychodynamics of the rapprochement subphase has helped to explain borderline psychopathology. Individuation itself has been used by such disparate schools as family systems theory. "The concept now seems to have emerged as a field of inquiry in its own right. This convergence of interest suggests its potential for integrating phenomenological, transactional, and intrapsychic concepts and for achieving a rapprochement between psychoanalytic and family systems orientations, and between individual and interrelational dynamic theories" (Harrison and McDermott 1980, p. 117).

Kohut (1971) compares his own formulations of early childhood development with Mahler's, calling her theories "not only the most persistently systematic but also the most useful and influential relevant contributions." He asserts that narcissistic transferences that occur during treatment are therapeutic activations of developmental phases which probably correspond to her symbiotic and separation–individuation stages. However, he differs with her in that he hypothesizes two separate lines of normal development: "one which leads from autoerotism via narcissism to object love; another which leads from autoerotism via narcissism to higher forms and transformations of narcissism" (p. 220).

Jacobson (1971) built her theories of depression partly on Mahler's explanation of the underlying conflicts of childhood psychosis. "The basic conflict seems to be of the same order in all depressed states: frustration arouses rage and leads to hostile attempts to gain the desirable gratification. When the ego is unable (for external or internal reasons) to achieve this goal, aggression is turned to the self image" (p. 183). Mahler's studies, according to Jacobson, show how the role of object relations, aggression, the drives in general, and the underlying hostility conflicts are related to infantile depression, and in particular show how the mother's lack of acceptance and "emotional understanding" of the child leads to a decrease in the child's self-esteem, to ambivalence, and to especially aggressive repetitive coercion of the parents. Such attitudes result in a turning of aggression against the self and in a feeling of helplessness.

All of these are visible in the case history of Violet. Her low self-esteem was evident in the slovenly way she looked and dressed, and in her lack of confidence in her ability to get what she wanted from the primary figures around her; her ambivalence and "especially aggressive repetitive coercion" of her parents could be seen in her attacks on the piano and in her insistence on her mother's getting gasoline out of the red rather than the green pump.

Greenberg and Mitchell (1983) give Mahler a mixed review. They credit her with being a major transitional thinker in psychoanalysis, but find a fundamental ambiguity in Mahler's theories of the autistic, symbiotic, and separation-individuation stages. They contend that in her efforts to draw "a developmental map" from the perspective of object relations or, in other words, to meld drive theory with object relations, she had to twist some things around. They call her work "an act of theoretical accommodation. To accomplish this she had to build upon, but also to revise and even distort, a broad range of drive model concepts: psychic energy, libido, the object, object relations, adaptation, the average expectable environment, narcissism, and so on" (p. 301).

For example, they say she:

changed the meaning of the word "object" from its original definition as a target of a drive (libidinal or aggressive) to anything that impinges on an infant's growth

expanded the concept of "narcissism" from a purely energic notion to a formulation that is both cognitive and energic

changed the concept of "environment" so that in her work it came to be synonymous with "mother"

derived both the capacity for delay of drive discharge and neutralization from interpersonal experiences

They wonder, "Has Mahler left the interpretive thrust of the drive model intact or has she introduced a fundamentally new vision of human growth and development?" (p. 301)

Gertrude and Rubin Blanck (1974) appreciate the light Mahler has shed on borderline psychopathology, asserting that "more than those of any of the other theorists, Mahler's contributions lend themselves to direct hypotheses about the nature of borderline phenomena and to transposition into technical procedures" (p. 53). They see as central to Mahler's theories her notion that optimal symbiotic gratification is essential to development. When symbiotic deprivation is severe (as it was in Violet's case),

the child regresses to symbiotic psychosis or secondary autism—
that is to an objectless existence. Such a child then continuously
attempts to merge with its "good" aspect and ward off reengulf-
ment by its "bad" aspect. In summarizing Mahler's scheme of
normal symbiotic development, the Blancks also explain Mahler's
therapy technique: "With an adequate symbiotic experience, however, ego building proceeds. The groundwork for formation of a
body image is laid. A rudimentary capacity to mediate between
inner and outer perception becomes operative" (p. 55).

Mahler was first and foremost a theoretician, and only secondarily a therapist—in contrast to Fromm-Reichmann, who was
primarily a therapist and secondarily a theoretician. Like Klein
and Winnicott, she emphasized the importance of the earliest infancy and of the mother's role, and her theories further elaborated
that role. However, by studying her case history of Violet, her
observations of the mother and the daughter, and her graphic
description of her tripartite treatment process, we can much better
understand her theories, for now we see them in the actual setting
in which they developed.

Mahler's detailed study of Violet's relationship with her
parents provides irrefutable evidence about how psychosis develops in childhood. It is interesting to note that as Violet got better,
her mother became worse. Her narcissistic rage had previously
been acted out on the child through her neglect and abuse, causing
her child to suffer the same kind of deprivation she herself had
experienced. When the therapist began reversing this process for
Violet, it aroused the mother's jealousy and rage, which had
formerly been taken out on Violet; that, too, had to be dealt with
in the therapy. Unfortunately, Violet's father was left out of this
whole process, which may be the only thing about it that might be
faulted.

Mahler's treatment differs significantly from that of her
predecessors in one important respect: She attempts to help the
child adapt to the idiosyncrasies of the parent. As Violet gets
better, she learns to deal with her mother's moods and rages. In a
sense, she now has to be a parent to her mother. Her ego becomes

more flexible than her mother's. This goal is quite different from the therapeutic aim of, say, Winnicott, who in the case of Philip had his whole family adapt to Philip's regressive needs. The irony is that Mahler's treatment aim of having the infant adapt to the mother reflects the line of development which, for Winnicott, would lead to a "false self." From this standpoint Mahler's therapy technique might be questioned. However, if you are dealing with a mother who is herself psychotic, it is easier to cure the child than the mother, since it is easier to reverse a recently developed process in a child than a deeply ingrained process in an adult.

It is interesting to note that Mahler's treatment approach for childhood psychosis parallels that used for narcissistic adults. In the first phase, the therapist attempts to make contact with Violet without being intrusive, allowing Violet to use her as a "mothering principle." Then, in the second phase, when she has established a rapport with the therapist, Violet begins reliving and understanding her traumatic experiences. This is similar to Kohut's (1979) approach but with different wording. In Kohut's initial phase of treatment, the therapist serves as a "selfobject"; once the patient has established an object transference, the therapist offers interpretations that bring about "transmuting internalizations" (see Chapter 9).

Finally, Mahler's work would also seem to corroborate Freud's contentions about infantile sexuality and penis envy. Violet's first genuine contact with her therapist was an exchange that had a sexual connotation: she giggled with pleasure when her therapist pushed a bubble against her naked belly. Later, when she began masturbating, she used a soap bubble to do so. At around the same time she began masturbating, she began expressing curiosity about penises, gave her dolls penises, drew pictures of penises, and started wearing her hair in a ponytail (a symbolic penis according to Mahler).

Mahler's case history about Violet and her mother is both a scientific document and, from a literary standpoint, a work of inspiration. Mahler spent her life attempting to unravel and understand the mother–child dyad, beginning with her observations of her own mother and younger sister. Perhaps she hoped that by doing so she could resolve her own feelings of childhood neglect. Whether she accomplished this we do not know. But we do know that she undoubtedly helped many others prevent or transcend the deprivations she herself had to endure.

6

THE DYNAMICS OF
MANIC-DEPRESSION

Edith Jacobson and Peggy (1971)

Edith Jacobson first began writing about the patient to whom she gave the name "Peggy M." in two papers, "Depression: The Oedipus Conflict in the Development of Depressive Mechanisms" (1943) and "The Effect of Disappointment on Ego and Super-ego Formation in Normal and Depressive Development" (1946). She later presented a more organized version of the case history in her book *Depression: Comparative Studies of Normal, Neurotic, and Psychotic Conditions* (1971), which included a twenty-five-year follow-up of the patient. The case is well known not so much for its description of technique but for its analysis of the dynamics of depression from the standpoint of ego psychology and object relations.

Although Jacobson, like Mahler, attempted to combine ego psychology with object relations, she is considered more of an ego psychologist than an object relationist, continuing in the line of development begun by Freud (1921) and extended by Hartmann (1958). Hartmann is regarded as the father of ego psychology. His work explored the functions of the ego with respect to adaptation, a function hinted at by Freud when he introduced the structural theory and delineated the workings of the id, ego, and superego. Jacobson carried on from where Hartmann left off, exploring in particular the dynamics of the superego in patients suffering from schizophrenia and depression.

Jacobson was born in the same year as Mahler—1897—in Hanau, Germany. Her father was a country doctor and encouraged her to become a physician. She received her medical degree in Munich in 1924 and trained as a psychoanalyst at the Berlin Psychoanalytic Institute, becoming a member of the German Psychoanalytic Society and, in 1934, a training analyst. Among the noted psychoanalysts at the Institute at that time was Hartmann, who came to have a strong influence on her.

When Hitler came to power, Jacobson escaped to Copenhagen. However, while in Copenhagen she heard that one of her patients had been detained by the Gestapo, so she returned to try to help her patient and was herself imprisoned. She was released two years later because of life-threatening thyrotoxicosis, a condition that was to afflict her for the rest of her life. While in prison she made good use of her time, formulating theories about depersonalization based on her observations of other prisoners. After her release she moved to the United States, where she became a member of the New York Psychoanalytic Society, eventually serving as its president. Mahler was also a member. The two of them, both born the same year, both Jewish refugees and noted European psychoanalysts, having immigrated to the United States, quickly became leading figures in the society, sometimes vying with each in a way reminiscent of the territorial battles of Anna Freud and Melanie Klein in England, only on a smaller scale.

From the outset of her psychoanalytic practice, she began extending and revising Freud's and Hartmann's theories, based on her observations of psychotic patients. In her major work, *The Self and the Object World* (1964), she revises Freud's concept of the undifferentiated matrix, proposing that not only the ego and id but also the libidinal and aggressive drives are undifferentiated during earliest infancy. This revision also changes the definition of primary narcissism and primary masochism (the death instinct), since these would now also be seen as undifferentiated in the beginning. Writing of primary narcissism, she relegates it to "the earliest infantile period, preceding the development of the self and object images, the stage during which the infant is as yet unaware of anything but his own experiences of tension and relief, frustration and gratification" (p. 15). Thus, in Jacobson's view, libido and aggression are not innate drives, but are brought into being by good and bad experiences with the mother or caretaker. She distinguishes between the ego (a psychic structure), the self (the totality of the psychic and physical person), and self-representations (the ego's internalized representation of the physical and psychic person). She also distinguishes between the self and object as experienced (the internalized representations) and the self and object in reality. Throughout her writing she attempts to make psychoanalytic terminology more precise. For her, "internalized object representation" was a more precise way of labeling what Klein referred to as "phantasies."

Although Jacobson was known as a "tough lady" with a warm heart, her therapeutic style and her writing were quite classical. In 1940, when Peggy entered treatment with her, Jacobson was a slightly gray, 43-year-old woman with somewhat masculine features and dark, cerebral eyes.

Peggy was 24 at the outset of therapy. Jacobson describes her (1971) as a "tall, attractive, and intelligent-looking" teacher "whose movements were retarded and who had a sad expression. Her friendly, gentle manner lacked spontaneity and warmth" (p. 207). In the beginning Jacobson diagnosed her as a hysteric, since she was able to cooperate, showed a good sense of reality and surprising insight, and developed an "excellent therapeutic alliance." However, later on Peggy harbored a transference psychosis, went into a severe depression, and suffered from experiences of depersonalization. Jacobson then diagnosed her as manic-depressive. During another period, when the patient's fantasies appeared delusional, Jacobson considered her schizophrenic. Eventually Jacobson decided that Peggy might best be classified as a border-line personality of the schizoaffective variety. She definitely had a severe mood-swing; when she was in her hypomanic state her coworkers called her "our little sunshine," and when she was depressed they were silently sympathetic.

"I'm afraid I'm going to lose my job," she told Jacobson during her first session. "I'm also afraid I'm going to lose my boyfriend." She said she had been deeply depressed for many months, and believed her depression was always related to disappointments in her love life. She had had a few unhappy romantic involvements in the past, and had recently begun her first sexual relationship with Sidney, a teacher and her supervisor at work. The relationship had been deteriorating for some time, as had her job performance. She was terrified of being rejected by him and fired from her job. "I need your help," she told Jacobson (p. 207).

Her father suffered from depression and compulsive symptoms. He had an inordinate fear of poverty and would wash his hands constantly, refusing to take food from Peggy because he assumed her hands were dirty. Her mother, a "warm but domineering woman," babied Peggy, protecting her from life and from her aggressive father. She told Peggy that her father had destroyed their home with his unpleasant behavior.

Peggy's analysis led back to a decisive period in her childhood when her brother was born and she was 3½ years old. Until then she had felt loved by both her mother and father, and she remembered taking walks and playing lovingly with her father. When her brother came, she told Jacobson, "everything was over and gone, and I had lost everything . . . as if I had died at that time. Life has been empty ever since" (p. 210).

After her brother's birth, her mother changed. "This was not my mother, it was a different person" (p. 210). Her father changed, too. He was so proud to have a son that he lost interest in Peggy. She sank into her first depression, filled with internalized rage at the baby. What made him so important?

It was his penis. Peggy saw this organ as a powerful, magical instrument that made men independent and aggressive. She hated and envied men for having such an organ, which can give the highest pleasure. She spoke of a feeling of emptiness in the vagina, like hunger. "There is something sad about this emptiness like about an empty life" she complained. A man could temporarily "fill up this defect by the presence of his penis" (p. 211).

Peggy grew up in competition with her brother. She became sweet and nice and smart to show up her brother, who was a charmer but was also a bed-wetter, a poor student, and a rebel. During adolescence she envied his aggressive and uninhibited behavior; she could not allow herself even the slightest aggression or sexual liberty, but clung and looked up to her pretty and competent mother.

At the age of 17 she made the first attempt to liberate herself from her family, failed, and went into a depression. She had tried to start dating, but her father interfered with her relationships. She could not study, could not work, slept badly, felt physically weak, and suffered from hypochondria and phobia.

At 24 she moved away from her family. By then she had completely changed her attitude toward her mother. "She developed an almost paranoid hostility toward the previously adored mother, whom she now held responsible for her sexual failures because 'she made me so dependent and weak'" (p. 208). She moved into the home of a divorced woman, who was living with a man and who "resembled the patient's mother in many ways" (p. 208). Influenced by girlfriends, she started her first sexual relationship—with Sidney, her supervisor.

Early on, Sidney had told her that he was also seeing an old girlfriend. Still she clung to him, feeling depressed after their occasional trysts, always expecting him to abandon her, fantasizing about his betrayal and her revenge. Each time he returned, however, her negative feelings melted and she could only comply. The relationship remained primarily a sexual one, even though intercourse gave her only mild pleasure; still she insisted it was "the only valuable thing" about life. She never had an orgasm, nor did she desire it, for to her orgasm meant "the end of something."

One day, when she had been in analysis for several months, Sidney informed her that his other girlfriend was pregnant and he felt obliged to marry her. They had sex, and then Peggy began to clutch him violently and cry for him not to leave her, not to "take it away!" Afterward she went into an even deeper, paralyzing depression, telling Jacobson everything was over and that she would never love again. Life was senseless, she moaned, melting away. She felt dead already. She felt a blankness like death. She felt alone in space, as though she was the only person in the world.

She had impulses to jump out the window or throw herself under a subway train. She was afraid of losing her job and of contracting tuberculosis. She feared open closets, closed rooms, and elevators. She was terrified of riding the subway, particularly when the train stopped. "Everyone seems to look like wax, all frozen," she said. "The next moment something terrible will happen. There will be a crash, and everything will end up in death and destruction" (p. 209). After a while she broke out of the depression, transformed into the elated "little sunshine," and started another love affair. This affair soon broke up, and was followed by another depression.

Throughout the first two years of the analysis, this pattern repeated itself. "In an elated condition she would start a love affair and throw herself passionately into the new bondage. There was always the same change from initial hopeful, exaggerated expectation to deepest disappointment and despair" (p. 210). It became apparent that her behavior was sabotaging her relationships. Haunted by jealous fantasies about her brother, she would act so cold and detached that she would frighten men into leaving her.

In analyzing Peggy's unsuccessful love life, Jacobson interpreted that it was associated with her envy of her brother and his penis. When Sidney left her—or whenever any lover left her—Peggy saw images of penises, often as large as those of horses. These images both attracted and frightened her, a manifestation of her ambivalence toward penises. She said that she wanted to have a penis in her vagina, even though it might destroy her, and she remembered hating and craving her brother's penis, occasionally dreaming about intercourse with him, once even molesting him when he was still an infant. She wished to deprive him of this organ as well as of the pleasure he got from his mother's breast. "Mother must have taken away my penis and given it to him," she said, "just as he got my mother's breast. I was not even allowed to suck my thumb" (p. 212).

She recalled that in her early childhood, at the age of 2 or 3, her mother had forced laxatives into her mouth, wrapped her body tightly in sheets and held her nose while she struggled. Later her mother compelled her to give up thumb-sucking by tying her hands to the bedposts and smearing bitter stuff on her fingers. The child cried out, "Please let me do it, please let me do it!" When she tried to masturbate, her hands were similarly tied and her body wrapped up. Again she begged, "Please let me do it!" Ever since then, she was never able to masturbate without anxiety, and could never reach orgasm. Bursting into tears, she would beg herself, "Please let me do it!"

The fantasy of throwing herself out the window represented, according to Jacobson, Peggy's impulse to escape the "overpowering psychic and physical tension of masturbation which stopped short of the climax. As if from a threat of suicide, she had to hold herself back on the verge of orgasm to avoid destruction" (p. 212). In addition, while she masturbated she had fantasies of urinating and defecating, which disgusted and frightened her. She had been so rigidly toilet trained, Jacobson explains, that she was clean by the age of 1. For years her mother routinely gave her enemas, which Peggy both feared and enjoyed, and which led to the formation of a passive homosexual relationship with her mother. This was acted out through anal games with a girlfriend at the age of 6 and 7, and became an aspect of her transference toward Jacobson. In their therapy sessions Peggy expected Jacobson to extract ideas from her brain and coax her to new insights, just as her mother coaxed her to defecate.

In the third and fourth year, more and more material came to the surface. With Jacobson's help, Peggy saw that her emotional detachment was linked to the severe restriction of her excretory functions. "She was not allowed to reveal her feelings of either love or hate; she had to hold them back like stool or urine, to deny that they existed" (p. 213). Her cold detachment was modeled after that of her father. He had treated her that way, and she in turn treated her lovers that way.

During a period in the therapy when she was talking about her brother sucking her mother's breast, Peggy's own breasts began to swell; she had cramps and held back her menstruation for weeks. She remembered that her mother had been sick for a while after she had come back from the hospital with the baby, and she was never again as happy as she had previously been. Peggy held the birth of the baby responsible for the change, and she linked her depression to her mother's depression during this period. She also hated her mother for taking away her penis, and she began talking about having a penis inside her cervix that might pop out during orgasm. During one of her sessions she had an anxiety attack as she imagined having an orgasm during which "everything inside her might pour out—penis, feces, urine, and blood—in an outburst similar to the explosion she had experienced when she was given an enema by her mother" (p. 214). Later she said that she had masturbated and had allowed herself to urinate and defecate at the moment orgasm was blocked, and she felt relief. She spoke of growing sensations of inner emptiness throughout her body that nothing could reach.

One day she remembered a traumatic event that had happened when she was 3, before her brother was born. She anxiously recalled sitting astride her father's lap in bed, playing see-saw with him. She thought she must have felt her father's erect penis and must have been aroused. She remembered feeling both excited and horrified and having a wish to take in his gigantic penis.

Suddenly she understood that her images of large horselike penises and her fears of being destroyed by orgasm were related to this scene, in which she as a little girl had felt a desire for, and fear of, her father's large organ.

A while later Peggy recalled another frightening scene from the time of her mother's pregnancy. For two weeks her mother had hired a "schizophrenic Negro housemaid" who one night entered the child's bedroom, carrying a knife and talking out loud to ghosts who were persecuting her. Peggy remembered her fright when she saw the black woman holding the knife, and then remembered her sadomasochistic wishes and fears concerning her mother's pregnancy: she imagined that her mother would take her and put her inside her belly instead of her brother, and she would be imprisoned there and tortured to death. "Mother might snatch up all children and penises around, and swallow them. That is how a woman gets pregnant," she told Jacobson (p. 215).

At one point Jacobson became sick for a few weeks and the treatment had to be interrupted. Peggy was informed of the illness by a physician when she came for a session. Her initial reaction was that Jacobson was a mean person who had left her alone, and was of no further value. Then she imagined that the physician was Jacobson's husband and fantasized taking him away from her. When she realized that she would not meet him again, she began devaluing him and looked forward to seeing Jacobson. She repeated this pattern several other times during the treatment, playing men she was seeing against Jacobson. When she felt disappointed by Jacobson, she would disparage her and talk with rapture about a man she was seeing; when the man disappointed or left her, she would disparage him and speak joyously of her relationship with Jacobson.

As she began to get more and more in touch with her anger and disillusionment with both her parents, she sank into a full-fledged depression that had deep narcissistic and masochistic features. Again and again she threatened to terminate therapy and live by herself, away from everybody. Then she remembered yet another traumatic scene—having witnessed her parents making love when she was 2½ years old. As she recalled this scene during the analytic hour, she became extremely anxious, dizzy, had diffi-

culty breathing, and felt as though she were dying. She saw a
picture of a woman with her head back, her mouth open, gasping
for breath, and sinking as if she were dead. Two other memories
came a short time later. When she was 5, she saw her mother lying
in bed, breathing heavily, almost dying of pneumonia; two years
later her own tonsils were taken out under anesthesia, and she had
a sinking feeling that she was going to die. These experiences were
linked to her fear of orgasm.

She had fantasies of killing both parents. She imagined helping her father tear down and kill her mother, sucking out her
genitals. She imagined killing her father, biting off his penis and
devouring his intestines. The destructive fantasies and urges grew
stronger. She also had schizophrenic notions that she had endowed
Jacobson with magical power; then she feared that this power
might vanish and she herself would collapse, since she depended
on Jacobson as her "only value." "In a frantic effort she tried to
build up the image of the analyst again, and to cling to it as to the
omnipotent goddess who might protect her from her archaic,
threatening superego which persecuted her with magic fears of
destruction" (p. 220). Her superego had been transformed by
frightening introjects. She felt that the objects she had physically
incorporated—bad mother, bad father, penises, babies, snakes—
would destroy her from within. She tried to suppress these objects, and the hostility bubbling up inside her, by assuming the
role of the good and powerful parents, but this did not work well.
She sank deeper into a depression, preferring to submit "to a
punishing superego, which promised future reconciliation and
happiness, than to a fatal liberation of her destructive impulses"
(p. 225).

Eventually, she could no longer hold on to the rage that
wanted to erupt inside her. She reached a point at which she
thought she would either go crazy or commit suicide. Jacobson
scheduled a four-hour session during which she finally unleashed
all the demons. Along with the release came an understanding of
how her defenses worked. Jacobson explains that she avoided her
psychic conflicts by pretending that she or the world was dead.

Her use of denial had first surfaced during the seduction by her father and in the observation of the primal scene; it had appeared again during the traumatic interruption of her masturbation. "It accounted for the detachment and coldness toward the love partner, the fading of sensation during intercourse, and the periods of blank depression with the feeling of complete inner death, of nothingness" (p. 221).

After about five years Peggy reached the critical stage of her analysis when she understood that her state of detachment protected her from her dangerous fantasy life. Finally her ambivalent feelings toward Jacobson broke through directly and could be analyzed. At the same time, she was able to achieve her first real love relationship, with the man she would eventually marry.

In reviewing the case, Jacobson hypothesizes that Peggy's psychopathology was brought about by experiences of disillusionment and abandonment at an early infantile stage. Peggy responded to these experiences with intense hostility, which made them all the more devastating. Such disillusionment at stages when the boundaries between object and self images are not yet firmly established, Jacobson contends, may lead to a severe pathology that impedes development of both object relations and narcissism. After recovery from primal depression, Peggy reached out again for her lost love objects and her narcissistic libido was thereby partly "retransformed into object libido." However, since her oedipal development was disrupted at the beginning of the genital stage, her object relations retained the features of preoedipal-narcissistic dependence and submission. She expected too much from the love objects as well as the self, and this could not be gratified. She overvalued and idealized the love objects and her ego ideal could not be attained.

Regarding Peggy's mania, Jacobson observes that in some types of hypomanic and manic conditions "the ego escapes into an illusion of power by an alliance with the id, but actually gives up its essential functions," while, in other forms, mania "represents a victory of love over destruction" that leads to a true growth of the ego (p. 227). In Peggy's case her slow recovery from depression and her transition into hypomania were related to the decline of her punishing superego and the rise of her "elated ego" as it pursued social interests, cultural strivings, and love relationships.

She terminated therapy in about 1945 to go to California to marry her boyfriend. However, since he did not propose to her right away, wanting first to earn enough money to support her, she suddenly left him (regressing to her repeating pattern) and returned to New York at her mother's behest. Peggy and her mother had a follow-up session with Jacobson, and Peggy soon went back to marry the man. As she did with many patients, Jacobson kept track of Peggy after termination, and she reported that Peggy "remained clinically healthy over the next twenty-five years . . . was happily married, and was successful in her work" (p. 320).

Never in robust health, Jacobson was nevertheless able to reach the age of 81, partly due to the care of her good friend and personal physician, Nora Gottschalk. She never married.

Interpretation

Jacobson became interested in the study of severely depressed patients from the moment she immigrated to the United States, and Peggy was one of the first patients to come to her. Although this case does not reveal very much about her therapeutic technique, one can glean something about the way she worked from the clues that appear along the way. We know, for example, that she generally used an ego psychology approach, eliciting and interpreting Peggy's infantile fantasies and memories. We know that she felt it was important for the patient to establish a good therapeutic alliance from the outset, and Peggy did. We know that she was willing to schedule a four-hour session toward the end of the treatment in order to accommodate Peggy's need to unleash the "demons" of her superego. It is also apparent that Jacobson encouraged Peggy's regression to a childlike state, in which Peggy could remember and report fantasies of wanting a penis, of being imprisoned and tortured inside her mother's body, of her mother snatching up "all the children and penises around," and so on.

In another chapter in *Depression*, Jacobson considers the technical issues of working with depressives, asking how can we let the intensely ambivalent transference of depressives develop sufficiently to allow its analysis while safeguarding against the patient's leaving treatment prematurely, as a result of having become either too manic or too depressed? She proposes several parameters for working with such patients. One is flexibility in scheduling appointments—the flexibility she showed with Peggy. "With regard to frequency of sessions, the prevailing attitude among analysts has been to give severely depressed patients daily sessions," she writes. "My experience has taught me differently. I believe that the emotional quality of the analyst's responses is more important than the quantity of sessions" (1971, p. 298). She advises scheduling three or four sessions a week instead of six or seven, observing that daily sessions are often seen as seductive promises or as intolerable demands that arouse masochistic submission to the therapist.

She elaborates on her belief that the analyst's emotional response is the crucial aspect of treatment with depressives, saying that what such patients need is "a sufficient amount of spontaneity and flexible adjustment to their mood level, warm understanding, and especially unwavering respect—attitudes which must not be confused with overkindness, sympathy, reassurance" (p. 299). At critical moments during the treatment, analysts must be prepared to respond with spontaneous gestures of kindness or brief expressions of anger, so as to help patients through dangerous depressive phases. However, she warns that depressives are frequently provocative and exasperating, so that any emotional response requires the most careful self-scrutiny and self-control. "The therapeutic success with depressives can best be gauged by their ability to remodel an unfortunate life situation which prior to analysis was bound to precipitate depressive states" (p. 301).

One can see in her work with Peggy how Jacobson strove to help her patient remodel her "unfortunate life situation"—the self-defeating pattern of her romantic life—by analyzing and interpreting its links with her unresolved infantile conflicts. In her use of emotional responses she is in agreement with Winnicott (1947) and Spotnitz (1985, see chapter 10). She also foreshadowed the work of Kohut (1971, 1977, see chapter 9), allowing Peggy and similar patients to form what Kohut would have called an idealizing transference without immediately interpreting it. At a certain point in the treatment, Peggy alludes to her idealization of Jacobson, expressing fear that the power with which she had endowed the analyst might vanish. Then, she herself would collapse. This marked a turn toward independence.

Greenberg and Mitchell (1983) also attest to the similarity between Jacobson's and Kohut's analytic techniques, noting that Jacobson addressed many of the same questions as Kohut—for example, whether the deepest pregenital fantasy material could and should be interpreted (both thought it could with some patients, and could not with others), and whether analysts should allow patients to "use" them. Citing another case history by Jacobson, in which she permitted a patient to use her in whatever ways and for whatever roles he needed, they suggest, "This constitutes a clear statement of the handling of what Kohut would call a self-object transference" (p. 324).

Commenting on her treatment of Peggy, Gero (1981) appreciates Jacobson's personal warmth and sensitivity, which he says comes through the clinical material. "One cannot help but admire Jacobson's courage, determination, and conviction that she could help this patient. I believe that the ultimate success of the therapy was as much dependent upon this quality of Jacobson's personality as it was upon her profound understanding of the pathological process" (p. 76).

Frosch (1983) believes that in working with psychotic patients, a therapist's personality is of crucial importance, noting that during the acute phase most successful therapists use their personalities to handle the vicissitudes of the transference. He observes that Jacobson, like Fromm-Reichmann, stresses that the analyst must become the "central love object" for some patients (as she did for Peggy), and wonders if a special, charismatic personality such as Jacobson's or Fromm-Reichmann's is necessary for success with such patients. He recalls an incident in which one of his own patients improved not because of the correctness of his interpretations but because, as she later reported, she liked the sound of his voice. Jacobson's work with depressed patients and her work on the theory of depression is, he believes, of the first rank. "In more recent years some of the most significant contributions on psychotic depression have been made by Jacobson," he says, adding that "she lays emphasis on the somatic substrate in much of depressive symptomatology" (p. 185).

Frosch differs with analysts such as Sandler, Glover, and Anna Freud, who argue that because Jacobson and others deviate from classical psychoanalytic technique, they should no longer call what they do psychoanalysis. He believes that "if one approaches a patient as an analyst, with an analytic attitude, if one uses an analytic way of thinking and deals with situations in the treatment within an analytic frame of reference, then this is part and parcel of the procedure" (p. 466). Analysts who make fine distinctions about what is or is not analysis, Frosch concludes, are carrying formalism to an extreme degree.

With regard to Jacobson as a theorist, Greenberg and Mitchell (1983) rate Jacobson somewhat below Freud. "As a result of her willingness to challenge all the essentials of psychoanalytic theory," they assert, "Jacobson's work overall constitutes what we consider the most satisfying drive/structure model theory after Freud's" (p. 306). However, they say that Jacobson's "recasting" of long-standing psychoanalytic hypotheses is not without a price. In her more theoretical writing, her prose is dense, "almost impenetrable"; there are apparent internal contradictions, and "hairs are split and resplit" until the reader loses interest.

Jacobson's theory, they say, consists of a complex mix of experiential and metapsychological concepts. "Although she insists that experiential concepts—pleasure as she has redefined it, the 'self,' and the 'object world'—are derived from innate, biologically given drives, her emphasis is on the phenomenological, and therefore relational side of things" (p. 325). They point to her use of the word "disappointment" instead of "frustration," as an example of how she has recast the terminology of drive/structural model thinking. Although they view Jacobson's attempt to derive metapsychological answers from phenomenological explanations as problematic, they believe that, ultimately, "the difficulties of her theoretical superstructure are as seminal and provocative as her insights are satisfying" (p. 326).

Kernberg (1975) agrees with Jacobson that the wide mood swings of manic-depressive personalities coincide with feelings of self-esteem. "Mood swings are the main indicators of self-regard at primitive levels of superego-determined regulation of self-esteem," he asserts. "At more advanced levels of superego functioning, more precise, delimited cognitive appreciation or criticism of the self replaces the regulation by mood swings" (p. 318). He also accepts Jacobson's analysis of the levels of superego development and their regulatory effects on the self: The superego regulates mood through its punitive feature, which provides criticism of the self, and through the ego-ideal (resulting from the introjection of idealized object and self images), which builds up the self and increases self-esteem when standards are met. The process could be seen in Peggy's history. "Clinically, it is dramatic to observe how overdependent some patients become on external sources of admiration, love, and confirmation when they suffer from an absence or inadequate integration of this particular superego structure" (p. 319).

The Blancks (1974) contend that one of Jacobson's major contributions is to emphasize—along with Spitz (1965) and Hartmann (1958)—the growth-promoting features of the aggressive drive. "Jacobson points out that, by the end of the first year, the child experiences not only frustration but also ambition, possessiveness, envy, rivalry, disappointment, failure. Through these he learns to distinguish his own feelings and the feelings of others" (p. 66). They also cite Jacobson's understanding of depression as the affective consequence of the primitive ego's inability to mourn early object losses. "Disillusionment and abandonment at an early age, when boundaries between self and object representations are not yet firmly established, may lead to depression, pathology in object relations, and narcissism. Objects become overvalued and overidealized. The wishful self images (ego ideal) cannot be realized. A brittle equilibrium may be . . . disturbed by later disappointment, leading to denigration of self and object" (p. 72).

The story of how Jacobson returned to Nazi Germany, despite the risks to herself, in order to come to the aid of a patient, says something about her character, about her strengths and weaknesses as a clinician. Returning to Nazi Germany was both courageous and stubborn. This courage later enabled her to reach patients other therapists might not have been able to reach, because she dared to try new interventions or to reveal herself emotionally; it also enabled her to tackle difficult theoretical concepts and expand them. Her stubbornness—which originally got her imprisoned and resulted in lifelong illness—caused her to take on more patients than she could handle (leading to overwork and the exacerbation of her illness) and to attempts at theoretical revision that could not succeed, because they entailed mixing two distinct systems of thought, metapsychological and phenomenological.

Ego psychologists in general often suffer from a kind of nearsightedness, as if they were looking at human behavior through a microscope. By focusing on drives, defenses, fantasies, and other psychic structures, they sometimes miss the overall picture—the object relations, the family system, the societal and cultural factors, the biological contributions, and the racial aspects. In addition, their writing is often bogged down with jargon and with "hairs split and resplit," as Greenberg and Mitchell aptly put it. Jacobson, like Mahler, made a bold attempt to break out of this nearsightedness, but she did not succeed entirely.

However, to the extent that she did succeed, she made key contributions to psychoanalysis. Just as Fromm-Reichmann's work with Joanna Greenberg and other schizophrenics broke new ground, Jacobson's analysis of Peggy and other depressives opened up new vistas in the understanding and treatment of patients with affective disorders. She will be remembered as a pioneer in charting emerging concepts such as *self-representations*, *depersonalization*, and *magical thinking*, and in exploring the permutations of the superego in psychotic processes. She will also be remembered as a human being of integrity, intelligence, and warmth, who devoted her life to the practice and study of psychoanalysis.

7

AN ANALYST
ANALYZES
AN ANALYST

W. R. D. Fairbairn
and Harry Guntrip (1975)

"I can't think what could motivate any of us to become psycho-therapists," W. Ronald D. Fairbairn once told his patient Harry Guntrip, "if we hadn't got problems of our own" (Guntrip 1975, p. 245). Guntrip went into treatment with Fairbairn in 1954, a few years after Fairbairn had published a book (1952) that proposed radical changes in psychoanalytic theory. Years later, when he was in his early seventies, Guntrip recalled his therapy with Fairbairn and compared it with his later analysis with Winnicott—the two giants of the object relations school of psychoanalysis. His paper, "My Experience of Analysis with Fairbairn and Winnicott," has since become a classic.

The importance of this paper lies in the fact that it provides an analyst's appraisal of his therapy with another analyst (for the purposes of this chapter we will concentrate on his appraisal of

Fairbairn), and that it is not an idealized portrait, such as most analysts present of their own work, but an objective description that shows Fairbairn as a somewhat rigid, authoritarian clinician who was not entirely successful in treating Guntrip.

Fairbairn was born in Scotland. He studied medicine and later practiced as a psychiatrist and as a psychoanalyst in Edinburgh. For a long time, he was the only psychoanalyst in Scotland. Early in his career he came under the influence of Klein, and his theories were very much influenced by her. However, perhaps due to his isolation, he was never psychoanalyzed himself, and Klein used this fact to put down his work when he stunned the British Society at a meeting in 1943 by declaring, in an epoch-making statement:

> . . . in my opinion the time is now ripe for us to replace the concept "phantasy" by a concept of an "inner reality" peopled by the Ego and its internal objects. These internal objects should be regarded as having an organized structure, an identity of their own, an endopsychic existence and an activity as real within the inner world as those of any object in the outer world. To attribute such features to internal objects may at first seem startling to some, but, after all, they are only features which Freud has already attributed to the Super-Ego. [Grosskurth 1986, p. 320]

After she had heard about these views, Klein reportedly scoffed that this upstart who had never even been analyzed was proposing theories similar to hers without giving her credit (Grosskurth 1986, p. 326). What Fairbairn was proposing was a radical new theory that, on one hand, dispensed with Klein's notion of the childhood "phantasy," and on the other, also discarded Freud's tripartite structural theory of the ego, id, and superego and substituted for it another tripartite system which seemed quite similar but employed different language. In Fairbairn's new system, there are three egos, which develop in response to three common types of mothers, as experienced by the infant: (1) The *infantile libidinal ego* develops as a reaction to the tantalizing mother who excites without satisfying. It hungrily and unceasingly craves love, approval, and sexuality; (2) The *infantile antilibidinal ego* develops in response to the rejecting, angry, authoritarian, antilibidinal mother. It is childishly moralistic, negative, hostile, self-persecuting, and resistant to relationships and therapy; (3) The *central ego* develops in response to the emotionally neutral, morally idealized mother. It attempts to maintain an equilibrium based on an idealized mother identification. Not only did Fairbairn (1952) displace Freud's structural theory, he also dispensed with the libido theory, stating that "the ultimate principle from which the whole of my special view is derived may be formulated in the general proposition that libido is not primarily pleasure-seeking, but object-seeking" (p. 137). In stating emphatically and clearly that the underlying motivation of a human being is to seek contact with other objects rather than to seek pleasure in and of itself, Fairbairn broke completely with Freud and established as a separate entity the object relations school of analysis.

Fairbairn's brilliance as a theoretician remains unquestioned; however, his skill as a clinician was questioned by Guntrip, who became a major figure in the object relations school in his own right through the publication of many papers and three books (1961, 1969, 1971). When his paper dealing with his treatment with Fairbairn and Winnicott appeared posthumously in the *International Review of Psycho-Analysis* in 1975 it became the cause of heated discussion among analysts, since it was written with an honesty that is rare for analysts (or for anyone else), and since it showed that Fairbairn as a clinician was much more Freudian than his writings had indicated.

Guntrip traveled by train from Leeds—where he taught at the university and conducted his own practice—to Edinburgh several times a week for about four years. Fairbairn lived in the country and saw patients in "the old Fairbairn family house," described by Guntrip in detail. He reports entering a large drawing room that served as waiting room, furnished with antiques, and proceeded to the consulting room, lined with a big antique bookcase. Fairbairn sat behind a large flat-topped desk, "in state" in a high-backed armchair. Guntrip lay on a couch with its head to the front of the desk. "At times I thought he could reach over the desk and hit me on the head" (Guntrip 1975, p. 148).

It struck Guntrip as odd that Fairbairn, who felt that the analyst could not be a blank screen but had to relate emotionally to the patient, should sit behind a desk in such a formal fashion. Later he realized that there was an upright chair he could have sat in, but he had *chosen* to lie on the couch.

Guntrip's first dream, a few weeks into the treatment, proclaimed the transference situation. The dream took place at his father's church—his father had been a Methodist minister—but instead of his father, Fairbairn appeared. Consciously Guntrip wanted to think of Fairbairn as his protective father, helping him to stand up to his aggressive mother, but unconsciously he felt otherwise. He dreamed:

> I was in Father's Mission Hall. Fairbairn was on the platform but he had mother's hard face. I lay passive on a couch on the floor of the Hall, with the couch head to the front of the platform. He came down and said, 'Do you know the door is open.' I said, 'I didn't leave it open', and was pleased I had stood up to him. He went back to the platform. [p. 148]

The dream was a thinly disguised version of Fairbairn's consulting-room. To Guntrip, the dream showed a clear negative transference of his "severe dominating mother" onto Fairbairn. Fairbairn interpreted it as "the one up and the other down bad parent–child seesaw relation. It can only be altered by turning the tables." According to Guntrip, Fairbairn continually interpreted his relationship to his mother as an oedipal problem, which Guntrip could not accept; this was further cause for Guntrip's casting Fairbairn as the dominating mother. However, after each therapy session, Fairbairn and Guntrip would have a "theory and therapy discussion period," during which Fairbairn could "unbend" and become "the good human father."

Guntrip says he went to Fairbairn to break through his amnesia surrounding the period of his brother's death to whatever lay behind it in infancy. Like most people, Guntrip had no recall of events in his early childhood, particularly those that had occurred before his third year, when his brother Percy had died. However, he did remember this episode, which became central to his treatment with Fairbairn.

Guntrip's mother had been an overburdened "little mother" before she married—the eldest daughter of eleven children, who saw four siblings die. Her mother (Guntrip's grandmother) was a "feather-brained beauty queen," who left her eldest daughter to manage everything, even when she was still a schoolgirl. She grew up with a "strong sense of duty," which impressed Guntrip's father. They married in 1898, but Guntrip's father did not know that his wife had had her fill of mothering babies and did not want any more. When he was 1 year old, his mother decided to put her energy into running a shop and Guntrip was left in the care of an aunt. (Later, in her old age, Guntrip's mother confided to Guntrip that she breast-fed him because she believed that it would prevent another pregnancy. She had refused to breast-feed Percy and when he died, his father blamed the death on this fact. After Percy's death, she refused to have sex with her husband.) "I ought never to have married and had children," his mother told him later. "Nature did not make me to be a wife and mother, but a business woman." On another occasion she said, "I don't think I ever understood children. I could never be bothered with them" (p. 149).

Guntrip recalled that when he was 3½ years old he had seen his younger brother lying naked and dead in his mother's lap. He rushed up, grabbed his brother, and said, "Don't let him go. You'll get him back!" (p. 149). His mother sent him out of the room and soon he himself fell "mysteriously ill" and was thought to be dying. The doctor on the scene said, "He's dying of grief for his brother. If your mother wit can't save him, I can't" (p. 149). His mother sent him to stay with his aunt, and there he recovered. Both Fairbairn and Guntrip felt that he would have died if his mother had not sent him away at that point.

Guntrip could remember very little of his childhood before his treatment with Fairbairn, but these traumatic events had "remained alive" in him, occasionally triggered off by widely spaced analogous events in his life. At the age of 26 he had a college friend who became a brother-figure. Once, when he had to leave his friend to go home for a vacation with his mother, he fell ill with a "mysterious exhaustion illness" that disappeared as soon as he returned to college. When he was 37, he became minister of a church in Leeds, and there he formed a close friendship with an associate minister. When the friend left "as war clouds loomed up," Guntrip again fell ill with the same mysterious exhaustion. Having at that point begun to study psychoanalysis, he could now analyze the illness and realize that it was related to his younger brother's death, and that he "lived permanently over the top of its repression" (p. 149).

The first few years of his analysis with Fairbairn, Guntrip says, seemed in some sense to be a revival of his situation after his younger brother had died. After Percy's death, from the time he was 3½ until he was 5, Guntrip sought "to coerce mother into mothering" him by repeated "petty psychosomatic ills, tummy aches, heat spots, loss of appetite, constipation and dramatic, sudden high temperatures . . ." (p. 150). From age 5 to 8, he changed tactics and became disobedient. His mother would fly into violent rages and beat him with a cane. When the cane broke she made him go out and buy another one. Finally, when he was 8, his mother's shop became more successful and she began to treat him better. By then, however, the damage had been done. In her old age she told him, "When your father and Aunt Mary died and I was alone, I tried keeping a dog but I had to give it up. I couldn't stop beating it" (pp. 150–151). She had not been able to stop beating her son, either.

Just as he had tried to coerce his mother into mothering him, so also did Guntrip try to coerce Fairbairn, in the first few years of their analysis, to become his protecting father. However, because of Fairbairn's broadly oedipal interpretations of his "internalized bad–object relations," this did not work. Also, there seemed to be a distinct difference between Fairbairn the therapist, and Fairbairn the colleague, with whom Guntrip discussed each of his therapy sessions immediately following their completion.

Fairbairn the therapist, Guntrip claims, fostered the negative transference through his "very intellectually precise interpretations." Once he interpreted Guntrip's dominating mother with the statement, "something forecloses on the active process in the course of its development" (p. 148). Guntrip thought to himself that he might have said the same thing in quite different language: "Your mother squashed your naturally active self" (p. 148). Although Guntrip felt that Fairbairn accurately analyzed his emotional struggle to force his mother to mother him after his brother's death, he could never accept Fairbairn's persistence in viewing this struggle in oedipal terms.

In his last paper, dealing with the aims of psychoanalysis (1958), Fairbairn had emphasized the "internal closed system" of broadly oedipal analysis, and he brought this technique soundly to bear on Guntrip's case. Fairbairn would repeatedly refer to the period of four years following Percy's death, during which he had tried to force his mother "to relate," as the "oedipal internalized bad–object relations period." When Guntrip's dreams became filled with this "bad–object relations" theme but were at the same time permeated by the "eruption" of "schizoid experiences," Fairbairn would steadily interpret them as "withdrawal" in the sense of "escapes from internalized bad–object relations." He would continually point out to Guntrip "oedipal, three-person libidinal and anti-libidinal conflicts in his inner world"—Kleinian object splits and Fairbairnian ego splits "in the sense of oedipal libidinal excitations" (p. 147).

When Guntrip complained about Fairbairn's insistence on interpreting this material as oedipal, drawing his attention to the fact that in his writing he had de-emphasized the Oedipus complex, Fairbairn retorted, "The Oedipus complex is central for therapy but not for theory" (p. 148). Guntrip was confused. He thought theory *was* therapy, and that the two could not be separated. He could not accept Fairbairn's oedipal triangle interpretations, which were probably about his wanting to get rid of his antilibidinal mother but at the same time winning his libidinal, exciting mother away from his brother. He probably could not accept that he had oedipal guilt about his brother's death. These differences of opinion between analyst and patient remained a point of contention between them, and at times Guntrip could no longer contain his anger.

When Guntrip "accidentally" knocked over Fairbairn's pedestal ashtray and kicked his glass doorstopper Fairbairn quickly interpreted that Guntrip was acting out transference anger. When, at another point, Guntrip tore some books out of his bookcase and threw them over the floor, Fairbairn interpreted that this act was symbolic of "tearing a response out of mother," and putting them back was symbolic of making reparation, à la Melanie Klein.

After the therapy sessions, when Fairbairn became the loving father, he would confess that one could go on analyzing forever and get nowhere. He would stress that it was the personal relation that was therapeutic. Science, he would contend, had no values except scientific "schizoid" values. It was useful for a time but then one had to get back to living. On one such occasion he said, "The basic pattern of personality once fixed in early childhood, can't be altered. Emotion can be drained out of the old patterns by new experience, but water can always flow again in the old dried up water courses" (p. 145). In these discussion sessions Fairbairn was a human being who professed a belief in the personal relation between therapist and patient but was nevertheless skeptical about the whole process. This contrasted to the rigid, nonpersonal analyst who sat "in state" behind his desk during the therapy sessions, striving for a cure.

The debate over whether his problem was oedipal or not came to a head when Guntrip brought in what he thought was the most striking example of a nonoedipal dream:

> I was being besieged and was sitting in a room discussing it with father. It was mother who was besieging me and I said to him: 'You know I'll never give in to her. It doesn't matter what happens. I'll

never surrender'. He said, 'Yes. I know that. I'll go and tell her' and he went and said to her, 'You'd better give it up. You'll never make him submit', and she did give up. [p. 148]

After three or four years of this, Guntrip became convinced that Fairbairn's contention that his brother's death and the years following it were central to his problems was not only wrong but was keeping him "marking time in a sadomasochistic inner world of bad object relations with mother, as a defence against quite different problems of the period before Percy's death" (p. 151). This deeper material, going back to his earliest infancy, kept pushing through. Then in 1958 Fairbairn fell ill with a serious viral influenza of which he nearly died, and he had to stop working for six months. While Fairbairn was ill, Guntrip began to "intellectualize" the problem he could not work through in therapy. He wrote several papers that later became the basis of a book. These papers took him "right beyond Fairbairn's halting point," and when Fairbairn returned to work in 1959, he "generously accepted them" as a valid extension of his own work.

He also gave Guntrip a telling interpretation. "I think since my illness I am no longer your good father or bad mother, but your brother dying on you" (p. 151). Guntrip suddenly saw the analytical situation in a different way. He knew that he would have to leave Fairbairn. Once Fairbairn had become his brother in transference, to lose him, either by ending the analysis or by remaining in treatment with him until he died, would be the symbolic death of Percy, which Guntrip feared would bring on a full scale eruption of that traumatic event, with nobody around to help him through it.

Since Guntrip had already decided to seek analysis with Winnicott, he began to phase out his analysis with Fairbairn that year. Ironically, it was Fairbairn who had first introduced him to Winnicott, asking Winnicott to send Guntrip a copy of one of his papers. Winnicott had included a note that said, "I do invite you to look into the matter of your relation to Freud, so that you may have your own relation and not Fairbairn's. He spoils his good work by wanting to knock down Freud" (p. 151). Apparently, these words by Winnicott had stayed in Guntrip's mind; perhaps they had even had an influence on his transference toward Fairbairn.

Later, after terminating with Fairbairn, he would discover in Winnicott a much more human and intuitive therapist who was able to be a "good mother," establishing a holding environment while Guntrip recovered his lost infancy. In their second session, Winnicott put his finger on the problem that had evaded Fairbairn, suggesting that he must have had an earlier illness before Percy was born, when he had first felt abandoned by his mother. "You accepted Percy as your infant self that needed looking after. When he died, you had nothing and collapsed" (p. 152). Because of Winnicott's "profound intuitive insight," Guntrip was no longer alone with "a nonrelating mother." Thanks to Winnicott, he began to realize that the first abandonment had occurred almost as soon as he had been born, and rather than a sibling rival, Percy had been, through identification, his "infant self," a companion against their "depersonalized" and "depressed" mother. When Percy died, it was as if Guntrip himself had died.

Winnicott also shed light on an aspect of the transference situation that had evaded Fairbairn. Noting that people were always commenting on Guntrip's ceaseless activity and energy, and that in sessions Guntrip did not like gaps of silence and talked ceaselessly, Winnicott commented, "You have to work hard to keep yourself in existence. You're afraid to stop talking, acting, or keeping awake. You feel you might die in a gap like Percy, because if you stop acting mother can't do anything" (p. 152).

Eventually, what Guntrip feared would happen during his analysis with Fairbairn *did* happen during his treatment with Winnicott: Winnicott passed away. But because of Winnicott's "good mothering," Guntrip had by then developed his own internalized good mother and was able to endure Winnicott's death without sinking into illness himself. Fairbairn also passed away soon thereafter, leaving Guntrip to carry on. He, too, would die a few years after recording his case history with them.

In summing up his experience with these two analysts, Guntrip states that each was of assistance to him. Fairbairn had helped him to understand Percy's death and its aftermath, and had assisted him in resolving the negative transference of his "dominating mother," eventually becoming another good father who had faith in him. Winnicott had entered "into the emptiness" left by his "non-relating mother," so that he could experience the security of being his own self.

He recalls that during his last session with Fairbairn, although the two had never shaken hands before, he had put out his hand and Fairbairn at once took it, "and I suddenly saw a few tears trickle down his face. I saw the warm heart of this man with a fine mind and a shy nature" (p. 149). Fairbairn invited Guntrip and his wife to tea whenever they were in town.

According to Fairbairn (1952), adult psychopathology, such as that described in this case, is the result of developmental failures—due to traumas and deprivations—to move successfully from the early state of infantile dependence and of the defensive reactions to these failures. The basic conflicts underlying these failures, he theorizes, borrowing from Klein (1932), are the schizoid ("to love or not to love")—wanting to love an object but fearing that the intensity of this love will devour and destroy the object—and the depressive ("to love or to hate")—wanting to love the object but fearing that the intensity of one's hate will destroy the object.

In contrast to Kernberg (see Chapter 11), who sees splitting as central to borderline personalities, Fairbairn feels that splitting is universal, to be found in psychotics and neurotics alike. According to Fairbairn, the infant splits the figure of mother into good and bad objects in order to diminish the experienced ambivalence of the object. The infant then internalizes the bad object—"to remove it from outer reality, where it eludes his control"—to the sphere of inner reality. The bad object is then further split into the exciting object and the rejecting object, which in turn become the libidinal and antilibidinal egos. However, these internalized objects are never completely integrated into an individual's psychic structure, for they have been implanted there as the result of developmental failures; they were not part of the "original pristine unitary ego"—that is, the healthy self.

The main task of therapy for Fairbairn is to exorcise the internalized objects and then discover what remains of the original pristine unitary ego. What Fairbairn suggests, in other words, is that humans are born whole and that parental rejection, deprivation, and frustration (and the infant's reactions to them) are the breeding grounds of psychopathology. Therapy seeks to make them free and whole again. This is apparent in his work with Guntrip, where Fairbairn focused on helping Guntrip to understand and rid himself of the antilibidinal mother who had let Percy die and had almost allowed Guntrip to die as well, while at the same time helping him to come to grips with the libidinal, exciting mother. He wanted to help him exorcise the bad internalized objects (the libidinal and antilibidinal egos) and allow him to rediscover his original pristine unitary ego so that he could feel whole. However, at the same time he was forever skeptical about how much analysis could accomplish.

In wrapping up the case history, Guntrip concludes that one must build one's theories from one's own personal experience. "The idea that we could think out a theory of the structure and functioning of the personality without its having any relation to the structure and functioning of our own personality, should be a self-evident impossibility (1975, p. 156). If the theory is flexible and progressive, Guntrip asserts, it will enable people to conceptualize their ongoing growth processes and throw light on the therapeutic possibilities. The flexible and progressive approach of Winnicott, in contrast with Fairbairn's "exactly intellectually defined theoretical constructs which state logically progressive developments in existing theory" (p. 156), opened the way to profounder exploration of the infancy period, where, regardless of a baby's genetic endowment, the mother's capacity to relate to her child "is the *sine qua non* of psychic health" for all infants. When there has not been good mothering, its substitute in the form of an analyst who can serve as a "good object" is essential for recovery.

"In analysis as in real life," Guntrip contends, "all relationships have a subtly dual nature. All through life we take into ourselves both good and bad figures who either strengthen or disturb us, and it is the same in psychoanalytic therapy: it is the meeting and interacting of two real people in all its complex possibilities" (p. 156). Addressing the question of whether a training analysis can be complete, he says, "In the last resort good therapists are born not trained, and they make the best use of training" (p. 145).

Interpretation

This unusual case history offers a built-in assessment from the analytic trainee, and as such it is not only a showcase for Fairbairn's theories and technique, but also for Guntrip's assessment and elaboration of that technique in comparison with Winnicott's. It also raises questions about training analyses required of all psychoanalytic candidates. Does a training analysis such as the one described in this case have the same impact as a regular analysis? Is it feasible to combine experiential and didactic work as Fairbairn did in his treatment of Guntrip?

Guntrip's main criticism of Fairbairn centers on the latter's rigidity and formality, his precisely worded, intellectualized interpretations, his insistence on viewing Guntrip's problems from an oedipal perspective (which seemed to contradict his theoretical writings on the matter), and his persistence in denying the importance of anything that came before Percy's death. Guntrip, however, had come into the treatment with an agenda, to break through the amnesia surrounding his brother's death, and to recall whatever lay behind it in the infancy period. This agenda may have impeded the treatment from the beginning, causing Guntrip to be unwilling to hear or take in interpretations that did not fulfill his underlying aim.

There were several other factors that were not considered by Guntrip. Throughout the case, Guntrip spoke of his anger at his mother, and at his transference of the "dominating mother" onto Fairbairn. Yet there was also an indication of a negative father transference of which neither Guntrip nor Fairbairn apparently became aware. Guntrip saw his father entirely in a positive light, as a loving and supportive figure; yet his dreams offer clues that there was unconscious anger and disappointment with his father. Guntrip interprets the first dream, in which Fairbairn is in his father's church but has his mother's hard face, as showing that he wanted Fairbairn to be his supportive father but the negative mother transference prevented it. Could this dream also be interpreted to mean that Guntrip was angry at his father (Fairbairn) for not rescuing him from his dominating mother? In the next dream, this theme is clear, as he has his father actually tell his mother to stop besieging him. Indeed, where was Guntrip's father during those first seven years, when his mother was besieging Guntrip and his younger brother? Was he off in the lofty clouds of religion, saving the souls of his congregation while ignoring the souls of his sons? It seems apparent that Guntrip wanted his father to rescue him from his mother, but that his father, although expressing support for his son, had been too weak to rescue him. Since his father's love and approval were his only means of survival during those early days, he needed to maintain an idealized image of his father and to protect him from anger, resentment, and contempt for his weakness. That anger, resentment, and contempt became part of Guntrip's negative transference toward Fairbairn but was never recognized as such.

Another factor that may have contributed to Guntrip's disappointment with Fairbairn was Winnicott's initial criticism of Fairbairn as somebody who "spoiled his good work" by having to attack Freud. From the outset Guntrip may have had it in his mind that Winnicott knew better than that upstart Fairbairn, and that at some point he would leave Fairbairn for Winnicott. Presumably Guntrip never told Fairbairn about this letter from Winnicott and so it was not analyzed; nor did they ever consider the possibility of a negative father transference along with the negative mother transference.

One also needs to question whether it was detrimental to the treatment for Fairbairn to mix therapy and didactic discussions. Guntrip's primary resistance to therapy involved his defiance toward the transferred bad mother. He says he tried in vain to get his mother to mother him and he also tried to get Fairbairn to mother him. This attempt, and Fairbairn's frustration of it, became a resistance to the treatment. There seems to have been some attempt by Fairbairn to analyze this resistance, but by conducting discussions after each therapy session he was in a sense giving in to the resistance and "feeding" Guntrip. The two were acting out the transference instead of analyzing it. Hence it never got properly analyzed or worked through, and so Guntrip's eventual termination from Fairbairn may be seen as another kind of acting out of this negative transference—walking out on the destructive mother *and* the weak father to go to his aunt—Winnicott.

This case history clearly highlights the fact that theoretical insight does not necessarily coincide with skill as a therapist. One case, naturally, cannot be taken as final proof that Fairbairn was a good theorist and a bad clinician, but in addition to Guntrip's own contributions to the failures of his analysis with Fairbairn, this case also shows Fairbairn to be somewhat rigid as a clinician.

Greenberg and Mitchell (1983) place Fairbairn as a theorist in the top rank of analysts. They suggest that Fairbairn's extension of the theories of Klein, as well as his countering her overemphasis on the role of innate aggression and phantasy with an opposite emphasis on reality and the destructiveness of parental deprivation, made an invaluable contribution to psychoanalysis. "His account of the conflicts accompanying the child's earliest relations with significant others, the internalization of disturbing aspects of those relations, and the centrality of the resulting internal object relations . . . impart to Fairbairn's work a lasting place and a seminal role in the history of psychoanalytic ideas" (p. 176). They also applaud Fairbairn for shifting his focus from *the person* and his internal drives to the person *within* his environment. They maintain that he, perhaps more than anybody before him, knew that a person cannot be understood in isolation.

Eagle (1984) commends Fairbairn for switching from the pleasure principle to the object-seeking principle, and cites experiments by Harlow (1958) that back up this switch. These now-classic studies of monkey mothers and infants showed decisively that the infant monkey's attachment to its surrogate mother was not derived from or secondary to the surrogate's association with the reduction of "primary drives" (hunger, thirst), but was rather based on the autonomous need for what Harlow called "contact comfort." Before the experiment, Harlow reasoned that if infant monkeys were attached to their mothers, due to drive satisfaction, then the infants would become attached to whichever mother-surrogate satisfied such needs. He then conducted an experiment in which infant monkeys were taken away from their natural mothers at birth and raised by both artificial wire and terry cloth surrogate mothers. In the experiment, the infants developed attachments to the terry cloth surrogate mothers who provided "contact comfort" while avoiding attachment to the surrogate mothers who satisfied primary drives but who were made of wire. Harlow concluded that the primary motivation was for contact, not for satisfaction of drives. Fairbairn anticipated Harlow's experiments, and the same phenomenon has since been observed in human infants (Stern 1977).

Jones, in his preface to Fairbairn's *Psychoanalytic Studies of the Personality* (1952), notes that "Dr. Fairbairn's position in the field of psycho-analysis is a special one and one of great interest. Living hundreds of miles from his nearest colleagues, whom he seldom meets, has great advantages, and also some disadvantages" (p. v). The main advantage, as Jones sees it, is that Fairbairn had not been subjected to any distractions or interference from colleagues and was able to concentrate entirely on his own ideas as they developed from his daily working experience. "This is a situation that conduces to originality, and Dr. Fairbairn's originality is indisputable" (p. v). The disadvantage of working alone, Jones adds, is that one has to do without the comments of one's colleagues and therefore risks going astray.

Kernberg (1980) is one of those who feels that Fairbairn did, indeed, go astray. Although he credits Klein and Fairbairn with helping to clarify the characteristics of primitive defensive operations and object relations, he believes that there are serious problems with their underlying theories of early development. "Confusing aspects of their overlapping and yet contradictory terminology forced me to develop my own operational definition of splitting and other related defenses" (p. 6). He feels that Fairbairn, following Klein, "ignored or neglected" the lack of differentiation between self and object representations that characterize earliest development. Hence he failed to consider the developmental stages that predate the differentiation of self- and object-components of his "schizoid position." This criticism affirms Guntrip's frustration with Fairbairn's unwillingness to consider events preceeding Percy's death. And, in fact, Kernberg alludes to this case, saying, "There is some irony in the protest Guntrip expressed at Fairbairn's adherence to classical psychoanalytic technique . . . in contrast to Guntrip's experience with his second analyst, Winnicott. In my opinion, Guntrip's criticism here speaks for Fairbairn" (p. 75).

Guntrip (1971), more or less in agreement with Kernberg, wrote elsewhere that although he would concede that Fairbairn should be recognized as the one psychoanalytic thinker who first unequivocally stressed object relations as the determining factor— "the all-important desideratum"—for ego development, he adds that as far as the ego goes, Fairbairn's theory "stopped at the analysis of ego-splitting, and still leaves open the final problem, that of the origins of the ego . . ." (p. 101).

Eagle (1984) is also critical of the "murkiness" of certain of Fairbairn's basic concepts, but overall he believes that what is important about Fairbairn's work are not the "specific, complex metapsychological formulations regarding internalized objects and split-off ego structures, but the broad emphasis on the importance of early object relations, the conception of psychological development in terms of differentiation between self and object, and progress from infantile dependence to mature dependence" (pp. 85–86). These theories, along with his rejection of Freud's instinct theory and the "explicit claim that object-seeking propensities are as primary and as biological as the sexual and aggressive drives" anticipated and were influential in the later ferment in these areas in psychoanalytic theory and practice.

Guntrip's paper, "My Experience of Analysis with Fairbairn and Winnicott," published by his wife after his death, is a remarkable document, a classic of its kind, that will continue to stir up debate on many issues. It may be that Guntrip was correct when he said that good therapists were born, not made. However, both Fairbairn and Guntrip will be remembered for this case, as well as for their advances in object relations theory.

8

A LIFETIME
ANALYSIS

Harold F. Searles and Joan Douglas
(1972, 1976)

One day a woman to whom Harold F. Searles later gave the pseudonym Mrs. Joan Douglas ran away from the Chestnut Lodge Sanitorium. She went to Washington, hired a horse, and rode up Pennsylvania Avenue to the gates of the White House, where she demanded an audience with the president. The police sent her back to the Lodge, and the FBI placed her name on a list of persons known to be a threat to presidents of the United States. A short time after that incident, Mrs. Douglas began her analytic treatment with Searles, and thirty-six years later, as this book was being written, she was still with him, making this case one of the longest, if not *the* longest, ever recorded in psychoanalytic literature.

Searles, like Lindner, is one of the few prominent psychoanalysts to be born in the United States and, again like Lindner, he writes in a simple, unpretentious style. He was born on September 1, 1918, in Hancock, New York. Of his mother, he has written that she was a dominating woman prone to psychotic episodes (Langs and Searles 1979), a fact that undoubtedly influenced his decision to work with schizophrenics. He received his medical degree from Harvard Medical School. He described his school years as extremely stressful. "I came to experience anxiety of such proportions as to leave in me an enduring fascination with, and desire to understand, the wondrously intangible thing which is human personality. . . ." (1965, p. 19). After graduating from medical school he served as a medical officer during World War II, after which he decided to specialize in psychiatry. He trained as a psychoanalyst at the Washington Psychoanalytic Institute, where his training analyst was Ernest E. Hadley, with whom he was in treatment for a number of years. "When . . . it finally became possible for me to find psychotherapeutic help in the form of a training analysis," he later observed, "I was well aware that I needed this for more than purely didactic purposes . . ." (p. 19). Although he often expressed appreciation for Hadley, he also related an incident when, during his analysis, he visited Hadley while the latter was in the hospital recovering from surgery. He was shocked when his therapist showed him his scar, thus revealing his penis (Langs and Searles 1979).

For fifteen years he was on the staff of the famous Chestnut Lodge—where other notable analysts such as Harry Stack Sullivan and Frieda Fromm-Reichmann had held court—and for a time he was clinical supervisor there. While at the Lodge he began churning out papers in his highly idiosyncratic style, papers that would signal his quick rise to the top of the psychoanalytic field. He also became a much-sought-after lecturer.

In both his writing and his personal appearances, he made relatively little use of psychiatric or psychoanalytic jargon, nor was he concerned with inventing new terms or redefining old ones. "Dr. Searles learned early in his work," Knight points out, "that all therapy . . . consists of deeply significant emotional experience in each of the two parties to the therapeutic relationship, and that progress toward a good outcome requires ruthless honest self-awareness on both sides" (Searles 1965, p. 17). His book, *Countertransference and Related Subjects: Selected Papers* (1979), is recognized as a classic in the field, and his *Collected Papers on Schizophrenia and Related Subjects* (1965), is standard reading in psychoanalytic institutes. He has also become known for dramatic demonstrations of his clinical approach with schizophrenics, presented at various conferences around the world.

A hallmark of Searles's style is an engaging self-honesty and humility. For example, in one of his best-known papers (1959), he asserts that one of the regular ingredients in the etiology of schizophrenia is an "effort to drive the other person crazy." He explains that in his clinical experience he has found that "the individual becomes schizophrenic partly by reason of a long-continued effort, a largely or wholly unconscious effort, on the part of some person or persons highly important in his upbringing, to drive him crazy" (p. 254), and he adds that through his own analysis he discovered that there was an aspect of his own character that wanted to drive not only his patients but everybody in his life crazy. Moreover, in his clinical experience and observations of fellow therapists, he found that therapists in general have an unconscious desire to drive their patients crazy. He points to a large percentage of therapists who possess an obsessive-compulsive character structure, the chief defense mechanism of which is that of reaction-formation. Consciously, therapists manifest a desire to help patients become less crazy; unconsciously, they sometimes want to drive them crazy. The chief motivation for this wish to drive others crazy, Searles believes, is "a desire to externalize, and thus get rid of, the threatening craziness in oneself" (p. 265). Just as we would not be surprised to find that a surgeon brings forth, during analysis, a powerful wish to physically dismember other people, Searles notes, "so we should be ready to discern the presence, in not a few of us who have chosen the profession of treating psychiatric illness, of similarly powerful, long-repressed desires to dismember the personality structure of other persons" (p. 278).

Searles first wrote about Joan Douglas in a paper published in 1972, and he continued to mention her in several succeeding papers. Admitted to Chestnut Lodge at the age of 36, she was "an attractive, well-groomed, healthy-appearing but actually highly paranoid woman who poured forth, at the slightest provocation, intensely threatened and threatening expressions of remarkably distorted delusional experiences" (1972a, p. 197). Her first analyst at the Lodge "quit in discouragement" after a year. A few months later, in January 1953, Searles took over.

Prior to Douglas's admission to the Lodge, she had spent a year at a psychiatric hospital specializing in somatic modes of treatment. During her stay there her paranoid delusions were neither diminished by psychotherapy, two courses of insulin-coma therapy, which resulted in at least seventy comas; nor by two courses of electroshock totaling at least forty-two treatments. A consultant advised a lobotomy, but Douglas's family obtained a second opinion, and were advised to transfer her to Chestnut Lodge for a "last-ditch attempt at psychoanalysis."

Searles last mentions her in a paper published in 1976, but in a follow-up interview in September 1989 he acknowledged that he was still working with her. For the first ten years he saw her in her hospital room (she steadfastly refused to come to his office); for the next five years, after he had left the Lodge to establish a full-time private practice, she was taken by taxi to his office, ten miles away. Only after fifteen years was she able to go to his office unescorted, although even then Searles claims that she was "still very delusional." Throughout her treatment Searles saw her four times a week, each session lasting fifty-five minutes. Sometimes he saw her for double sessions. After thirty-six years he had spent about 7,000 hours of his life with her, and she had gone from an attractive woman in her late thirties to a grandmother, 72 years old, who wore false teeth. She is one year older than Searles.

It was not until the age of 33 that Douglas became "overtly psychotic," although Searles suspects that she began to suffer from unrecognized schizophrenia at an early age. Her mother had been a highly unstable woman, subject to constantly changing moods that Searles guessed were of a manic-depressive nature. She also seemed to have a highly fragmented personality and, in the words of Douglas's brother, she "loved to dominate" her daughter. Her brother described how their mother would return from Mass in a beatific mood, and moments later would be throwing a pot at one of the children. The father was said to be a distant, head-in-the-clouds person whose complete disregard for his daughter also contributed to her psychosis. At the time her own overtly psychotic behavior began to appear, Douglas was married and had four children of her own, whom she dominated in the same way that her mother had dominated her.

From the beginning of her stay at the Lodge, Douglas refused to acknowledge the existence of her husband or her children and for prolonged periods refused to open gifts or letters from them. Her husband and children had visited her immediately prior to the beginning of her analysis with Searles, but the visit had been a disaster. Five years later her husband divorced her, and only ten years later did her two older children try to visit her again; each found her so "disturbingly crazy" that neither ever returned.

Throughout the first several years Douglas made a number of "frighteningly serious, intendedly homicidal" attacks on various people in the Lodge, and Searles himself often felt afraid of her. Mainly, however, her murderousness was expressed through unconscious verbal communications that had the effect of "doing violence to one's sense of reality" and causing identity confusion. "There were times, particularly in unusually stormy sessions during the early years," Searles claims, "when I felt so threatened and enraged that I was seriously afraid lest I lose control of my own murderous feelings, and kill her" (Searles 1972a, p. 199). It took sixteen years before Searles felt that he had established any kind of therapeutic alliance with her; until then he lived "with the bitter knowledge" that were he to become discouraged and quit, she would be far from grieved; "she would count it, I knew, as simply one more triumph, and a not particularly notable one at that" (p. 198).

Over the years, Searles points out, "a truly staggering multitude of staff personnel" tried to help Douglas, while trying to suppress, "as I have, myself," their tremendous investment in her remaining psychotic. These included ten psychiatric administrators, ten psychiatric social workers, numerous nurses, occupational and recreational therapy personnel, and a far larger number of attendants—in addition to fellow patients. Searles mentions this in order to "indicate what awesome demands the psychoanalytic treatment of a chronically schizophrenic patient can make upon the best efforts of a multitude of professionally trained persons" (p. 200).

From the beginning, she manifested a great deal of "ego dedifferentiation and ego fragmentation" (or, in Kleinian or Kernbergian terms, splitting). Searles interpreted these to be unconscious defenses against such emotions as guilt, grief, and love, and as attempts to realize strivings for omnipotence. For a long time Douglas was convinced that there were 48,000 Chestnut Lodges among which she was constantly being shifted. There were many "doubles" of everyone, including herself. (When a male aide left the sanitorium she did not miss him, for she was convinced that there were thirteen more of him in various guises.) She harbored the notion that there was a chain on her heart and machinery in her abdomen, and that her head and Searles's head were repeatedly being replaced by other heads. She often experienced both herself and Searles, "bodily and *in toto*," as being replaced by a succession of other persons during therapy sessions. She felt unfairly accused by people about her more destructive acts, which she was convinced were done by her malicious doubles. "Well, there were nine hundred and ninety-seven tertiary skillion women [doubles]," she once protested, "associated with Chestnut Lodge; so why should *I* be blamed for everything everybody did?" (pp. 200–201).

In the beginning she misidentified herself and others repeatedly, and had only "splashes of memory" of any experiences prior to her hospitalization. Once, when she went on a shopping trip with an aide, she later reported to Searles that she had experienced a succession of different aides. Searles interpreted this as being her own changing emotions toward the aide being split off and projected onto the aide. Douglas asserted that she had never had a mother or father or husband or children, and when Searles once asked her something about her mother she protested, "Whenever you use the word 'mother,' I see a whole parade of women, each one representing a different point of view" (p. 201).

Douglas was unable to differentiate between figurative and concrete modes of thought, animate and inanimate objects, human and nonhuman forms of life, males and females, adults and children, ideas and persons, and real and imagined events. She believed that everything had once existed in the form of a person who had been turned by the malevolent outer forces (such as Searles) into inanimate objects such as trees, airplanes, buildings, and the like. She did not experience memories of people from her past, but was convinced that the image in her mind was "the flesh-and-blood person," who had been shrunk and imprisoned in her head.

As the years went on, Douglas became more and more isolated in the Lodge as personnel members and fellow patients, who at first found her crazy talk engaging, gradually "became thoroughly alienated by reason of their helplessness to feel at all predictably related to her in any meaningful way" (p. 203). Nevertheless, Searles plodded on, himself experiencing "a quite terrible feeling of unrelatedness" that made him feel at times that he was trying to communicate with an extraterrestrial. Part of this unrelatedness had to do with her belief that she had neither a body nor a mind. Once, when Searles mentioned her mind, she replied, "You see, my mother was my mind" (1975, p. 404), implying that when she lost her mother, she lost her mind. (It was immediately after her mother's death that she had become overtly psychotic.)

Searles was eventually able to decipher her language and discern that she was involved in two "all-absorbing tasks." One was a struggle to be born—that is, to leave her existence as "a boundless element, variously specified as light, or electricity, or air, or water"—and to obtain a body of her own to inhabit. This struggle to be born was related to her infantile relationship to her mother. Once she told Searles, "I recall where I met you once, millions of years ago when I was Pamela of Britain. I went—uh—inside my *self*. You were then living in a—on a farm in my bosom, my right breast, and you took one look at me and you said, 'Oh, you're *sun*" (p. 214). Searles replied that he did not know that he had the power to cause her to assume different forms. She paused and then answered:

> Well, my *mother* . . . uh—before she was a baby, I mean when she was a woman, she could think herself—as herself, and hold her face . . . and look very well, and then she would give it to me and *I'd* look very well; but I was a *baby*, and she didn't teach me how to really *do* it, so, uh, it would *stay* that way, 'cause I was always in a soul—I never had a—really had a body, until—no, it's all *soul* material. But it fleshed, uh, and that's where we live, on my *soul*.
> [p. 215]

Douglas's other task was to differentiate what was outside of her (reality) from what was inside (fantasy). However, this task was made extremely difficult by her psychotic defenses, which included dedifferentiation, ego fragmentation, projection, introjection, and denial. Only after Searles began to realize "the awesome extent to which her experienced world, so remarkably delusional" was based upon actual real components of himself—his expressions, his moods, his words—was he able to help her with this task.

In working with Douglas, Searles was required to join with her in a state of what he terms "therapeutic symbiosis," which he describes as partly based on delusional transference and partly based on their real relationship, a relationship that involved a symbiosis participated in by both. He notes that she needed him to play an "omnipotent-creator transference role," which he for many years shied away from because he was threatened by her holding him omnipotently responsible for her delusional world and by "the unconsciously gratifying lure of omnipotence" (p. 212). She needed him to play this role because in her early childhood her mother had evidently attributed to her a godlike malevolence, holding her responsible for all anguish, no matter whether real or psychotically created, in the older woman's life.

Douglas's attempt in the transference to get Searles to be the malevolent god represented a reversal of the symbiotic state between her mother and herself, a reversal that Searles hoped would enable her to separate from her mother. With her help, he overcame his reticence, and, after several years, was able more effectively to play this role.

In the early years Searles kept a written record of the case; after Douglas had begun to see him privately, he started audiotaping her sessions. His notes from these recorded sessions provide a deft portrait of her personality and an outline of the progress of the case over the years. He describes her as often pacing about during sessions, changing her clothes in front of him—exposing her nude body to him—and taunting him about never making a pass at her. If she sat near him she had to keep busy with knitting or sewing so that she could have large needles and scissors nearby in case Searles tried to rape or kill her, "which she was convinced I had done innumerable times" (p. 206). During the ten years he saw her in her room at the Lodge, the door often had to be kept locked during the sessions lest she run away. After he began seeing her privately in his own office, he often worried that she would become physically unmanageable.

In his notes about selected sessions he observes that on May 7, 1965, during the second year of treatment conducted in his private office, she wondered what he would do if someone broke into mercury droplets. At the next session she spoke of hundreds of men standing around in her head, and a few sessions later she experienced olfactory hallucinations arising from what she called "God-rot," which Searles interpreted as being traceable to "the decay of omnipotent introjects." A short time later she told him, looking both deflated and relieved, "I used to be God; now I'm a woman" (p. 217). Searles saw this announcement as a turning-point in her struggle to be born, to grasp reality.

On December 11, 1965, she looked into Searles's eyes intently, as she often did, and perceived "a changing succession of different figures," some real persons from her past, some from world history, some nonhuman creatures. A few sessions later she told him that she was going to put into him the multitude of dead people who inhabited her. The next session, two days later, Searles experienced a transitory feeling of being insane—a sense of confusion and estrangement, which he believed was related to her "impregnating" him with the fragmented products of the "God-rot."

On April 29, 1970, she spoke of them as being two babies sitting in a perambulator and expressed pleasure that she and Searles were having sexual intercourse by talking. Several weeks later he suddenly felt shattered by her searching gaze. It mobilized all his guilt about her long illness. He became aware of sadistic and lustful feelings toward her and felt guilty of exploiting her and her illness for research purposes.

During this session she called him a "baby-raper" and "Lucifer-Eternal Rest," which Searles interpreted to refer to his "genuinely diabolical" qualities as well as to his never making any sexual overtures to her.

On May 27, 1970, she told Searles with sympathy that there was no room in her family for him, treating him as though he were an orphan boy. Five days later he found himself feeling "unprecedentedly diabolical" toward her, and experienced this as being to some extent linked to his own "inherent, basic fiendishness." He was quite disturbed.

On September 22, 1970, she was silent most of the session, which he found more exasperating than usual. Calculatedly, he told her he felt sorry for Satan, for when she died and went to hell, as he was sure she would, Satan would have to spend even more time with her than he'd spent. He observes that in the following session she was more collaborative, explaining that she almost invariably thrived when he vented his harshest feelings on her.

In his classic 1975 paper, "The Patient as Therapist to His Analyst," he provides an update of his treatment of Douglas, emphasizing how she—and all patients—need to be a therapist to their therapist. Just as Douglas had once wanted to heal her mother—particularly after the mother had gone through a nervous breakdown—in order to help her mother become a better mother for her, so now in the transference relationship she strove in various ways to "cure" Searles so that he could better play the transference role of the omnipotent mother.

Of a session in the seventeenth year of treatment, Searles (1975) writes that her "consciously lovingly concerned, and unconsciously murderously competitive, efforts to bring surcease to various mother-figures were evident" (p. 408). He had begun to realize by then that she felt overwhelmed by his therapeutic devotion to her—"devotion which presumably contains more of murderous competitiveness than I can yet integrate" (p. 408). Identifying with the aggressor, she spent this session, as she did others, preoccupied with how to rescue her mother (Searles), while feeling continually frustrated in this attempt.

In the nineteenth year of treatment, he describes a session in which for ten minutes she gazed at him with an expression of helplessness, troubled feeling, bewilderment, vulnerability, and uncertainty as to whether to trust him. Then she began to lambast him in her highly delusional way, which Searles nevertheless knew alluded to their immediate situation. One of her main complaints was her feeling that Searles did not need her in any way, nor feel entertained by her. "My mother . . . she doesn't seem to need me for nothin' . . ." she said at one point. Six minutes later she said, "I amuse *her*" (p. 412). Searles understood that she had a need for him to see her not simply as a psychotic, but also as a helpful, entertaining human being. As he thought about it, he began to see her from another point of view, to appreciate her confusion "as a truly breath-taking creativity, far more fascinating, wondrous and, of course, alive than, for example, a beautiful and intricate Persian rug." At the same time he also became more receptive to "her tremendous wit and her indomitable sense of humor" (p. 413). For many years he had not been able to appreciate these things because he had been so desperate to help her that he had been unaware of how concerned she was with helping him, entertaining him, and giving him relief from his own depression. The more he allowed her to help him, the more she allowed him to help her.

At about this same time he noticed that she had become more and more capable of grieving. In earlier years, she had defended against her sadness through her paranoid defense mechanisms. Whereas formerly he had feared that she would commit violence against others, now he increasingly feared that she would do violence to herself.

During a session at Christmastime 1973 after they had been together nearly twenty years, he found her to be "more psychologically *here*" than ever before, and also more related to him. She acknowledged to him at one point that both her mother and her father had regarded her as worthless, as giving nothing worthwhile to either of them. He found out from a nurse that when she returned to Chestnut Lodge from the session, she cried for the first time in this nurse's several years of experience with her. Two sessions later she spoke about her mother's hatred of her: "But I can't get over why she hates me so much . . . my mother doesn't like me" (p. 420).

She now recalled new, realistic memories of her childhood. Her mother had gone to Italy several times to study opera, leaving her and her siblings in the care of "a chaotic myriad of ill-remembered" baby-sitters and surrogate parents. On many previous occasions she had derided their sessions as her "baby-sitting" with him.

In January 1974 Searles, an acknowledged authority on the psychotherapy of schizophrenic patients, gave a demonstration at a professional conference in another city. He characterized this appearance as "nothing less than triumphant," but when he returned to his session with Douglas, he found himself again feeling totally inept and deserving of her scorn. It was dawning on him, he observes, that he had a need for her to confirm his lowest feelings of self-esteem—to reassure him that he was as worthless as he often privately felt. He adds, however, that for various reasons his "hunger for vilification" had lessened recently and he was therefore better able to tolerate her insults and maintain a realistic, collaborative rapport with her.

Later that year Douglas's sister paid her a three-day visit. When Searles interviewed the sister toward the end of her stay, she said she saw impressive indications of progress on Joan's part, although there were still signs of her psychosis. During a session with Douglas, she in turn evaluated how much progress "her patient"—her sister—had made, caricaturing and mimicking certain of her sister's most notable traits. However, she still spoke of her sister as "the Mrs. Bradleys," perceiving her to be multiple figures. After more than twenty years of work, Searles himself concludes that Douglas was somebody who had come, after a long, tragic struggle, into kinship with others, "but had yet to come to nonpsychotic terms with the conflict between her omnipotence-based murderousness toward her fellow human beings, and her at least equally intense loving and therapeutic concern for them" (p. 426).

In a paper published in 1976, "Transitional Phenomena and Therapeutic Symbiosis," Searles again refers briefly to his work with Douglas, recalling how he used the tape recorder during their sessions as though it were a third person. He cites, as an example, times when, because he was feeling "furious" at her for her attacks on his character, he would turn to the recorder and deliberately talk "in a coldly clinical, lecturing fashion" about her schizophrenia. At other times, when he was feeling fond of her and noticed that she was frightened by this warmth, he would turn to the recorder and talk to it warmly, as though it were a companion. He was convinced that taking advantage of the presence of the recorder promoted group relatedness and ego integration.

In a session on April 3, 1974, during which he had made many comments into the recorder, she mentioned the name of an acquaintance of hers and said, "She can come and join our group therapy" (1975, p. 555). On July 17, 1974, she referred to herself as "this group," and confirmed, when Searles questioned her, that she meant herself, Searles, and the tape recorder. He saw this as one of many indications that she was improving, changing from her sense of herself as discontinuous, unrelated, and shifting unpredictably from day to day and moment to moment, to a sense of identity which, "while still multiple, involved a group of 'selves' simultaneously existing in group relatedness" (p. 555).

This paper, published when the treatment had reached the twenty-three-year mark, is one of Searles's last written reports of his analysis of Douglas. However, Searles was interviewed by telephone in September 1989. He told the author that he was still working with Douglas. At that time Searles was 71 years old and his patient was 72. Asked if he thought this was going to be a lifetime case, he hesitated and then replied, "I would say so." He then agreed to write an update of the case, which is quoted in its entirety below:

Mrs. Joan Douglas has been in psychoanalytic therapy with me for more than thirty-six and a half years, and I expect that she will need to be in such treatment, whether with me or another therapist later on, for the remainder of her life.

Since I last described, in 1979, the way her treatment was progressing (see Searles 1986, pp. 243–247), she has improved a great deal. I say this even though, in each session, delusional thinking is evident at least several, and often many, times. In June of 1979 she was able to move to outpatiency and has maintained that status ever since. A relative who has visited her over the decades was marveling to me, at a relatively recent visit, that whereas she used to be irrational about 90 percent of the time, now she is so only about 10 percent of the time.

In April of 1979, as part of a concerted attempt to help her move out of the hospital, her administrative psychiatrist started her on a major tranquilizer. This was reduced, because of problems with hypotension, to Haldol, 1 mgm per day, and she has been on that dosage since then. I believe that the Haldol has been a useful adjunct to the treatment, but not to be compared, in fundamental treatment-importance, to her work with me and with a succession of administrative psychiatrists, nurses, social workers, attendants, and other persons—very much including those family members who have kept in contact with her over the years, and who have supported this long treatment endeavor.

With her knowledge, I have sound-recorded all of our sessions for more than twenty years. My playbacks of these tapes, during such research time as I can find in my schedule, reassures me of the great value of our work together, and helps me to see wherein I am being useful to her and wherein, on the contrary, I am unconsciously interfering with her striving toward better ego-integration and fuller individuation from me.

Three months ago, my discontinuing Saturday work with patients meant a decrease in our time together from four to three and a half hours per week.

For many years now, she has made no secret of the fact that our sessions mean a great deal to her. But also for many years now, she has had available to her the ability to form meaningful relationships with many other persons, and I know that if, for any reasons, I become no longer able to be her therapist, she is quite able to carry on her treatment with another one. I expect to be in practice for at least several more years, and I shall count it both a very fulfilling pleasure, and a privilege to go on working with her.

At the time of the interview Searles was devoting himself to his practice, to his wife Sylvia, his three children, his grandchildren and was looking forward to retirement.

Interpretation

Searles is noted for his contribution to the understanding of transference psychosis, which has been variously defined but which he has redefined as any type of transference that distorts or prevents a relatedness between the patient and therapist as "two separate, alive, human and sane beings" (Searles 1965, p. 669). He breaks it down into four varieties: In the first, traceable to the autistic phase of infancy, the patient has not yet built up part-object relationships nor an image of self and mother as separate objects, and so the therapist feels unrelated to the patient. In the second variety, clear relatedness has been established, but the relatedness is of a deeply ambivalent nature, with fear of annihilation accompanying the patient's wish to join the therapist. This causes the therapist also to fear annihilation and loss of sanity. In the third category, the patient wishes to complement the therapist's personality or to help the therapist to become established as a separate and whole person.

In the fourth type, deeply and chronically confused patients, who in childhood were used to their primary caretakers doing all their thinking for them, try to perpetuate this symbiotic relationship with their therapists.

The case of Joan Douglas would seem to demonstrate at least three and perhaps all four of these varieties of transference psychosis during its long course. Searles notes that during the first fifteen years or so neither he nor anybody else on the staff of Chestnut Lodge felt related to her in any way, and that at times relating to her was like trying to communicate with "an extraterrestrial." At the same time, he also experienced fears for his own life because of her murderous rage, observing that "there were times, particularly in unusually stormy sessions during the early years when I felt so threatened and enraged that I was seriously afraid lest I lose control of my own murderous feelings, and kill her." These descriptions would seem to match up with the first two types of transference psychoses. As for the third type, Searles thoroughly documents in "The Patient as Therapist to His Analyst" the many ways in which Douglas attempted to cure him of his grandiosity, his depression, and his need to keep her crazy and himself sane. It also appears that she manifested the fourth type of transference psychosis as well. At one point she says to Searles, "You see, my mother was my mind," implying that her mother had done her thinking for her, and that Searles, as her transference mother, would have to do likewise.

What stands out about this case, however, is not so much Douglas's everchanging transference psychosis, remarkable as it was, but Searles's even more remarkable countertransference responses (some might call it a "transference psychosis") and what he did with them. Nowhere in the psychoanalytic literature will one find more startling confessions than are found in this case. Searles writes of "murderous feelings," of "the unconsciously gratifying lure of omnipotence," of wanting to keep her psychotic for both "deeply personal as well as scientific reasons," of "sadistic and lustful feelings," of an "inherent, basic fiendishness," and of "devotion which presumably contains . . . murderous competitiveness." He contends that his ability to feel these things in himself and to admit that they were not simply identifications with her projections but, to some extent, his actual feelings, was instrumental in working successfully with her. He used his countertransference feelings to understand her, verbalized them to her to achieve therapeutic progress, and acknowledged them to himself and to his readers to free himself of their unconscious effect on his behavior.

The other thing that stands out about the case is, of course, its length. On one hand, Searles had the tenacity to stay with one of the most exasperating patients ever recorded in the literature. Why he chose to stay with her, while terminating with other patients when he left Chestnut Lodge, is a question that perhaps only he can answer. But stay with her he did, for thirty-six years, all the while putting up with a relentless nonrelatedness, bitterly facing the knowledge that if he had become discouraged and quit she would have counted it as "simply one more triumph, and a not particularly notable one at that," tolerating her ceaseless threats to murder him, submitting to violence to his "sense of identity," endless scorn, and many other forms of resistance. Nevertheless, some would criticize Searles for mishandling the transference and his own countertransference in this and similar cases; others might question the validity of this case, or any case, that lasted a lifetime.

Jacobson (1967) believes in allowing schizophrenic patients like Douglas to use her, noting that, "If we understand their defensive devices and the different roles in which they cast us, we can, at least during certain critical periods of our therapeutic work, lend ourselves to assuming these roles" (p. 50). However, she stops short of the kind of "therapeutic symbiosis" advocated by Searles, noting that "although I admire the frankness with which he discusses his own countertransference manifestations, I must admit that I consider countertransference problems a private matter. Except in very general terms, their open discussion and public exhibition do not seem to me to be particularly useful" (p. 60). Such problems, she asserts, should be recognized and controlled in one's self- or re-analysis. She adds that therapists who permit themselves to establish a parent–child relationship with patients that "includes not only feelings of fondness and affection but even parental incestuous desires" may at a certain stage regress along with the patient into a mutually symbiotic dependency and find themselves "in dangerous situations which, in my opinion, are of no therapeutic value" (p. 62).

Frosch (1983), while not openly disagreeing with Searles, quotes extensively from Jacobson, and acknowledges that in his own work with schizophrenics he tries to make himself available "as a fulcrum" and to establish a therapeutic relationship during a patient's acute delusional periods. But during quiescent periods he tries to reach "a rational part of the ego" and provide interpretations "within a psychoanalytic atmosphere" (p. 467).

Jacobson speaks for many, if not most, psychoanalysts. She does not see Searles's public honesty as useful, and suggests that he work it out in his own analysis. She is also cautious about the dangers of regression. I would disagree with her on all counts. Public honesty is always useful because it demonstrates for everybody, therapists and patients alike, that therapists are as completely human as everybody else. There is a universal tendency among human beings, as Searles has noted, to externalize their own craziness and attribute it to others. It is this very tendency that leads to madness, as well as to other social problems. (See Searles's "Unconscious Processes in Relation to the Environmental Crisis," 1976, pp. 228–242.) Searles's public honesty serves two important purposes: it attacks this universal tendency of human beings to deny their own craziness, while modeling a more honest, less hypocritical attitude; and it allows Searles to reveal publicly his troublesome thoughts and urges and thus provides him with a safeguard against acting them out. As to Jacobson's suggestion that Searles should work these things out in his self- or re-analysis, I would reply that one can never be totally objective about oneself, and therefore self-analysis is not reliable in handling countertransference, especially the extreme varieties of countertransference induced by working with psychotics. Nor is additional psychoanalysis necessarily an answer, for very often training analyses—as the case of Fairbairn and Guntrip shows (see

Chapter 7)—fall short of the mark. Jacobson's next point, her fear of the dangers of regressing along with a patient, may provide us with an explanation of why so many training analyses fall short— they remain intellectual. Jacobson's contention that Searles's "therapeutic symbiosis" may become a dangerous dependency reflects, perhaps, her own fears of letting go, as well as a misinterpretation of Searles's work. My impression is that although Searles writes of symbiosis, he never loses sight of reality—unlike Lindner (1955), who in his work with Kirk Allen ventured into the dangerous territory of which Jacobson writes (see Chapter 3).

Those who are critical of any analysis that goes on for a very long time, and particularly critical of one that lasts a lifetime, usually take the position that the therapist is unconsciously creating a dependency and exploiting the patient. In this instance, they even have Searles's own confession about feeling guilty that he might be exploiting Douglas and keeping her psychotic for research purposes. "You see?" such critics may exclaim. What such critics are unable and unwilling to understand, however, is that Searles's very confession is proof that he is aware of this himself and is trying to do something about it by confessing to it in public. It is human to have such thoughts, and those who would deny them, who would never utter them in public, are the very ones would be most likely to live them. The question remains: why has Searles spent an entire lifetime with Douglas? My answer is a simple one: because she needed it. Her psychosis was of such a severe nature that neither insulin nor electroshock therapy had any effect. Nor, in my opinion, would large dosages of psychiatric drugs have helped her. They might have made her more calm, so that she could have been maintained in a psychiatric setting for the rest of her life with less money spent on psychotherapy. But if we speak about actually curing her, I not only agree with Searles that her case required a lifetime treatment, I also commend him for his loyalty and endurance.

Balint (1968) is also among Searles's supporters. As I pointed out (Schoenewolf 1990), in Chapter 6 on Ferenczi's experiments with regression, Balint considered the rift among psychoanalysts with regard to the therapeutic use of regression as having begun, tragically, with Ferenczi. He notes that Searles and others at Chestnut Lodge were among the few who, since Ferenczi, were interested in regression and saw its positive value in therapy. But, he observes, "all these analysts, including myself, belong—not to the 'classical' massive centre—but to the fringe. We are known, tolerated, perhaps even read, but certainly not quoted" (p. 155).

Pao (1979), commenting on Searles's treatment of Douglas, compares it with his own approach. Citing his work with "Tina," he describes how changes in the content of Tina's delusions were invariably related to things that were going on in their therapy sessions. "In his [Searles's] description of the patient's realistic perception of the therapist in delusional transference, Searles implicitly presented a view similar to the one offered here" (p. 242). He also credits Searles for illuminating the manner in which a therapist registers and organizes his emotional responses to his patient "as well as how he uses the material in the therapeutic setting" (p. 342).

Volkan (1981), though not alluding directly to the Douglas case, expresses appreciation for Searles's clinical vignettes showing "the affective flow between the early mother and her child, and, in a later stage of development, between the patient and his therapist." Such interactions have been beautifully described by Searles, Volkan notes, "especially in connection with severely regressed patients" (p. 318).

Tauber (1983) looks at the limitations of classical analysis with regard to countertransference and calls attention to Searles's notions on this subject. "In brilliant fashion, he reveals how his own methods are at variance with the classical technique. He makes a powerful case for forthrightness, for spontaneity and for avoiding emotional evasiveness" (p. 66). He notes that the challenge of working with very disturbed persons deeply and "inescapably" shakes the foundations of our concepts and "forces us to resolve" not only questions of therapy but of human existence as well.

In Robert Knight's preface to one of Searles's books (1965), he expresses awe at Searles's honesty and humility, pointing out how Searles allows readers to see, again and again, his personal feelings, impulses, and fantasies as they are evoked during stressful sessions with schizophrenic patients. "The reader who is unaccustomed to seeing such highly personal revelations may now and again be startled. My guess is, however, that he will wind up with a heightened respect for, and perhaps even a little envy of, the therapist-author" (p. 17).

Searles's analysis of Mrs. Joan Douglas was, and continues to be, a turning point in the history of psychoanalysis. He is a pioneer in the treatment of schizophrenic patients, particularly in the use of countertransference thoughts and feelings in their treatment, and this case more than any other crystallizes his innovative techniques. His work with Douglas, moreover, undeniably proves that there are indeed cases where a lifetime analysis is necessary.

9

THE TREATMENT OF NARCISSISM

Heinz Kohut and Mr. Z. (1979)

During the second half of the twentieth century, narcissism became one of the primary subjects of investigation by psychoanalysts. At the same time, narcissistic patients began to appear more often in therapists' offices. Indeed, while in the early days of analytic therapy most patients were hysterics or obsessive-compulsives, by the time Heinz Kohut began his practice in Chicago in the 1950s, many, if not most, private therapy patients tended to have narcissistic disorders. Kohut devoted his life to the study of narcissism, founding a school of therapy which he called the "psychology of the self."

Kohut was born in Vienna in 1913, the only child of a well-to-do business executive and his wife. His father, to whom he had never really been close, died of leukemia when Kohut was in his early twenties. Kligerman (1982) relates an anecdote about Kohut's boyhood that may foreshadow his curiosity about the human psyche. Kohut had an older friend, a college student, who served as what he would later call a "selfobject." They used to play a complex game of Twenty Questions that took the form of "if

157

some event had or had not happened then what would be the present state of affairs?" For example, if Socrates had not lived, what would be the state of architecture in Vienna? Kohut's adeptness at this game, which required him to look into the mind of his friend, reveals the beginnings of his interest in the workings of the mind.

Kohut studied medicine at the University of Vienna, obtained his medical degree in 1938 at the age of 25, and then entered into analysis with August Aichhorn. He came to the United States in 1940, trained in neurology and psychiatry at the University of Chicago, and became a candidate at the Chicago Psychoanalytic Institute, graduating in 1950. In 1948 he married Elizabeth Meyer, and they had a son, Thomas, two years later. He remained married for thirty-three years, until his death.

Kohut began as an ego psychologist in the classical tradition, but by 1971, when he wrote *The Analysis of the Self*, he had broken with tradition to develop his own theory of narcissism. He elaborated on this theory in his next two books, *The Restoration of the Self* (1977) and *How Does Analysis Cure?* (1984), as well as in his now classic case history, "The Analysis of Mr. Z." (1979). In these and other works he delineated the "narcissistic personality disorder" as a diagnostic entity with its own developmental origin, and argued that such patients, contrary to classical tradition, could be treated analytically.

For Kohut, *self* has a different meaning than it did for Jacobson (1971). His *self* is no longer a representation, nor a product of the activity of the ego (Hartmann 1958), but is itself a functioning agent of the psyche. The beginnings of the self emerge during the narcissistic stage of development (roughly equivalent to Mahler's symbiotic stage), when "the baby's innate potentialities and the [parents'] expectations with regard to the baby converge" (Kohut 1977, p. 99). During this stage the child relates to the mother as though she were part of himself, not a separate person or object. Kohut devised the term "selfobject" to denote this kind of relationship. Kohut postulates two separate lines of healthy development: (1) from autoerotism to narcissism to object love, and (2)

Psychotherapy Book Club

members get a

FREE BOOK

when they sponsor a new member.

New members get a

FREE SUBSCRIPTION to the

Psychotherapy Book News,

a 64-page magazine featuring

books from all

publishers at

discounts up to

95% off.

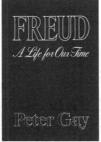

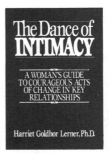

Each time you order a book at regular member's price, you can choose a Special Discount selection at tremendous savings. Recent offers include:

 $27.50/**$3.95**

 $39.50/**$5.95**

 $27.50/**$3.95**

 $19.95/**$7.95**

 $22.95/**$2.95**

 $35.00/**$5.95**

 $50.00/**$5.95**

 $29.95/**$5.95**

 $19.95/**$1.95**

The Psychotherapy
Book Club Guarantee

- There is no minimum purchase required.

- You receive a **FREE SUBSCRIPTION** to the *Psychotherapy Book News.*

- If you want the main selection, do nothing. It will automatically be sent to you.

- If you want another book or no book at all, you simply mark the reply card and return it by the specified date. If you receive a main selection without having at least 10 days to notify the Book Club, you may return it for full credit.

- You pay only the low member price for each book plus shipping and handling.

NEW MEMBER APPLICATION

☐ **YES,** send me a **FREE SUBSCRIPTION** to the *Psychotherapy Book News,* and begin my membership in the Book Club according to the Guarantee described above.

Name _____

Address _____

City _____ State _____ ZIP _____

New Member's Signature _____
                                      (Signature required)

Sponsors can choose their **FREE BOOK** from the most recent issue of the *Psychotherapy Book News.*

Sponsor's Name _____

Account # _____

Address _____

City _____ State _____ ZIP _____

FREE BOOK Code # and Title _____

_____

PI0100

Psychotherapy Book Club

members get a

FREE BOOK

when they sponsor a new member.

FOLD, SEAL AND MAIL

from autoerotism to narcissism to higher forms and transformations of narcissism. Pathological narcissism is the result of failures of empathy and inadequate mirroring by the parents during this narcissistic stage. A parent, usually the mother, may idealize her child, in which case the child's personality will become organized around a grandiose, exhibitionistic idea; he or she will continue to need such idealization from people in later life and will suffer narcissistic injuries (a loss of self-esteem and a rage reaction) whenever people cannot fill that need. A parent may demand that the child idealize her (the child is great because of his or her relationship with a great person, the parent). In either case, the child remains fixed at this stage, as he is not able to develop a self separate from his parent's, or, as Kohut put it, the "transmuting internalization" does not occur, and he or she never advances to the point of being able to relate to another person as a separate object.

Kohut defines the analytic process with narcissistic personalities as an attempt by the analyst to help the patient achieve the transmuting internalization (roughly equivalent to Mahler's "separation-individuation") that was blocked during childhood. In a narcissistic transference, the analyst becomes a selfobject to the patient, serving either as an idealized or an idealizing object (one who mirrors the patient's grandiosity). Kohut (1977) states that a "fundamental claim of the psychology of the self [is] that the presence of an empathic or introspective observer defines, in principle, the psychological field" (p. 32n). By "empathic or introspective observer," Kohut meant analysts, who are no longer neutral in the classical sense but allow themselves to be idealized by the patient or to mirror the patient's grandiosity until such time as he or she has developed a more cohesive self. Once that has occurred, standard technique can be employed.

In his paper "The Two Analyses of Mr. Z." (1979), Kohut describes two separate analyses with the same patient, each conducted five times a week and each lasting about four years. He provides no dates for either analysis. In the first analysis, Kohut claims to have used a traditional classical approach, while in the second, more successful analysis he utilized his newly developed self-psychology technique. The patient first consulted him when he was a graduate student in his mid-twenties. Kohut describes him as handsome, well-built, and muscular with a pale and sensitive face that was in contrast to his athletic appearance, and who spoke in a halting manner. Mr. Z.'s initial complaints were vague: he talked about extrasystoles, sweaty palms, feelings of fullness in his stomach, and alternating periods of constipation and diarrhea. He said that he felt lonely, was unable to form lasting relationships with women, and, he thought, was functioning below his capacities at school.

For a time Mr. Z. had relieved his loneliness by going out with a friend. Sometimes he and the friend would be joined by Mr. Z.'s mother. His father had died when Mr. Z. was 21, leaving behind a tidy inheritance, and Mr. Z. had since lived with his mother, who painted and had a variety of artistic interests. After the father's death, his friend and his mother had been his main companions; then the friend became attached to an older woman and excluded Mr. Z. from his new relationship. This sent Mr. Z. to analysis.

As the analysis proceeded Mr. Z. revealed, haltingly and with shame, through his fantasies, a masochistic attitude toward women. In his fantasies he abjectly performed menial tasks for a domineering woman, who forced him to perform the sexual act. "At the moment of ejaculation he typically experienced the feeling of desperately straining to perform in accordance with the woman's commands, similar, as he explained, to a horse that is made to pull a load that is too heavy for its powers and is driven on by the coachman's whip to give its last ounce of strength . . ." (p. 4).

In recounting his early childhood, he portrayed the first three years of his life as happy. When he was 3½ "certain events of far-reaching significance" took place. Mr. Z.'s father became ill and had to stay in a hospital for several months. During his stay, he fell in love with a nurse and went to live with her after he had recovered. The affair lasted about a year and a half. When his father returned, Mr. Z. was 5 years old and had grown used to having his mother to himself. Family life was restored, but the marriage was an unhappy one thereafter.

The main theme of the first year of analysis was "a regressive mother transference." Treating Mr. Z.'s narcissism from a classical standpoint, Kohut saw the patient as an unrealistic, grandiose individual who demanded that his therapist let him have complete control of the analytic situation and admire and dote on him as his mother had done, particularly before his father's return when the child was 5 years old. Kohut repeatedly presented Mr. Z. with reconstructive interpretations of his behavior. He would explain how Mr. Z. transferred his mother onto his analyst, and expected special treatment from him, and this need for special treatment could be traced back to a time when he had his mother all to himself, with no preoedipal sibling rivals and no father who might have been an oedipal rival.

"He blew up in rages against me, time after time," Kohut writes. "Indeed the picture he presented during the first year and a half of the analysis was dominated by his rage" (p. 5). He would rage about Kohut's interpretations concerning his "narcissistic demands" and his "arrogant feelings of 'entitlement,'" or because of weekend interruptions, scheduling difficulties, or vacations.

"You don't understand me!" Mr. Z. would erupt again and again.

Kohut would counter with another interpretation.

After a year and a half the patient abruptly became calmer and less demanding. Kohut assumed that the interpretations had been successful and said so, telling Mr. Z. that the working through of his narcissistic delusions was now bearing fruit. The patient disagreed, but in a calm and friendly way. "The change has taken place not primarily because of a change in me," Mr. Z. said, "but because of something *you* did. Remember when you began one of your interpretations about my insatiable narcissistic demands with the phrase, 'Of course, it hurts when one is not given what one assumes to be one's due'? That's what did it." Kohut did

not take the patient seriously at the time, thinking that "by denying the effectiveness of my interpretation he was putting up a last-
ditch resistance against the full acceptance of the delusional nature
of his narcissistic demands" (p. 5).

From then on Kohut focused on Mr. Z.'s infantile sexuality
and aggression—"his Oedipus complex, his castration anxiety, his
childhood masturbation, his fantasy of the phallic woman, and,
especially, his preoccupation with the primal scene" (p. 5). Gradually more material emerged. Mr. Z. had witnessed his parents' love-
making from the time he was about 5 until the time he was 8.
During the time his father was away, he had slept next to his mother
in his father's twin bed. After his father returned he slept on a couch
at the foot of his parents' beds, from where he could hear them
having sex. They fought frequently during those years, and in his
memories Mr. Z. thought of their sexual intercourse as another form
of fighting. More material also emerged about Mr. Z.'s own sexual
activity. He had been an obsessive masturbator for as long as he
could remember, and his sexual fantasies had been stimulated by a
book his mother had read him, *Uncle Tom's Cabin*, which was about
black slaves. From the age of 5 to 11 he imagined himself being
bought and sold like a slave by women. "He was ordered about,
treated with great strictness, had to take care of his mistress's excre-
ments and urine—indeed, in one specific, often repeated fantasy, the
woman urinated into his mouth, i.e., she forced him to serve her as
an inanimate vessel such as a toilet bowl" (p. 6). Finally, material
emerged about a two-year-long homosexual relationship Mr. Z. had
had with a camp counsellor during his preadolescent years. Mr. Z.
idealized this friend, and Kohut interpreted that this relationship
was "a reactivation of the bliss of the pre-oedipal, pregenital relation
to the idealized mother" (p. 7). The relationship ended when Mr. Z.
reached puberty and at the same time "gross sexuality" entered the
picture; for the first time in the relationship, the counsellor tried—
unsuccessfully—to penetrate Mr. Z. anally, and then had an ejaculation as Mr. Z. caressed his penis.

Kohut's approach throughout this first analysis was "fully in
tune with the classical theories of psychoanalysis" (p. 7). He

interpreted Mr. Z.'s masochism as sexualization of his guilt about the preoedipal possession of his mother and rejection of his father. Mr. Z. had to create the imagery of a domineering phallic woman, Kohut contended, to assuage his castration anxiety. This imagery denied the existence of human beings who had no penises by giving women power over him (penis = power), and it asserted that his mother was more powerful than his father and could protect him from his father's wrath.

Gradually, as he worked through the underlying conflicts, Mr. Z.'s masochistic preoccupations diminished. He moved out of his mother's house, began dating a woman a year older than he, and had satisfactory sexual relations with her. Although Kohut noticed that there were still reactivations of his narcissistic attitudes, expectations, and demands during the last two years of analysis, he interpreted them with "increasing firmness," telling the patient these new reactivations were resistances to deeper fears about masculine assertiveness and rivalry. Mr. Z. seemed calmed by these interpretations. Kohut believed that the deepest conflicts were finally reached after three and a half years of therapy, when Mr. Z. brought in a "significant" dream:

> In this dream—his associations pointed clearly to the time when the father rejoined the family—he was in a house, at the inner side of a door which was a crack open. Outside was the father, loaded with giftwrapped packages, wanting to enter. The patient was intensely frightened and attempted to close the door in order to keep the father out. [p. 8]

Again, Kohut interpreted this dream classically, stressing that it referred to the boy's ambivalent attitude toward the returning father, his castration fear, and his tendency to retreat from competitiveness and male assertion to the preoedipal attachment to his mother and to a submissive or passive homosexual attitude to the father.

As the termination phase wound down, Kohut felt that something was not quite right, but he was not sure what it was. Only later, upon recollection, did he realize that the entire terminal phase was "emotionally shallow and unexciting" in contrast to the rest of the treatment, which was full of strong emotion from Mr. Z. Nevertheless, the first treatment ended with a warm handshake "and the expression of gratitude on his part and of good wishes for his future life on mine" (p. 9).

Four and a half years later Mr. Z. wrote Kohut to congratulate him about a professional office he was currently holding (Kohut once served as president of the American Psychoanalytic Association) and to acknowledge that he himself was not doing so well and was interested in resuming analysis. During the intervening years he had had a succession of relationships but they all seemed shallow and unsatisfactory. He was successful at his profession (Kohut does not say what it was), but his career seemed more a burden than a pleasure. Also, since he had moved out of his mother's house, her health had taken a turn for the worse, and she had become paranoid. Kohut concluded that the patient's masochistic propensities had been suppressed rather than resolved by the first analysis, and had shifted to his work and life in general. Six months later the second analysis began.

At the beginning of the second analysis, as in the first, Mr. Z. idealized Kohut, just as he had idealized his mother; this time, unlike the first, Kohut did not interpret this idealization. "In harmony with my then newly acquired insights about the analyst's correct attitude vis-à-vis a narcissistic transference *in statu nascendi*, I did not interfere with the unfolding of the patient's idealization of me" (p. 11). After about two weeks this idealization began to subside and was replaced by a mirror transference of the merger type. Mr. Z.'s glow of well-being faded and he became "self-centered, demanding, insisting on perfect empathy, and inclined to react with rage at the slightest out-of-tuneness with his psychological states, with the slightest misunderstanding of his communications" (pp. 11–12). While in the first analysis Kohut had looked upon such behavior as defensive, tolerated it as unavoidable, and then confronted it with interpretations; in the second analysis he saw it as "an analytically valuable replica of a

childhood condition that was being revived in the analysis"
(p. 12). This new approach eliminated the patient's "unproduc-
tive rage reactions" and led to the penetration of a formerly
unexplored part of Mr. Z.'s personality—his narcissistic attachment to his mother.

Not only had Kohut's theoretical outlook changed since the
first analysis, but, more importantly, his analytic stance had
changed as well. During the first analysis he had wanted to help
the patient relinquish his narcissistic demands and grow up. In the
second he set aside goal-directed therapeutic ambitions and re-
stricted himself to the task of reconstructing the early stages of
Mr. Z.'s experiences, particularly as they related to the pathological personality of his mother. In addition, Kohut's view of the
mother–son relationship had also changed. In the first analysis he
had seen the patient's idealistic attachment to his mother in terms
of an unconscious incestuous tie, while in the second analysis the
actual character of the mother came more sharply into focus. She
was a person who "held intense, unshakable convictions that were
translated into attitudes and actions which emotionally enslaved
those around her and stifled their independent existence" (p. 13).
In exchange for idealizing her son, she demanded that he submit to
her total domination of his life. He was not allowed to have any
other significant relationships, particularly with other women. As
his mother's character came to light, Kohut and Mr. Z. understood
why his father had gone to live with the nurse: it was a flight from
the mother's intense and pathological possessiveness. "As the patient saw it: the father had tried to save himself, and in doing so he
had sacrificed the son" (p. 13).

While the patient got in touch with more of his memories of
"the serious distortion" of his mother's personality, he became
more resistant. He began retreating from the analytic task. "I
wonder whether these memories are really correct," he would say.
"Perhaps I'm slanting this presentation for you, because it's what
you want to hear." Kohut interpreted this resistance in terms of
fears about the loss of his mother as "an archaic selfobject." Mr. Z.
was afraid that if he gave voice to these long-repressed negative

thoughts, feelings, and memories about his mother, she would no longer idealize him, and his self would disintegrate. It was almost as though she were in the room with him, listening to his every word. Slowly and painfully Mr. Z. was able to shake off his mother's indoctrination and the aura of sacrosanctity with which she had enveloped their relationship. He began to see that while she had seemed to be in empathic contact with him, in reality she had used him as a selfobject, to serve her forever. Even when she spoke in glowing terms of how successful he would be in life, her assumption was that she would always be there at his side.

A new well of memories emerged about his mother. Until he was 6 she had taken an intense interest in his bowel movements, insisting on inspecting them after each sitting. Then, when he turned 6, she abruptly stopped these inspections and began to be concerned with the skin on his face. The ritual of inspecting his face for blackheads took place every Saturday until he moved out. This ritual had two phases. In the first she would describe to Mr. Z. disapprovingly and in great detail what she saw; in the second she would proceed to remove the ripest of the blackheads. "The mother, who frequently expressed her pride in her long and hard fingernails, described to her son its extrusion and showed him the extracted plug of sebum—a faecal mass in miniature—with satisfaction, after which she seemed gratified, and Mr. Z. too, experienced some temporary relief" (p. 15).

Kohut asserts that during the first analysis he might have diagnosed the mother as an obsessive-compulsive with "anal-sadistic drive aims." However, during this second analysis he saw her differently. She was, he contends, a borderline narcissistic personality. He believed she had a psychotic core, a "central pre-psychological chaos" in her personality, and that this "central hollowness" of her self caused her to compulsively maintain a strict control over her selfobjects, whom she needed in order to restrain her self. Though superficial acquaintances saw her as normal, those who knew her "soon felt the lifelessness that lay underneath the appearance of normality" (p. 15).

At this point in the second analysis, Kohut asked himself why all this crucial material about Mr. Z.'s mother had not surfaced during the first analysis. Kohut claims that it was because during the first analysis he was biased by his classical orientation; he was so intent on discovering infantile drives and conflicts between id, ego, and superego that he did not pay attention to the mother's narcissism. Moreover, Kohut's seemingly unshakable convictions about these drives and conflicts became for the patient a replica of the mother's distorted outlook on the world, to which the patient had adjusted in childhood and accepted as reality. That attitude of acceptance and compliance had become reinstated with regard to Kohut, and the success of the first analysis was, Kohut now decided, merely a "transference success." The patient improved because Kohut told him to.

As Mr. Z. overcame more and more of his "disintegration anxiety" (the fear of losing his mother as a selfobject) the analysis plunged forward. Now Kohut was able to reinterpret two other sets of childhood experiences which, during the first analysis, had been interpreted in terms of drives and conflicts: his obsessive masturbation, and his preoccupation with the primal scene. "We realized not only that neither his masturbation nor his involvement in the primal scene had ever been enjoyable, but that a depressive, black mood had pervaded most of his childhood" (p. 17). Mr. Z. now understood the primal scene as a demand by his mother that he witness even her most personal interactions and be absorbed by them, a demand to which he submitted "via the masochistic relinquishment of his independence" (p. 18). Since he could not genuinely experience a sense of being alive, his self having not separated from his mother, his masturbation was an attempt, "through the stimulation of the most sensitive zones of his body, to obtain temporarily the reassurance of being alive" (p. 18). In discussing his memories of masturbation, Mr. Z. now recalled, not without a great deal of shame, that he had engaged in "anal masturbation" and had smelled and even tasted his feces. He came to understand "in empathic consonance with another human being" that these childhood activities were not bad or disgusting; these too were attempts to reassure himself that he was alive.

The "second phase" of the "second analysis" turned to a consideration of the role of Mr. Z.'s father. Mr. Z. now remembered the primal scene from his father's angle, seeing him as a weak man dominated and subdued, sexually and otherwise, by his mother. He remembered the friend who used to go out with him and his mother, whose abandonment led to his first entering treatment; he saw this friend also as a weak man, running from Mr. Z.'s mother. However, he remembered the camp counsellor, with affection and respect, as a strong and admired man.

With respect to his interpretation of Mr. Z.'s relationship to the camp counsellor, Kohut's view had also changed since the first analysis. At that time he had said that the relationship represented a regression to the phallic mother; now he believed that the counsellor had been a "yearned-for figure of a strong fatherly man, perhaps the admired older brother he had never had" (p. 19).

While Mr. Z. still complained about his father's weakness, and about the friend who had abandoned him, he also began to express an intense curiosity about Kohut.

"What was your childhood like?" he would ask. "What are your interests? Where were you educated? What's your family life like? Do you love your wife? How's your sex life? Do you have any children?"

"Your curiosity about me is a replication of your curiosity about your parents during the primal scene," Kohut interpreted.

"You misunderstand me," Mr. Z. retorted (p. 19).

Eventually Kohut agreed that he was misinterpreting Mr. Z.'s motivations. His patient was not, he realized, expressing a revival of sexual voyeurism, but was attempting to find out if Kohut was a strong man, who had a healthy relationship with his wife, and who could serve as a strong father-figure for his children. When he gave Mr. Z. this new interpretation Mr. Z. seemed pleased and dropped his insistent demands for information. From then on the analysis began to focus on Mr. Z.'s father, and for the first time Mr. Z. spoke of his father with "a glow of happiness," stressing the positive features in his personality. This was, Kohut believed, the turning point of the treatment.

As he focused on "the discovery of the strong father," Mr. Z. had recurrent attacks of severe anxiety, dreams about his mother turning her back on him, nightmares about desolate landscapes, burned-out cities, and heaps of piled up bodies, dreams that featured images similar to those of the concentration camps he had seen on television. Kohut interpreted these dreams and nightmares as indications that Mr. Z. "was now relinquishing the archaic self (connected with the selfobject mother) . . . in preparation for the reactivation of a hitherto unknown independent nuclear self (crystallized around an up-to-now unrecognized relationship with his selfobject father)" (p. 19).

Mr. Z. began recalling positive things about his father—his charm, his attractiveness to people around him, and the skill and resoluteness with which he handled his business affairs. He dwelled in particular on a memory of being with his father at a resort in Colorado. His mother had to take care of her sick mother at the time, so it was one of the rare occasions she had allowed the son and father to spend time together. One night his father, having indulged in drink, went on stage in a nightclub and took over for the orchestra's regular singer, to rousing applause. A woman came over and congratulated him afterwards—somebody his father evidently knew—and the boy thought that perhaps his father was having an affair with her. This memory of his father's personality when he was away from his mother, and the male bonding that took place during their trip, was very important to Mr. Z. He realized that up to that point in the analysis he had seen his father only through his mother's distorted lens.

The termination phase of the second analysis began in the same way as had the terminal phase of the first—with an interpretation of the dream about his father returning home with gifts, one which highlighted the dream's new meaning:

The new meaning of the dream as elucidated by the patient via his associations, to put his message into my words, was not a portrayal

of a child's aggressive impulse against the adult male, accompanied
by castration fear, but of the mental state of a boy who had been all-
too-long without a father; of a boy deprived of the psychological
substance from which, via innumerable observations of the father's
assets and defects, he would build up, little by little, the core of an
independent masculine self. [p. 23]

By the end of the second analysis Mr. Z. had essentially
broken the "deep merger ties" with his mother and forged a link
with his father's "maleness and independence." He could now
pursue his life goals not in a masochistic way but joyfully, as the
activities of "an independent self." He spoke of plans for a major
work, and after termination this work came to fruition and established him in his field. A few years later Kohut received a postcard
saying that Mr. Z. had married, and another several years later
announced the birth of a daughter. Kohut heard that Mr. Z.'s wife
was a "well-balanced, warm-hearted, socially outgoing person,
without a trace of the paranoid certainty and need to control that
had characterized Mr. Z.'s mother" (p. 26).

As for Kohut, he himself went on to become a major contrib-
utor to his own field, and those who knew him say that his
personality changed over the years as he went from being a shy,
modest young man to end up the grandiose founder of a psychoanalytic school. Always in frail health, he passed away at the age
of 68, two years after the publication of "The Two Analyses of
Mr. Z."

Interpretation

After its publication, "The Two Analyses of Mr. Z." became the
focus of much controversy. At the center of this controversy is the
issue of whether or not interpretations based on self psychology
tend to avoid patients' aggression, gloss over sexual and oedipal
material, and lead patients away from their nuclear oedipal conflicts. In addition, there has been a debate over whether the first

analysis should be considered a classical analysis or simply a bad one.

Ostow (1979) asserts that in the first analysis Kohut was not discerning enough. He did not notice the contrast between the idealized relationship Mr. Z. described himself as having with his mother, and the hostility he exhibited in the transference and in his masturbation fantasies. The transference was full of rage suggesting hostility to the mother, according to Ostow, and this hostility was confirmed by the sadomasochistic masturbation fantasies about being enslaved to a phallic woman. Ostow believes this oversight was made not because Kohut was using a classical approach, but rather because he was not using it competently.

A New York psychoanalyst is quoted by Malcolm (under the pseudonym of "Aaron Green") as saying about Kohut's Mr. Z., "The first analysis, which he calls a 'classical analysis,' just didn't make sense. In the second, 'Kohutian' analysis, he finally did what any one of us 'classical' analysts would have done in the first place." He adds that Kohut's description of the first analysis reads "like a caricature of analysis, while the second analysis is made to seem rich and profound, subtle and empathic, humanistic and humane" (Malcolm 1980, p. 118). He alludes to a trend of these kinds of case histories, in which one therapeutic approach is made to look bad in contrast with another approach, which the writer just happens to be advocating.

Edelson (1984) echoes these sentiments, arguing that the history of Mr. Z. does not validate Kohut's therapeutic approach, since the case material can be interpreted in any number of ways. Indeed, Edelson chastises Kohut, implying that he is naive and shows little understanding of what is required to make a convincing argument for the hypothesis he is presenting.

Chessick (1989), while generally in agreement with Kohut about the efficacy of self psychology, nevertheless demonstrates that the central dream by Mr. Z. of his father coming home with gifts can be interpreted in a number of ways other than the two presented in the history. Looked at from the Kleinian perspective, the gifts might represent part objects—breasts, penises, etc.—or "all-good self and object representations that the patient yearned to incorporate inside himself in order to neutralize his own bad inner self and object representations" (p. 173). Perceived from a phenomenological angle, an interpretation might focus on the struggle between the patient and his father, taking the dream at face value. "It is possible these are gifts that have been given to the father, thereby emphasizing his power, his genitals, and his other possessions (perhaps the mother), all of which he is potentially able to give to the patient should he wish to do so" (p. 174). The interactive point of view might stress the transference nature of the dream. "In it the patient is attempting to keep from being penetrated by the therapist; the patient is in a passive, frightened, submissive homosexual attitude toward the therapist" (p. 174).

Ornstein (1981) supports Kohut's claim that the case demonstrates the superiority of the self-psychology approach with narcissistic patients. By interpreting the father dream near the end of the first analysis in terms of oedipal rivalry, Kohut had cut off further investigation. In the second analysis, when Kohut used a more empathic approach, he was able to understand that Mr. Z. needed to acquire the idealized male strength of his father. In effect, Kohut had shifted to a point of view in which he identified with the patient, rather than with the patient's mother. Hence the patient was no longer seen as a demanding tormentor, but as someone tormented.

Meyerson (1981) also hails Kohut's treatment of Mr. Z., but believes that the second analysis was successful not because of greater empathy, but because of the language used by Kohut. Kohut guided Mr. Z. to the realization that it was all right for him to have negative feelings about his mother and to express his rage, his masochism, and his exhibitionism during his sessions. This helped him to consolidate his "true self." According to Meyerson, Kohut was simply being fatherly, in the best psychotherapeutic tradition.

Kohut (1984) answered his critics, asserting that he was not the victim of countertransference in the first analysis, nor did he deliberately distort his report of the technique he used in that analysis in order to make the second analysis seem superior. He admits, though, that some gifted classical analysts might have worked with Mr. Z. as he did in the second analysis. However, then he seems to hedge a bit, adding, "Even if I had emphasized certain features of my behavior, played them up, as it were, in order to make a point with special clarity, I would see nothing in such a move that would be out of keeping with our scientific communications" (p. 90). He explains that for him case histories are simply ways of illustrating his theses, and are not intended to be taken as scientific proofs; "they are a special means of communication within the professional community intended to clarify scientific information from a clinical researcher to his colleagues" (p. 89).

With regard to Kohut's theory of narcissism, Greenberg and Mitchell (1983) contend that in his effort to add to Freud's depiction of neurotic psychopathology based on the psychodynamics of object libido, "Kohut has stretched the concept of narcissism past the point of usefulness, setting it apart from other features of interpersonal relations. This has led to a blurring of crucial distinctions between mirroring of grandiosity and realistic caring and recognition, and between idealization and respectful commitment" (pp. 371–372). They further criticize Kohut for setting narcissism apart from object love (the realm of classical structural neurosis) and viewing everything as deriving from disturbances of narcissism.

Spotnitz (1985) gives Kohut credit for identifying narcissistic rage as a "specific manifestation of aggression that arises when the self or the object do not live up to the expectations directed at their function" (p. 56). This phenomenon was graphically illustrated in Mr. Z.'s case when Kohut did not live up to his expectations and treat him the way his mother had treated him—that is, when he did not mirror his grandiosity. However, Spotnitz differs with Kohut in that he actively encourages the patient's verbalization of aggression, whereas Kohut considers aggression a by-product that might be avoided if the therapist is empathic enough, as he points out in contrasting the beginning phase of the first analysis, when Mr. Z. was prone to frequent rages, with the beginning phase of the second analysis. (See Chapter 10.)

The Blancks (1974) praise Kohut for his boldness in making a foray into an unknown territory, but contend that only history will determine the validity of his theory. "It is our opinion . . . that, at our present state of knowledge, it is premature to attempt to delineate specific diagnostic entities for which specific courses of treatment may be prescribed" (p. 87). They cite ongoing infant observations that continually reap new insights into the many-faceted aspects of mother–child interaction in the critical early months.

I quibble with Kohut, as well as with others such as Kernberg (1975) and Hartmann (1958), who distinguish between normal and pathological narcissism. They define normal narcissism as the libidinal investment of the self, whereas pathological narcissism is seen as resulting from disturbances in this normal investment of the self, springing from environmental failures in early childhood. In my view, any libidinal investment of the self is pathological. The normal state of affairs is for the libido to be directed outward to another object. Healthy self-esteem does not spring from narcissism, but from a strong, well-balanced ego. I object to giving two meanings to narcissism just as I objected in an earlier book (Schoenewolf 1989) to Freud's distinction between normal and pathological masochism with respect to female sexuality. One of the reasons psychoanalysis has bogged down in the complexity of its terminology is because terms like "narcissism" and "masochism" keep being defined and redefined and, as Greenberg and Mitchell note, stretched beyond usefulness. Kohut, of course, is known for his needlessly dense and complicated writing style, as though he were trying to demonstrate superiority through his use of arcane language.

One of the charges made against Kohut is that he himself was narcissistic, and his psychology of the self was simply an outgrowth of his own narcissism, a grandiose creation of his grandiose self. There has even been talk by informed sources in the analytic community that Mr. Z. was Kohut—that he was writing about his own analytic experiences with Aichhorn and then his later self-analysis. If one compares the basic facts of Kohut's background with Mr. Z.'s, they generally match up: both Kohut and Mr. Z. were only children; both of their fathers died when they were in their early twenties; both lived with their mothers; both were physically large but had timid personalities as young men; both had friendships when they were boys with older men; both married rather late (at 36), and both had one child (although Mr. Z. had a daughter while Kohut had a son). Then there is the major project that Mr. Z. begins at the end of his second analysis, which will establish him in his field. Kohut could well have said the same about his first book. A certain vagueness in the details of the case, and the fact that Kohut did not provide dates for the two analyses, also lend support to this speculation. Freud admitted to writing about himself in *The Interpretation of Dreams* (1900), and in various other papers. Kohut, however, never commented on the rumors about the identity of Mr. Z. Perhaps we will never know.

No matter how one views the case of Mr. Z., it cannot be denied that Kohut's insights into narcissism led the way toward the understanding of one of the leading problems of the modern era. He provided a detailed picture of how narcissism develops, the forms in which it develops, and the forms in which it reappears in the therapist's office. Understanding these forms, therapists are better able to cope with modern patients, many of whom are either narcissistic or have narcissistic features in their characters.

10

THE PARADOXICAL ANALYST

Hyman Spotnitz and Fred (1976), and Harry (1988)

While Kohut concentrated on narcissism in general, Hyman Spotnitz explored its more severe forms, including schizophrenia. While Kohut focused on narcissistic grandiosity and the idealized or idealizing selfobject, Spotnitz emphasized the importance of narcissistic rage, both as an etiological factor and as a crucial matter to be dealt with in therapy. And while Kohut described the various forms of narcissistic transference, Spotnitz delineated the forms and utilization of narcissistic countertransference.

Spotnitz was born in Boston in 1908, the eldest of five children. His father owned a candy store, his mother was a housewife. He graduated from Harvard in 1929, then attended medical school at Friedrich Wilhelms University in Berlin, obtaining his medical degree in 1934. He returned to receive his doctorate in medical science from The College of Physicians and Surgeons, Columbia University, and was then accepted as a candidate at the New York Psychoanalytic Institute. However, Spotnitz fell into disagreement with the New York Psychoanalytic Institute about his control case. He wanted to analyze a schizophrenic, but the Institute considered such patients unsuitable for control cases. Always somewhat of a maverick, he broke with the institute and went his own way. He was in analysis with Lillian Delger Powers for five years (five to six times per week), and was supervised by Herman Nunberg and Sandor Rado during his analytic training.

Spotnitz's interest in schizophrenia began at the time he did his psychiatric residency. His first patient was "a beautiful young woman," who suffered "an acute schizophrenic episode" immediately after her marriage (Spotnitz 1976, p. 106). As she sat in a corner of the ward in a catatonic stupor, eyes gazing off at nobody, cigarette stubs burning her fingers without her being aware of it, Spotnitz stayed at her side. He remained with her several hours a day, five to seven days a week:

> I listened to her sympathetically, drawing her out on her symptoms laughing with her when she laughed at her own wisecracks, and making numerous other efforts to get her to make some emotionally significant communication. This made her no better.
>
> Then, during a session when I said some harsh words to her, she immediately came out of her stupor and hurled a glass ashtray that missed my head by an inch. The miss was intentional, she later told me, but she had felt like killing me. [p. 106]

He had made the discovery that would be the key to his therapeutic approach. A sympathetic response had simply increased the patient's defensive posture, while giving her back a dose of her own aggression brought her to life. He encouraged her to continue to express any aggressive feelings she had about him— but verbally. From that point on he was able to work successfully with her, and within six months she was released from the hospital as cured.

Spotnitz went on to found a new school of psychoanalysis— Modern Psychoanalysis—with its own particular perspectives on the nature of schizophrenia (which is considered in the modern psychoanalytic literature as a severe form of narcissism) and psychotherapy. His major writings have been collected into four books, *The Couch and the Circle* (1961), *Psychotherapy of Preoedipal Conditions* (1976), *Treatment of the Narcissistic Neurosis* (Spotnitz and Meadows 1976), and *Modern Psychoanalysis of the Schizophrenic Patient* (1985). In addition, *Modern Psychoanalysis*, the journal he helped found, devoted an entire issue to a case he supervised—"Treatment of a Pre-Schizophrenic Adolescent" (1988).

According to Spotnitz, individuals become "defective" to the degree that their maturational needs are not met in their interchanges with "natural objects" during their childhoods, particularly during their first two years of life. These maturational failures arouse a rage reaction in the child, and this rage is suppressed by parents; the children then withdraw into their own world, protecting primary objects and themselves from this rage and erecting an illusory world in which they are in some way powerful in order to compensate for their feelings of powerlessness.

Spotnitz (1985) developed a carefully designed approach for working with schizophrenics and narcissistic personalities, worded in the languages of science, medicine, and psychoanalysis. This approach is aimed at unleashing the patients' dammed up aggression and helping them talk. "The analyst's participation in resolving resistance is consistently one of providing communications that will enable the patient to verbalize freely all impulses, feelings, thoughts, and memories" (p. 104). For patients who have formed only a narcissistic transference, he recommends from two to five units of communication [sentences] per session; for those who have attained an object transference he recommends from 10 to 100 units of communication. Too much communication—"excessive sensory input"—with patients who are in a narcissistic transference may impede patients' verbalizations or, as Spotnitz puts it, cause "inadequate motor output." Similarly, too little communication may have the same result. As to the forms of communication which the analyst utilizes, Spotnitz has devised a range of interventions for every possible therapeutic situation—from "object-oriented questions" (questions that direct a narcissistic patient's attention to the therapist) to "ego-oriented questions" (questions that direct the patient's attention to his own functioning, used only after a patient has attained an object transference); from "ego syntonic joining" (agreeing with a patient who feels abused by her husband) to "ego dystonic joining" (agreeing with a patient who continually devalues himself); from "commands" (with out-of-control patients) to "explanations" (for facilitating better rapport). All such interventions are termed "maturational communications" or "verbal feedings."

Spotnitz's most famous, and most controversial, maturational communication is the "toxoid response," an elaboration of Winnicott's concept of objective hate (1947), Reich's character analysis (1933), and Jacobson's timed expression of anger (1971). In his classic paper "The Toxoid Response," originally published (1976) in *The Psychoanalytic Review*, Spotnitz writes that "in cases of schizophrenia, psychotic depression and other severe disturbances, one encounters resistances, chiefly preverbal, that do not respond to objective interpretation. Their resolution is thwarted by toxic affects that have interfered with the patient's maturation and functioning" (Spotnitz 1976, p. 49). He asserts that such resistances yield to an "emotional working-through process" rather than to customary "working-through on an intellectual basis"; one way this emotional working-through can be accomplished is by a "toxic response." He compares this process to the science of immunology, wherein individuals are injected with a mild case of a disease in order to immunize them against it. When a narcissistic patient begins acting out rage toward the analyst, the analyst develops a narcissistic countertransference—becoming infected with the patient's feelings. The analyst then conducts a self-analysis to ensure that the rage has been induced by the patient (objective countertransference) and not by his or her own unresolved psychopathology (subjective countertransference). If it is determined that the rage has been induced by the patient, the analyst may decide to administer a dose of this rage back to the patient. The patient "is given verbal injections of the emotions he has induced in the analyst, carefully 'treated' to destroy their toxicity and to stimulate the formation of antibodies," Spotnitz (1976) explains. "In brief, *the induced emotions are employed as a toxoid*" (p. 50). Spotnitz cautions that this intervention is not to be used indiscriminately, for it can cause damage to the patient if the therapist is not sure that his countertransference is objective.

In his most famous case history, about a schizophrenic patient he calls "Fred," Spotnitz demonstrates the use of not only the toxoid response but a full range of maturational communications. Fred's case, detailed in several chapters of *Psychotherapy of Preoedipal Conditions* (1976), probably took place during the 1950s, when Spotnitz was still formulating his technique. When he entered treatment, Fred was a "highly intelligent young man" of 20, on the verge of "a full-blown psychosis." He had a history of suicidal attempts, sexual escapades, arrests for reckless driving, and disputes with teachers and classmates that had led to his dropping out of college.

From the first session on Spotnitz lost no time in helping Fred to verbalize his aggressive feelings. During the first session, Fred spoke nervously about the "breakdown" that had ended his college career, about his parents, and about his childhood. Then, becoming agitated, he started questioning Spotnitz. What was he interested in? What were his hobbies? These questions were interspersed with provocative remarks, such as, "This couch must be older than I am" (p. 132). Spotnitz countered by asking him similar questions, and making similarly provocative remarks. "The more I talked as he did," Spotnitz explains, "the more secure he felt, and his mounting feelings of security enabled him to verbalize a great deal of anger" (p. 133). By the end of the second session, he threatened to tear Spotnitz's office apart. Spotnitz asked Fred what he would do, and he replied that he would break the windows and smash the desk lamp. Spotnitz reminded him that he was supposed to verbalize his feelings, not act on them.

When this instruction was repeated during the third session, Fred retorted that he had no intention of cooperating. He said that

his father had forced him to come, and he did not want to be there
anyway. Spotnitz then used the technique of "ego syntonic joining."

> "Then why don't you stop?" I asked him. "If you don't want
> to be treated, you don't have to be."
> "You're only saying this because you know my father won't
> let me stop," he replied. "You know I can't buck him."
> "No, I'm serious about this," I told Fred. "If I tell your father
> that you should stop, he will believe me." [p. 133]

They haggled over this issue for two more sessions before
Fred was convinced of Spotnitz's sincerity. Then Fred shook his
hand and started to leave; Spotnitz told him to be sure not to come
back unless he really wanted to be treated. This series of interventions, according to Spotnitz, was a therapeutic maneuver designed
to increase "the insulative capacity of Fred's ego" so that he could
stand up to his father and verbalize his negative feelings about
therapy. Two days later Fred's father called, and Spotnitz told him
that Fred should not come unless he himself wanted to. Ten days
later Fred called, pleading for an immediate appointment. Spotnitz
arranged a session for that same day.
     Fred's anger at Spotnitz abated for a few sessions, then
emerged again. He would talk about wanting to get off the couch
and attack Spotnitz, then lapse into silence. Spotnitz tried to get
him to continue to verbalize such feelings, but it was a struggle.
"Feelings of guilt about what he might say clammed him up. He
also had strong fears that talking about his impulses would force
him to act on them. He was convinced that his destructive urges
proved that he was incurable" (p. 54).
     Spotnitz began noticing that Fred's threats were arousing a
great deal of resentment in him. When Fred boasted of how his
fantasies of violence made him unique, Spotnitz felt more resentment. He decided to give Fred a toxoid response. The next time
Fred threatened Spotnitz, Spotnitz threatened Fred back, but inef-

fectually. "Don't try that stuff," Fred countered. "You're repeating what I say but you don't really feel it" (p. 55). Spotnitz had the impression that Fred was egging him on and so he bided his time, allowing the induced rage to build up inside him. A short time later, Fred exploded during the middle of a session, shouting, "I'll bash your head in."

"No you won't," Spotnitz exploded back, "because I'll bash yours in before you can get off the couch" (p. 55).

Fred was awed, exclaiming that he thought Spotnitz really did hate him as much as he hated Spotnitz and could be even more vicious. Spotnitz believed that Fred garnered relief and security from such emotional responses. As he did so, he became less and less terrified of his destructive urges and they gradually lost their toxic quality. He saw that somebody he respected and relied on could accept and verbalize such urges, and that he himself could dwell on these "long-outlawed feelings and thoughts" without acting impulsively.

At another point during the treatment, toward the end of the first year, Fred walked in wearing a new suit and called Spotnitz's attention to it. It was the first suit he had ever picked out for himself. Spotnitz praised him for making such a good purchase. As Fred lay on the couch, he reflected that his face was ugly. Spotnitz silently interpreted that he was "really telling me: Though I want to be admired, I don't deserve to be" (p. 110).

Spotnitz replied, "You do look somewhat beast-like."

Fred laughed, and said he knew Spotnitz was exaggerating, but he liked it when Spotnitz agreed with him, because whenever he had put himself down to his parents, they had always tried to build him up and it disturbed him. (Being regarded as an ugly beast, Spotnitz understood, gave Fred a "feeling of protection" in the presence of "a frustrating object," who would therefore be warned of Fred's dangerousness.) Fred recalled that during the previous session, when he had said he was stupid, Spotnitz had told him, "Why not be stupid?" He said he had felt relieved to hear this, for it meant he did not have to be intelligent, to con-

stantly reassure himself that he was not a moron. Spotnitz interpreted that being told to be stupid gave him permission to be a
happy infant.

"I feel like a nude baby looking himself over," Fred said. "I
feel just like wiggling my ears and hands and saying 'wiggle-
woggle'" (p. 110).

Fred's allusion to being a baby harkened back to his birth and
infancy. His mother had almost died during childbirth, and had
made him feel guilty for being born, and for being a boy instead of
a girl. He had spent his life "punishing himself, to expiate the
suffering he had brought to his mother" (p. 111). Shortly before
the end of the session, he said he wanted to be a male with a vagina
and asked if Spotnitz would cut off his penis. Spotnitz asked how
that would give him a vagina. Fred began rambling about fears of
castrating himself or torturing himself. "Maybe I'll die," he said.
"That would make things right with mother. I'd walk down the
stairs, throw my balls on the table and say to everybody, 'There—
that is reality'. . . . Who the hell knows what I'm talking about? I
ought to show you the wonderful pictures I have of sharks and
snakes" (p. 111).

Fred continued to be preoccupied with castration. One day,
when he asked Spotnitz if he should cut off his testicles and
present them to his mother, Spotnitz asked him, point-blank,
"Would you cut off your testicles for me?" Fred went speechless
with terror. "Why don't you get furious at me for asking you such
a question?" Spotnitz continued. "If your mother or anybody else
ever makes such a demand on you, you should tell them to go to
hell!" (p. 112). Fred laughed for ten minutes, and after that his
thoughts of castration ceased.

In the next few sessions, however, the rage that lay beneath
the fear of castration, the deep rage at his mother for unconsciously making this demand on him, began to build up and
became displaced onto Spotnitz. He shrieked that Spotnitz had
never done a thing for him except give him horrible feelings he had
never had before, that Spotnitz enjoyed being hated by him, and
enjoyed his misery. He said Spotnitz was a faker and a thief and

that he was going to report him to the AMA. Then he ran out of the office. For a few sessions after that he clammed up again. When he launched another attack of verbal abuse at him, Spotnitz reflected his abuse and gave some back to him. "He heard me out without saying a word. Then Fred got off the couch and solemnly shook my hand. 'If you can take what I've dished out here and give it back to me,' he said, 'you're my friend for life'" (p. 112).

The efforts to control Fred's assaultiveness continued for several years. Once, in a moment of fury, Fred reached for a bronze ashtray and shouted, "Stop this stalling and talk to me." Spotnitz calmly reminded him that he was to verbalize his feelings, not act them out.

As Fred's assaultiveness waned, he no longer verbalized the wish to attack Spotnitz, but rather expressed his resistance in less destructive ways. One day he talked about wanting to take a trip to California, going from there to Alaska.

"That sounds like a wonderful idea," Spotnitz told him. "But why limit yourself to this continent? There's so much more to see in the rest of the world. Why not make the trip really worthwhile by taking a boat to Australia, especially New Zealand?" (p. 134). By reflecting Fred's resistance pattern, Spotnitz hoped to convey, emotionally, that he was aware of both Fred's misery and of his attempt to run from treatment. By giving him permission to resist, Spotnitz also took the pleasure out of it.

Often Fred would plead with Spotnitz to relieve him of his emptiness and misery. When Spotnitz asked why he *should* relieve him, Fred replied, "I hate you for permitting me to go on tormenting myself" (p. 134). His narcissistic demand for verbal feeding was again and again frustrated by Spotnitz, leading to explosions, although the explosions were fewer and further between as the treatment wound down.

By the end of treatment, which probably lasted about five years, Fred's narcissistic preoccupations had diminshed considerably. (Spotnitz does not say exactly how long Fred's treatment lasted, nor how frequently he attended, but most modern analysts see patients once or twice a week.) He was "conditioned to the verbal discharge of his object interests," and felt secure enough to "attach himself to new objects." He became more interested in his work, his studies, and social activities. Years later, Spotnitz reported, "Fred is now a comparatively well-adjusted human being, married, and earning a good salary. He is regarded by himself, his family, and others who know him as a healthy and happy person" (p. 109).

Spotnitz's book-length case history, "Treatment of a Pre-Schizophrenic Adolescent" (1988), while not as interesting as his case about Fred, nevertheless conveys a somewhat more subdued picture of modern psychoanalysis. In this case Spotnitz served as supervisor, while the actual therapy was done by Leo Nagelberg. When he was 13, "Harry" was brought by his mother to the agency with which Spotnitz and Nagelberg were associated.

"I'm so worried," the mother told the initial interviewer. "Harry keeps on telling me he loves me so much he has to kill me. Sometimes he twists my arm or laughs hysterically as he says it. And he seems to enjoy hurting me. . . . Sometimes he jumps on my bed, covers my face with a pillow, and shouts that he's going to choke me" (p. 9).

Harry's treatment lasted four years. During the first three years he met with his therapist once a week; during the fourth year they met twice a week, for a total of 179 sessions. In his first sessions he spoke haltingly, in muffled tones. Although he was a brilliant student, he was losing interest in school. He wanted to stay in bed all day and listen to the radio, sometimes with a sheet over his head. He had nothing to tell the therapist. "I was born and I'm still living," he mumbled. The therapist told him he did not have to come if he did not want to. Harry came, and eventually he talked.

Harry's father had died when he was 5 years old. Afterwards, he and his mother had moved in with his grandparents for a while. The grandfather doted on his daughter and her son, but the grandmother was jealous and hostile toward them and, according to Spotnitz, set out to make their life a torment. Harry's mother eventually was forced to move into a furnished room with her son. There she surrounded him with constant flirtatious attention. Though they had separate beds, they slept close to each other. On weekends they exchanged beds. They dressed and undressed in front of each other, and they would push each other on the bed, sometimes playfully, sometimes angrily. The mother often provoked fights; then, as if in retaliation, she would slap her son or spit in his face. Sometimes she would lock herself in the bathroom. After scenes of violence, she would write poems to Harry asking that he enter "a harmonious relationship" with her, as a mother and her son should have.

During the beginning phase of treatment, Harry tried to come to grips with his violent impulses toward his mother and his frequent bouts of nausea (he had been throwing up since he was 6). In his fourteenth session, for example, he said that he had stayed in bed all morning, argued with his mother and, after supper, vomited. The therapist asked what the argument was about. Harry said that sometimes his mother told him she was not his mother. And she was always telling him to get out of the house, to go on an errand, to visit a friend. On that day he was trying to practice his clarinet:

> I was in the living room practicing. She told me she couldn't stand hearing me. She wanted me to take the clarinet into the bathroom. I offered to take off the mouthpiece and just to practice with my hands, but she said I just shouldn't practice in the living room. We argued some more and hit each other. Then at suppertime I threw up.
>
> Dr T.: Why does your mother tell you that she is not your mother?
>
> Harry: I used to tell her I wished she wasn't my mother, so she told me she would grant my wish. [p. 33]

Harry was caught between the "crossfire" of his mother's seductive and her rejecting behavior. He was disturbed by his aggressive and sexual feelings about her. "Vomiting is a way of getting rid of her, along with what she has fed him" (p. 33).

As Harry verbalized his violent urges toward his mother, they began to abate. Then for many sessions he talked about masturbation and "peeping" at his mother and at other women, seeming to want the therapist to intervene in some way. The therapist did intervene, suggesting that Harry cut down on his masturbation as an experiment, to see if he could control himself. The therapist understood that the boy needed a father-figure to help him learn to accept the frustration of his sexual drives. Harry's strong drive to masturbate and his fantasies of incest, served to isolate him from other human beings. His therapist hoped that by helping him learn to control his drives he might help him learn to feel more normal.

The therapist had biweekly supervisory conferences with Spotnitz. "After hearing his review of the material obtained from Harry and his own reactions to it," Spotnitz writes, "I functioned in the role of an accessory ego to increase his awareness of the totality of his emotional response to Harry and to help him deal with the problems that Harry presented" (p. 196). He instructed Nagelberg to mirror the patient (behave somewhat like him) in order to convey the message that "nothing dangerously new" would be injected into their relationship. Occasionally Spotnitz recommended specific interventions. Harry had begun to insist, session after session, that Nagelberg teach him psychology. One day he brought in a psychology book and read from it for almost the entire session. Then he told Nagelberg that while the book he was reading taught him many things, the therapist did not teach him anything. "The supervisory conference at this point," Nagelberg wrote in his case report, "was the most crucial one in the course of the whole case in terms of making me feel more comfortable" (p. 196).

Spotnitz suggested to Nagelberg that he ask Harry, "What would I get out of it if I teach you psychology?"

When, a session later, he put the question to Harry, it turned Harry's thinking around. "I can see your point," he said. "You would get nothing out of it. I wouldn't be giving you anything. I don't help you at all, but only myself. Well, never mind, I'll talk about myself anyway; I want to help myself" (p. 68). This intervention was a way of mirroring the boy's demandingness and letting him know, indirectly, that if one wants something in life, one must offer something in return. It also helped the therapist to feel more comfortable and to release the countertransference feelings Harry had induced in him. Finally, it made it clear to Harry that his wish to be taught psychology was an attempt to control the therapist, and the gratification of that wish would not truly benefit him, while discussing his problems would.

Later, during a period when Harry was insisting, again and again that Nagelberg adopt him—resulting in a long impasse—Spotnitz again advised Nagelberg to use a paradoxical mirroring technique. "In the supervisory conference preceding the ninety-seventh interview, I suggested that [he] turn the question around—that is, ask Harry why he did not adopt the therapist. The boy would then be able to view the situation from the position of the adult who can give rather than that of the child who needs" (p. 197). When the therapist did so, Harry expressed surprise at being asked such a question, then revealed that his mind was no longer set on being adopted.

Harry gradually managed to separate himself from his mother and to model himself after his therapist. Meanwhile, Harry's mother was also seeing a therapist at the agency, and she became more aware of her contribution to Harry's problems. Both steadily improved. During the 162nd session, Harry reported that he had had a conversation with his mother in which she had expressed remorse about what had happened when he was younger, saying she had done the best she could.

"From my viewpoint, I was right to feel rejected then," Harry told the therapist, "but from hers, she was right and she did not reject me" (p. 179).

Harry became more involved at school and with his peers and stopped staying home with his mother. Eventually he graduated from high school with honors and received a scholarship to a university. After the last session, his therapist noted that Harry was making good progress at home and at school, learning to relate to his peers as well as to his mother and his therapist. "Infantile urges still cause him some difficulty, but there is now a good margin of safety between his impulsiveness and his capacity to release his energy into socially acceptable behavior. Hence, he can plan for the future with some serenity, and move into it with considerable confidence" (p. 193). He concluded that Harry was now "an emotionally integrated" person who could function harmoniously with others.

Referring to the case as "the reconstruction of an ego fragmented by rage," Spotnitz concludes that although there were certain shortcoming of supervision and therapeutic technique, the treatment was successful overall. It achieved "structural change" through the use of "psychological reflection" and other joining approaches, demonstrating the efficacy of modern psychoanalysis.

Interpretation

While Spotnitz founded a new school of analysis and became a cult figure somewhat in the manner of Kohut, his writings were almost entirely ignored by the psychoanalytic establishment. There is no mention of him or his writings in the literature, except in those books written or edited by analysts of the modern psychoanalytic school. His supporters, usually other modern psychoanalysts, tend to idealize him, while his detractors tend to dismiss him as a "wild analyst." In truth, he is neither the prophet some followers make him out to be, nor the wild man his critics would have him be.

Why, then, has he been so ignored? The psychoanalytic establishment is a conservative lot, and it tends to veer away from anybody who is too liberal, too flamboyant, or too popular. For a long time, the establishment did not refer to the writings of Ferenczi, perceiving him as having gone astray. After Reich was sent to prison and went mad, the establishment did not mention his writings or his name for many years. (The irony is that psychoanalysis was itself once considered wild and pornographic by the psychiatric establishment and is still so thought of by some.) Spotnitz's use of paradoxical techniques, particularly the "*toxoid response*," is viewed by the establishment as misguided, just as were Ferenczi's active therapy and Reich's character analysis. The suspicion is that Spotnitz did not neutralize his own aggressive tendencies, and he therefore inflicted his aggression on his patients, justifying such abuse under the rubric of "maturational communication." Spotnitz contributed to this state of affairs by breaking with the New York Psychoanalytic Institute— an act of defiance that cast him as a heretic in the eyes of the establishment, as someone who could be dismissed as not having the character to finish "basic training." He contributed further to his rejection by the establishment by allowing himself to become a cult figure and publishing his most important book, *Modern Psychoanalysis of the Schizophrenic Patient*, in a bright red cover (it is referred to as the "red book," in an allusion to the sayings of the former dictator of China) and by conducting flamboyant demonstrations of his work at modern psychoanalytic conferences.

Ethan (1989), a psychoanalyst of the classical mold, privately summed up his objections to Spotnitz by saying, "Every modern analyst I've ever met seems to live, eat, and breathe Spotnitz. Yet what has he really done? Everything he claims he discovered was in reality discovered by others before him. His followers all idealize him, hang on to his every word, like infants at their mother's breast. And they have an attitude that modern analysis and only modern analysis is the correct way to do therapy. But they haven't really proven anything."

Supporters, however, claim that Spotnitz is misunderstood. They claim that most analysts have not adequately worked through their aggression; most deny their own aggression and resist confronting the aggression of their patients, a point made previously by Ferenczi (1933), Reich (1933), and Winnicott (1947). Hence, Spotnitz's theories are threatening to them.

Supporters also contend that Spotnitz made lasting contributions to the field. Margolis (1986), for example, asserts that "the writings of Hyman Spotnitz . . . provide the most authoritative formulations of the techniques [of joining and mirroring] and offer striking examples of their use in psychoanalytic therapy" (p. 21). Referring to the case histories—such as Fred's—in *Psychotherapy of Preoedipal Conditions*, Margolis explains that Spotnitz gradually evolved the notion of *joining* after painstaking work with schizophrenic and other narcissistic patients. He found that when the therapist aligned himself with the patient's resistance, the patient would invariably begin to cooperate. "The patient perceives joining as support of his innermost impulses and needs. He is thereby induced to let down his guard and enter a narcissistic relationship with the analyst, ultimately leading to the forthright expression of feelings" (p. 32).

Elsewhere, Margolis (1987) notes that Spotnitz's principal contributions to psychoanalysis were the treatment procedures he devised. "On the model of the mother–infant couple, the modern analyst treating the narcissistic patient occupies himself not merely with making the unconscious conscious, but with all the multifarious activities and interests of his patient, within and without the office framework" (p. 165). In modern psychoanalysis, Margolis asserts, the concept of management has been broadened to include not only the management of the therapeutic environment and the patient, but also the management of the patient's external environment (family, work situation, and so forth). It attempts to recreate for the patient the mother–infant situation, so that he can safely regress and experience a "normal unfolding of preordained maturational continuities" in the therapist's office. "Spotnitz may thus be said to have enlarged the purview of psychotherapy to cover all aspects of treatment of the narcissistic patient, management among them" (p. 165).

Meadow (1987) compares Spotnitz's distinction between objective and subjective countertransference to Winnicott's concept of "objective hate" and Racker's concordant and complementary countertransference. She notes that Spotnitz, more than anybody else, pondered the question of whether or not analysts could tolerate helping patients to say absolutely everything. Meadow claims that most of the difficulty that analysts have with this lies in the range of feelings that they can tolerate before taking action during the patient's sessions; for example, leaving the session before the time is up, throwing the patient out, or making hostile interpretations. "Spotnitz has written extensively about the negative narcissistic transference, in which the punitive pregenital aggression and the archaic wish to triumph over the hated object are aroused. Like Kohut, Spotnitz used an echoing technique, but rather than echo the words, he chose to echo emotionally the patient's hatred" (p. 135). Meadows asserts that this technique brought about a major improvement in the analyst's ability to help the patient feel understood.

Epstein (Epstein and Feiner 1979) credits Spotnitz, along with Winnicott (1947) and Searles (1955), with understanding that patients have a specific therapeutic need for the analyst's hateful feelings at certain times. In agreement with Spotnitz, Epstein says there are definitely times when a patient has a maturational need to experience feelings from his analyst, and this need challenges traditional analytic detachment. Epstein backs Spotnitz's contention that when a therapist meets a patient's hate with forbearing silence or sympathy, it makes the patient worse, setting up a vicious circle. "The patient is destructive; the therapist is kind and forbearing; the patient is in danger of recognizing the therapist as good and himself as bad; fearing devastation by guilt and self hatred, he hates the therapist all the more for provoking this dangerous situation" (p. 227). In other words, Epstein asserts, when a therapist responds to hate and contempt with benign understanding, such a response weakens the patient's ego. The patient feels guilty and bad for hating the therapist. "Suicidal impulses gain in strength; paranoid anxieties mount; manic and schizoid defenses are called into play" (p. 228).

Marshall (1979) finds Spotnitz's division of countertransference into objective and subjective countertransference useful. He goes even a step further, dividing each of them into conscious and unconscious components. A therapist, for example, might feel jealous of a patient because that patient arouses feelings the therapist had for his younger sister, yet be unaware of these feelings. In that case he would be said to have *unconscious subjective countertransference*. Or he might feel jealous and be aware of it. In that case he would have *conscious subjective countertransference*. Then again, he might feel jealous because this is the feeling that the patient is inducing in him (the feeling having nothing to do with the therapist's younger sister), yet not be aware of it. This would be *unconscious objective countertransference*. And if he were aware of it, he would have *conscious objective countertransference*. I would add here that there are some instances where there might be a combination of subjective and objective countertransference—when a patient is inducing a feeling in the therapist, and this feeling at the same time arouses something from the therapist's past. It is these instances, where there is a mixture of subjective and objective countertransference, that give a therapist the most difficulty.

Spotnitz (1988), answering his critics, notes that for many years psychoanalysts were convinced that it was impossible to reconstruct a psychotic ego. He refers specifically to Eissler's article about "psychoanalysis with parameters," which stipulated that modifications of the classical technique "must never transgress the unavoidable minimum" and that the "final phase of the treatment must proceed with a parameter of zero" (1953, p. 111). He then cites recent articles in the *International Journal of Psycho-Analysis* by Boesky (1988) and Beland (1988) that stress the importance of the negative transference, negative countertransference, and the feasibility of working with psychotics.

Notwithstanding the endorsements of his followers, Spotnitz is open to criticism in several areas. Theoretically, his writing is inconsistent. At times he attempts to mix neuropsychology with psychoanalysis, while at other times he writes on a strictly metapsychological level. Moreover, although he has attempted to formulate a new school of analysis that specializes in working with narcissistic patients, particularly schizophrenics, he has not developed an adequate theory of the development of narcissism. The theory he has developed is sketchy; he speaks of failures of "maturational communication" during childhood that lead to the build-up of rage, but he does not provide examples of such failures. His emphasis on the build-up of rage as an etiological factor and on the working-through of this rage in therapy seems a bit simplistic without more of a theoretical base.

His case histories also suffer from this flaw. The case of Fred is sketchy. He does not tell his readers exactly how long he treated Fred or how frequently Fred attended sessions (although, to his defense, such information is often not given in shorter histories). More important, there is not enough background information about Fred's childhood and about how he got to be the way he is. In addition, Spotnitz does not adequately explain why he does what he does and why his therapeutic approach works. His explanations about "insulating the ego," and supplying Fred with the maturational communications he needs are a step in the right direction, but leave the reader wanting to know more. How does the "toxoid response" really bring about change? His analogy with immunology—injecting individuals with a small dose of a disease in order to immunize them against it—is confusing. In modern psychoanalysis, the therapist is injecting the patient with a small dose of a disease the patient already has, while in immunology, the patient is injected with a disease he does not have. In essence, Spotnitz is giving the patient "a dose of his own medicine," to use the vernacular. This, of course, is "housewives' psychology" (a term that was once used to describe Freud's methods); it may be valid, but it is not adequately explained or documented. Spotnitz leaves it for others to fill in the gaps in theory.

In contrasting Spotnitz's treatment of Fred with Kohut's work with Mr. Z., I wonder how one method can seem so successful in dealing with rage, while another method seems just as successful. Could Kohut have treated Fred just as successfully by being an empathic selfobject? Could Spotnitz have analyzed Mr. Z. by reflecting his rage back at him? It may well be that both treatments could be effective, and that the crucial aspect of therapy is not so much the technique as the personality of the therapist.

Finally, Spotnitz's notion that the psychoanalyst should "manage" not only the patient but the patient's external environment does not stand him in good stead with the establishment. For example, modern analysts have been known to take stands on certain moral issues, as when they order a patient not to get an abortion. Here Spotnitz and his followers seem more aligned with Milton Erickson (see Haley 1973) than with Freud. I, too, question whether an analyst ought to intercede in such ways or take such moral stances. On the other hand, family systems theory shows that it is difficult to effectively treat isolated individuals without taking into consideration the system in which they function. The point is debatable.

However, despite these criticisms, Spotnitz has made important contributions to analytic therapy. Freud raised our consciousness about the ways we deny and act out our sexuality. Spotnitz raised our consciousness about the ways we deny and act out our aggression. Indeed, he has shifted the emphasis from sexuality to aggression. According to Spotnitz, it is frustrated aggression, rather than frustrated sexuality, that leads to psychopathology: one cannot achieve genitality unless one has worked through the aggression. Although many classical analysts have said the same thing, nobody has said it more directly than Spotnitz.

Spotnitz has also made an important contribution to analytic technique. His carefully elaborated, detailed approach for working with schizophrenics and borderline narcissists is as useful to therapists as is Kohut's delineation of the types of narcissistic transferences. And, following Ferenczi, Reich, Winnicott, and Jacobson he has shown that there are times when it is necessary for the analyst to express an emotion to a patient—when withholding such an emotion, or responding with empathic understanding, would, in effect, "kill the patient with kindness."

11

DEALING WITH THE BORDERLINE PATIENT

Otto Kernberg and the Rebel (1976), the Suicidal Patient (1989), and Miss B. (1989)

Druck (1989) tells a story about a woman drifter who loudly demands, again and again, of a female therapist, "Tell me to have a nice day, tell me to have a nice day, tell me to have a nice day. . . ." When the therapist finally does tell her to have a nice day, the drifter glares at the therapist and exclaims, "You're ugly!" This story, Druck says, illustrates the dynamic of a Kernbergian patient (p. 7).

During the second half of the twentieth century, a new diagnostic category—borderline personality disorder—was created in order to classify this kind of patient. This type has actually always existed—indeed, some analysts now believe the Wolf Man was a borderline personality—but it has proliferated in recent years. As more of these personality types have appeared, so have psychotherapists specializing in handling them. The psychoanalyst who perhaps became most famous for working with these difficult types was Otto Kernberg.

Kernberg was born in Vienna in 1928 and spent his early childhood there. His well-to-do Jewish parents immigrated to Chile after the Nazis took over Austria. He grew up in Chile, where he attended the Institute for Psychoanalysis in Santiago and went into analysis with Ramon Ganzerain, a noted Chilean psychoanalyst of the Kleinian mold. After his psychoanalytic training he and Ganzerain moved to Topeka, Kansas, where he headed a research project and eventually served as supervisor and training analyst at the Topeka Training Institute for Psychoanalysis. Later he served in the same capacities at the Columbia University Psychoanalytic Institute, while also functioning as professor of clinical psychiatry at the Columbia University College of Physicians and Surgeons. For many years he held the position of Director of General Clinic Services for the New York State Psychiatric Institute. His wife Paulina is also a psychoanalyst. They have several children.

From the earliest days of his training, Kernberg demonstrated a flair for working with borderlines. Although some have referred to this diagnostic category as a garbage can into which therapists throw all who do not fit into any other category, while others define borderlines as individuals whose mode of functioning is about halfway between neurotic and psychotic, Kernberg, perhaps more than anybody else, precisely delineated the psychodynamics and treatment of borderlines. In his major works (Kernberg 1975, 1976, 1980, 1984; Kernberg et al. 1989), he defines borderlines as individuals who suffer from an excess of aggression stemming from either genetic or environmental causes. Writing in language borrowed from Jacobson (1964) and Klein (1932), by whom he was greatly influenced, Kernberg explains that the excessive aggression of borderlines is warded off through the defense mechanism of splitting and the associated defenses of primitive idealization, omnipotence, devaluation, denial, and projective identification. By splitting (dissociating) themselves from their negative self and object representations, borderlines are able to protect their positive self and object representations, but as a result they do not establish a strong ego. Neutralization of aggression never takes place, as the integration of positive and negative self and object representations cannot occur when splitting predominates. Kernberg distinguishes borderlines from neurotics, whose major defense is repression, and from psychotics, who use extreme forms of dissociation to defend against fears of merger with threatening objects.

Kernberg devised a method of vigorous confrontation and interpretation for dealing with borderlines. Although he never wrote a major case history demonstrating his technique, his books are sprinkled with vignettes that offer telling examples of borderline acting-out and how he handles them.

Typical is the case of "Rebel," a name I am using for a 20-year-old man who came to him because of "serious school failure, chronic rebelliousness at school and at home, minor difficulties with the law, and a generally chaotic lifestyle, all of which seemed beyond the understanding and control of the parents and school authorities" (1976, p. 173). Kernberg diagnosed him as a "narcissistic personality functioning on a borderline level, with antisocial features," and began analytic therapy three times a week. He says that "some degree of external structure" was provided by a psychiatric social worker. This may allude to Kernberg's well-known practice of seeing some patients with a co-therapist, who fills in during Kernberg's frequent conferences, meetings, and other professional absences.

The Rebel's principal characteristics were grandiosity and bravado, interrupted only intermittently when one of his grand schemes fell through, or in some other way he crashed against an "unpleasant and undeniable aspect of reality." Then he fell into a momentary state of panic and despair and used Kernberg as a lawyer or advisor on how to deal with dangerous, unmanageable authorities. Kernberg writes:

> As soon as the crisis was over, his grandiose, derogatory, man-of-the-world facade would take over. Rather than sit in any other chair

in the office, he usually sat in my analytic chair, stretched himself to full length, and started the hour by condescendingly asking me how I was doing. (As this was a face-to-face psychotherapy, formally there was nothing wrong with his sitting in my chair—as the patient correctly remarked.) [p. 174]

His facade was so convincing that other patients commented to Kernberg on what a healthy-looking young man the Rebel was, and wondered why he was seeing a therapist.

For a long time he filled his hours with complaints about the stupidity, ignorance, and unfairness of various authorities, relatives, and friends. When Kernberg confronted him with the fact that he always complained about everybody else, but held himself to be impeccably innocent and righteous, the Rebel smiled incredulously. When Kernberg insisted on this interpretation, the Rebel reacted with "outright indignation."

Kernberg also pointed out to him, on numerous occasions, that he found himself having to play a certain role. "I find myself in the curious position," he told the Rebel, "either of listening to you silently—with the implication that I am agreeing with you—or, if I dare to question any of your statements, of becoming one more example in your world of unfair grownups and, particularly, unfair grownups in a position of authority, with whom you are struggling at all times" (p. 174).

He then added "You must have realized from my various comments that I often question what you are saying and that I have opinions or ways of looking at what you say that are different than yours" (p. 174). Kernberg pointed out that the Rebel must also have experienced Kernberg's silence as criticism or even hypocrisy, which put the Rebel in the uncomfortable position of being in therapy with a hypocrite or an "angry authoritarian ally" of his parents. When he wondered, along with the Rebel, what he was getting out of therapy, Rebel responded that he felt Kernberg was understanding, honest, and knowledgeable. "Although I'm not getting anything at all out of therapy," Rebel told him, "it's nice for a change to meet with a person with those qualities" (p. 174). Kernberg did not believe him.

At times Kernberg openly challenged the Rebel's grandiose assumptions, which elicited attacks of rage against him, "the intensity of which I at first found almost frightening." He gradually came to realize the Rebel used this rage to shut off any view of himself or of reality that contradicted his own. "I had rarely experienced a more effective control over my psychotherapeutic efforts in the treatment of a nonpsychotic patient," Kernberg notes (p. 175).

As time went on, Kernberg realized the patient was lying to him when he told him about instances of his antisocial behavior. For example, he did not tell him the truth about the drugs he was taking; Kernberg found out about this from other sources. When Kernberg confronted him about lying, the Rebel at first tried to explain it away as a misunderstanding. However, eventually he admitted that he was lying. Kernberg then pointed out to him that there was a contradiction between his avowed admiration of Kernberg's honesty, understanding, and knowledge, and his own dishonesty. "Your dishonesty makes a caricature of any understanding and knowledge I could acquire about you," was the way he put it. "And treating me in dishonest ways belies any interest that my honesty could have for you" (p. 175). Over a period of time he stated, again and again, that he now had to question everything Rebel had told him so far, including his appreciation of Kernberg as somebody who was knowledgeable and honest.

"What's in it for you to lie to me?" Kernberg asked him (p. 176), and wondered if the Rebel might feel that he and Kernberg were involved in a con game in which the Rebel was paying for phony services, money that his parents were actually providing for his psychotherapy. Kernberg wondered if, in exchange for this money, he was giving Rebel an alibi for his difficulties in school, or hours that became a cover for other activities. He said he was hesitant to say these things, not wanting to sound harsh and critical like other authority figures; but if he did not say them, he would be dishonest or ignorant and "feed into the con game situation." Eventually the Rebel began to listen and to improve.

Kernberg explains that he was careful not to make such comments when he was feeling so frustrated or angry that he could not tell if he was motivated by concern or by the need to get rid of his own feelings. However, he asserts that when the transference is predominantly negative and tends to destroy human interaction, it needs to be interpreted.

> The therapist's focusing on whatever remnant of a capacity for an authentic human relation remains is very important under these circumstances. In this case, I tried to convey by my attitude of respect, by my acknowledging how hard it was for the patient to listen to anything contradictory to his thinking, that I appreciated his effort and courage in nonetheless keeping his appointments with me. I would, however, never attempt to foster, establish, or even tolerate a pseudopositive relationship based on an acceptance of the patient's corrupted and corrupting superego pathology. [p. 176]

In general terms, Kernberg uses this case to illustrate the need, "even under these rather extreme psychotherapeutic circumstances," to explore the causes of "meaninglessness" in the interaction between the patient and therapist. He stresses that the understanding of even very primitive transferences depends on reconstructing significant human interactions and conflicts "out of the general dispersal, destruction, suppression, or distortion of them that is characteristic of borderline patients" (p. 177).

The case shows how Kernberg differs with Spotnitz in that he does not attempt to provoke a patient's aggression, nor does he believe in expressing anger to a patient. He agrees that a therapist should focus on the negative transference, but he feels that the patient's expression of anger in sessions should be limited. The negative transference needs to be confronted, he contends, because the borderline patient's splitting causes him to distrust the therapist; hence he acts to destroy the help that is given him—that is, to "bite the hand that feeds him." However, it must be confronted in such as way as to minimize the expression of anger, since that expression gratifies an instinctual need linked with "severe, preoedipal aggressive drive-derivatives" characteristic of borderlines. "It is this gratification of instinctual needs which represents the major transference resistance" (Kernberg 1975, p. 86).

The case of the Rebel also highlights another of Kernberg's techniques, that of gratifying a borderline's demands, especially during the beginning phase of treatment. Borderlines are known to make demands for such things as frequent telephone calls, extra sessions, contact during vacations, hugs, and the like. The Rebel tacitly demanded that he be allowed to sit in the analyst's chair, and Kernberg gave in to this demand. He viewed it as an appropriate manifestation of structural difficulty in the patient's capacity to function on his own, and therefore went along with it until the patient had developed a more mature mode of functioning.

In his most recent book (Kernberg et al. 1989), Kernberg includes a vignette that demonstrates his technique of confrontation with a suicidal patient. In a session following a suicide attempt, the therapist began by asking the patient what was on his mind. The patient, an intelligent and articulate young man, replied that there was nothing on his mind. The therapist informed him that he had been talking with the patient's brother, and that the latter told him that the patient had attempted suicide and would not be able to come to the session because he was in the hospital. "Of course, this immediately raises the question about whether you're really being able to go through this. You didn't call me; you didn't explain anything," the therapist said (pp. 42–43).

The patient interrupted to say that he *did* call. The therapist reminded him that he called after his brother had and only because he was afraid that the therapist would be annoyed at him. The patient answered that he had been too "out of it" to call. The therapist insisted that he should have taken the initiative anyway. The patient interrupted again to say that he was so out of it that he did not know what day it was. The therapist then shared with him the information his brother had provided—that the patient was on drugs, and that was why he was out of it. The patient now admitted that he had taken an overdose of Elavil and Valium.

"From experience you know that once you take drugs you are out of it," the therapist pointed out, "and you should have called me saying, 'I am about to take those drugs and I am not showing up on Tuesday'" (p. 45).

The patient protested that it is not normal to call somebody up and tell him that he is going to take an overdose. The therapist replied that in that case they had to talk, because "unfortunately that would have to be normal procedure" if the patient wanted to go through with the psychotherapy treatment. He reminded the patient that in order for him to fulfill his commitment to the treatment to come regularly twice a week, he would have to take responsibility for his daily life. The therapist then began to spell out what he saw as a minimum requirement for "really carrying out" the psychotherapy. The patient listened.

The therapist brought to the patient's attention the fact that he had attempted suicide often in the past and that these attempts must be taken very seriously.

> "So what I would expect for you to do is whenever you feel that you are about to make such a gesture, regardless of the reason for it, at that point you go into a hospital immediately."
> "I won't go into a psychiatric hospital."
> "OK, then I won't be able to treat you. (Pause.) Then we have reached the end of the beginning." [pp. 46–47]

The patient argued with the therapist about this point. The therapist stood his ground, maintaining that "there are certain minimal preconditions" for successful therapy. After a while the patient agreed to this condition, and the therapist asked if he wanted to hear the rest of what he had to say. The patient said that he did. The therapist then outlined three possible paths of action. If the patient was feeling suicidal and could not control it, he was to go into a hospital. If he had already taken drugs, he was to call the hospital, or the police, or his family, or a friend to get him to the hospital. If he decided he could control it, he could wait and discuss it with the therapist.

The patient questioned the therapist as to various other possibilities. "What if I have taken drugs, and that necessitates medical attention as opposed to psychiatric attention?" (p. 48).

The therapist replied that in that case the patient would have to go to the emergency room first, and then be transferred to a psychiatric hospital. The patient did not feel it would be necessary for him to go into a psychiatric hospital. The therapist replied that once he was out of control, somebody had to evaluate whether he needed further hospitalization. The patient asked why the therapist could not do that. The therapist reminded him that his responsibility as a psychotherapist was "to help you understand what this is all about, and the only way in which I can do that is by staying totally away from all the management and the administrative issues regarding your suicide" (p. 48).

And so the patient's acting out was confronted and the therapeutic contract was reaffirmed.

In this case, the therapist deviated from the stance of neutrality because the patient's behavior threatened the treatment. For the moment the therapist lay aside any attempt to interpret the patient's behavior in order to concentrate on drawing the patient's attention to the fact that his behavior impinged on his ability to participate in therapy, and that he was required to take responsibility for the treatment. Only after this treatment-destructive behavior was under control could they go back to standard procedure, which for Kernberg means emphatically interpreting the here-and-now transference situation and the patient's outside life and then, usually much later in the treatment, linking the transference interpretations to the patient's childhood. Note that in contrast to Spotnitz, who will sometimes take actions designed to help manage a patient's outside life, Kernberg believes in letting others manage such things.

In the case of Miss B. (Kernberg et al. 1989), Kernberg shows how the interpretation of major defenses such as primitive idealization, projective identification, omnipotent control, denial, and devaluation, facilitates therapeutic progress. He also deftly illustrates how a therapist can use countertransference feelings to benefit the therapy.

Miss B. went to considerable lengths to get an appointment with a therapist whose reputation she claimed to admire; however, as soon as he agreed to see her, she began expressing doubts about whether she wanted to begin the treatment. She did not like the little town where she would have to live during the treatment, a town that would destroy her with its "ugliness, provincialism, lack of stimulation, and horrible climate." She preferred New York or San Francisco, and "raised questions about the professional insecurity of the therapist, reflected, as she saw it, in his remaining in such a small town" (p. 94).

One day, after several weeks of therapy, she came to a session all dressed up. She spoke of a male friend, a prominent lawyer in San Francisco, who had invited her to move there and live with him. She went on to describe her current lover as "ridiculously inexperienced" in bed, and said that she had decided to drop him. He was nice, she said, but average and without refinement. She added that after her first visit to the therapist, her mother had wondered whether she would not be better off with a younger and more energetic therapist who would be firm with her. The therapist had impressed her mother as friendly, but "plain and insecure."

"What are your thoughts about your mother's comments?" the therapist asked.

"She's a very disturbed person, but at the same time intelligent and perceptive" (p. 95).

The patient smiled apologetically and said that she did not want to hurt the therapist's feelings, but that she agreed with her mother. The therapist, she said, dressed in a provincial way and lacked the quiet yet firm sense of self-assurance she liked in men. He was friendly but did not possess intellectual depth, and she doubted that he would be able to tolerate her being open with him.

The patient said all this in a friendly way, and it took the therapist a few minutes to recognize the underlying tone of condescension. She then went on to talk about her plans for meeting her friend in San Francisco.

As she spoke, the therapist began feeling dejected. He remembered that this patient had already seen many other therapists, and several had described her as incapable of committing herself to therapy. He decided now that it was probably not going to work out with him either. He felt like giving up. Then he realized that he was acting just as the patient had suggested, when she told him that he was incapable of intellectual depth. He also found that he felt physically awkward, and identified with the boyfriend the patient had just dismissed as sexually inept. In fact, he had become another devalued man.

As he silently analyzed the situation during the course of the session, it gradually dawned on him that he stood for all the men she had first idealized and then rejected.

He now remembered the patient's expressed anxiety in the past over his not taking her on as his patient, her desperate sense that he was the only therapist who could help her, and the intense suspicion she had expressed in the first few sessions that he was interested in learning all about her difficulties only to dismiss her, as if he were a collector of rare specimens of patients toward whom he had a basically derogatory attitude. He decided there was an act of revenge in the patient's devaluation, the counterpart of her sense in the past that he would assert his superiority and devalue her. [pp. 95–96]

As he thought more about this, he became aware that he was feeling much the same way she had described herself as feeling in her relationships with men—inferior, despairing, stupid, uneducated, and inept. He also saw the patient's devaluation of him as a replication of her mother's devaluation of the daughter when she made fun of her because of the inappropriate men with whom she became involved.

During the following session, the young woman again spoke of plans to move to San Francisco and complained again about her current lover and the small town where the therapist lived. The therapist now found himself hating the town and thinking of it critically; then he realized that "the town also stood for him in the transference, and the town and himself also represented her own devalued self image projected onto the therapist" (p. 96). Meanwhile, the patient was now identifying with her mother, and enacting an aspect of her grandiose self, while projecting onto the therapist the devalued parts of herself and, at the same time, living out her mother's efforts to destroy her attempt to get involved with a man who might care about her.

At last the therapist formulated an interpretation and presented it to her. He told her that her image of him as an intellectually inferior and awkward person stuck in an ugly town was her image of herself when she felt criticized and attacked by her mother; her attitude toward him had "the quiet superiority, the surface friendliness, and yet subtle devaluation" that she had, in fact, experienced so painfully from her mother. He added that by reversing roles in this way and devaluating her therapist, she might also be frightened that she would succeed in destroying him and that she might have to escape from the town to avoid the "painful disappointment and sense of loneliness that would come with this destruction of him as a valued therapist" (p. 97).

The woman heard him out and replied that she had been feeling those things about him, and actually *did* feel dejected after their last session, and maybe she was afraid of losing him as a valued object. She said she felt better now that he had given her this interpretation, and inquired if he could help make the visit to her friend in San Francisco a success, so that he wouldn't ridicule her for living in such a small, unattractive town.

Kernberg notes that she had now reverted to a dependent relationship with the therapist—almost without transition—and had begun to project the "haughty, derogatory" aspects of herself (her identification with her mother) onto the man from San Francisco.

This case, he explains, illustrates the mechanism of projective identification: the patient projected an intolerable aspect of the self, and by doing so induced in the therapist a corresponding internal attitude. The patient thereby had a subtle control over the therapist, by derogating and dismissing him, keeping him "temporarily imprisoned in this projected aspect of herself" (p. 97). It also illustrates the projection and reprojection of the grandiose self. When she was seeking the therapist for treatment, she projected her grandiose self onto him (idealizing him); then she "reintrojected" it (devaluing him); still later, after his interpretation, she "reprojected" it onto the San Francisco boyfriend.

Kernberg also explains that in this case, as in the previous cases, he limits his interpretations to the here-and-now. "The primitive transferences of borderline patients must first be integrated in more cohesive representations of the patient's self and significant others before they can be directly related to their unconscious origins in the past" (p. 98). Hence, his aim with Miss B. was to provide her with insight that would assist her integrative process and help transform her primitive transference to an advanced or neurotic transference.

Interpretation

Kernberg became a pioneer in working with borderlines. These are difficult patients who can at one minute idealize a therapist and in the next devalue him, and for whom dependency is generally a loathsome thought, fraught with fears of self-annihilation. In contradistinction to narcissistic and neurotic patients, in whom the most intense transferences come only after lengthy analytic work, with borderlines primitive transferences may emerge within the first days of treatment and must be dealt with immediately. His approach was to confront such patients early in the treatment with interpretations of their ego-syntonic acting-out. Most therapists, including Kohut (1979), do not believe in interpreting resistances that are ego-syntonic, so in this respect Kernberg went against prevailing thought, and in so doing stirred up a controversy. However, he had much success with his method.

Stolorow and Lachmann (1980) are among those who criticize Kernberg's approach. As followers of Kohut, they feel that Kernberg's approach is not empathic. In fact, they contend, his confrontive approach induces a negative transference and acting out because he interprets too soon and too deeply. This form of confrontation may even be experienced by the patient as a repeat of the original traumatic situation with his primary figures. According to Stolorow and Lachmann, such an unempathic approach may result from "a failure to recognize the arrested developmental aspects of the patient's psychopathology so that vital developmental requirements revived in relation to the analyst have once again met with traumatically unempathic responses" (p. 191).

Calef and Weinshel (1979) accuse Kernberg of departing from basic psychoanalytic principles such as free association and the corresponding freely suspended attention of the analyst. Instead of utilizing freely suspended attention, Kernberg views patients through "a prism of prefabricated ideas," and, they say, his treatment is predicated on his diagnostic labels and preformed ideas about patients. This approach is dangerous because it "is based not so much on the analyst's responsibility to maintain the analytic process but on his preconceived notion of what the patient *must* be like and by a greater tendency to permit the analyst's own value judgments to intrude on the analytic work and the analytic process" (p. 489).

Druck (1989) also chastises Kernberg for his emphasis on confronting the patient's negative transference. He believes the patient may interpret the therapist's confrontation as an "invitation to battle" that leads to the patient viewing the therapist in a paranoid manner. In addition, by confronting the patient the therapist may unwittingly get the patient to agree with him "as a form of masochistic submission to superior force." Druck explains: "A narcissistically vulnerable patient will certainly find it more difficult to engage in painful self-exploration when there is the possibility of narcissistic rebuff" (p. 256).

Druck adds that if the therapist begins working with the patient's aggression too early in the treatment, the patient may feel that his already weak good self-representation has been destroyed. "The therapist will be prematurely attacking a necessary defense before the patient is able to use the therapeutic alliance for support" (p. 257). Also, early confrontation might provoke malignant regression; that is, the patient may regress to the form of acting out that was originally invoked during early childhood. Rather than confronting the negative transference, Druck recommends that therapists focus on the ways in which the patient feels that the therapist is hateful and stay with an inquiring approach.

Another criticism by Druck centers on Kernberg's stress on the patient's adaptation to objective reality. Druck points out that Kernberg expects patients to assume all the responsibilities of reality—including higher forms of reality testing and secondary process functioning—when "this may be, in itself, the basic treatment issue" (p. 259). He claims that Kernberg does not take seriously certain feelings and experiences of borderlines, such as their narcissistic wishes and their demands that the therapist act as an external holding object. These, he contends, may need to be acknowledged and allowed to change at their own pace in order for the therapy to succeed.

Finally, Druck sees as hypocritical Kernberg's insistence on a neutral stance when he is enlisting third parties to aid the patient, as in the case of the suicidal patient. In this case the therapist attempted to preserve neutrality by enlisting the aid of other parties (the brother, the family, friends, social workers, and so forth) to help with managing the patient's outside activities. Druck notes that "in actuality, the assistance provided by the third party must be understood as coming from the therapist, who has diagnosed that the patient needs more than just interpretation. Thus the therapist is, in effect, involved but denying his involvement, and on some level the patient knows this and responds to the hypocrisy of the situation.

However, Druck disagrees with those who criticize Kernberg as being unempathic. Empathic listening, he says, has unfortunately become "a code phrase" for doing psychotherapy within a self-psychological mode, and it implies that therapists who are not self psychologists are unempathic. Druck asserts that there are certain patients for whom Kernberg's confrontive approach may be more supportive and empathic than so-called "empathic listening." "Through confrontation, Kernberg acknowledges and is empathic to the patient's angry, orally hungry self. If this approach is correct with a given patient, the patient will respond to confrontation and interpretation by feeling understood and held" (p. 263). The patient will also feel that his rage and badness are accepted by the therapist; they will not destroy the therapist, and therefore they can be accepted by himself.

Greenberg and Mitchell (1983), on the other hand, take Kernberg to task for his theoretical formulations about borderline psychopathology and personality development in general. Like Jacobson (1964) and Mahler (1975), Kernberg has attempted to combine drive theory and object relations, but, according to Greenberg and Mitchell, unsuccessfully. They believe that Kernberg has drastically changed drive theory. While Freud and most other drive theorists view drives as biologically determined, Kernberg does not see man as innately sexual and aggressive; rather he sees him as "innately responsive." He takes the view that early interpersonal experience is crucial to what individuals become and that experience gives rise to defense systems (such as splitting) that express sexual and aggressive aims. "Good theory can be derived from these premises," they conclude; "good classical psychoanalytic drive theory cannot" (p. 340).

Some of the criticism leveled at Kernberg is similar to that directed at Spotnitz. There are similarities in their approaches. Both see the necessity of confronting the negative transference. Spotnitz confronts through mirroring, Kernberg through interpretation. Druck joins in this criticism of Kernberg, but then does a flipflop by saying that many patients may require this kind of confrontation. I agree with Druck's second opinion.

In the beginning phase of treatment, borderlines tend to act out in ways that are destructive to the treatment. There is no way to get around the fact that at this point they need a firm hand. The therapist is forced to either confront this destructive behavior or lose the patient. As Druck and Kernberg point out, the patient needs to know that his aggression cannot destroy the therapist, and being confronted by the therapist makes him feel understood. In addition, by mirroring or interpreting the patient's acting out, the therapist takes away the patient's power to devalue and enrage the object. To quote an old proverb, "the jig is up." What was formerly an ego-syntonic resistance now becomes ego-dystonic.

Those who, like Druck, maintain that Kernberg's early confrontation of borderline patients interferes with the formation of a working alliance do not properly understand borderlines. In fact, early confrontation strengthens, rather than destroys, the working alliance. Borderlines come into therapy full of distrust for the therapist. Through projective identification, the therapist is seen as a dangerous adversary to whom they must not at any cost submit. In addition, borderlines have weak egos and the attendant problems in impulse control, poor frustration tolerance, and a limited sublimatory capacity; these also contribute to a very bad working alliance from the beginning. Through vigorous confrontation and interpretation, Kernberg is able to break through the wall and establish genuine communication. When, for example, he points out to the Rebel the discrepancy between his stated admiration for his therapist's honesty and the fact that the Rebel is lying to him, this establishes a bond. Perhaps for the first time somebody has called the Rebel's bluff. In the case of the suicidal patient, the therapist not only confronts the patient with his irresponsibility, but also lays down the rules in no uncertain terms. If the patient will not follow these rules, he is told the therapy will have to end. This kind of firmness seems absolutely necessary to establish a working alliance with an acting-out borderline; nothing short of that will do. Miss B. had already gone through many therapists, rapidly idealizing and devaluing them. It is a good bet that at least some would have been seen as empathic. Kernberg's approach of immediately interpreting the grandiose self may have been just the thing that kept her in therapy for the first time. (Kernberg, however does not provide information about what happened following the session described in the vignette.)

Druck proposes an alternate method for dealing with aggression early in the treatment. He suggests that the therapist focus on how the patient feels the therapist is hateful and stay with the "usual inquiring approach." This suggestion assumes that the patient is in touch with his feeling that the therapist is hateful and is willing to acknowledge it. Most borderlines are nowhere near that place; confrontation brings them there.

Finally, Stolorow and Lachmann's contention that Kernberg's confrontive approach may foster malignant regression is unfounded. If a therapist genuinely cares about a patient, and if he is capable of a mature relationship with the patient, then the confrontation will be perceived by the patient in that light. However, if the therapist is acting out a subjective countertransference stemming from unresolved issues from his own past, then that confrontation may bring about a malignant regression. On the other hand, the patient may simply be one of those described by Balint (1968) who are prone to malignant regression without any inducement by the therapist.

All in all, Kernberg has provided many original insights into the workings of the borderline mind and useful techniques for treating the borderline. He has helped solve one of the most baffling problems facing modern therapists. He has been thorough and systematic in his consideration of all aspects of the problem, including the etiology, psychodynamics, transference picture, and the countertransference problems related to borderline personalities. Continuing in the tradition of psychoanalytic defense analysis begun by Reich (1933), his approach may well be the most rigorous yet devised for that particular way of doing therapy. It is, indeed, a heroic approach. It is easier to "let sleeping dogs lie" than to awaken them. This, in effect, is what Kernberg does. He directly confronts the patient's mad behavior and thereby risks getting bitten himself.

The tragedy is that there are not enough Kernbergs to go around. Borderlines are becoming more the rule than the exception—in and out of therapy offices. They may be a symptom of the overall decline of Western society and of the general deterioration of empathic parenting, a self-perpetuating cycle in which borderline parents beget borderline children, generation after generation. But Kernberg and others have shown the way.

12

ANALYTIC THERAPY

What Is Analytic Therapy?

In discussing classical technique, Freud (1912) once said, "I must, however, expressly state that this technique has proved to be the only method suited to my individuality; I do not venture to deny that a physician quite differently constituted might feel impelled to adopt a different attitude to his patients and to the task before him" (p. 109). Each of the therapists in this book took Freud's disclaimer to heart. They bent psychoanalytic technique to their own constitutions, as well as to the personalities of their patients. If there is a key to all successful therapies, it might well be—as Shakespeare put it—"to thine own self be true."

In analytic therapy, as in other things, the sum is greater than the parts. The analysts described herein saw things from their own perspectives, based on their own particular constitutions and upbringings; each devised a particular way of understanding human behavior and a particular way of doing therapy. Each contributed to psychoanalytic theory and to therapeutic technique, but none can or should claim to be the final authority. Analytic therapy is the sum of all their contributions, a growing science of behavior, based on clinical participation–observation research. There are some theories that have become generally accepted as laws—such

as those involving transference, countertransference, and resistance—while others, involving the etiology of narcissism or aggression, are still being debated. But the practice and the research
continue.

Analytic therapists are human. They may be overly permissive or aggressive, they may go mad, they may have affairs with
their training analysts, they may divorce, they may become es-
tranged from their children, they may bicker among themselves
and vie for power and leadership, and in general behave in the ways
human beings have always behaved from the beginning. They do
not live perfect lives, have perfect marriages, or raise perfect children. What they have in common, however, is the capacity for self-
honesty about these matters. Because of their own analyses, they
can acknowledge their frailties and not allow them to get in the
way of doing therapy. This may well be the highest ideal to which
human beings can aspire. Hence, what analytic therapists model
for their patients are not perfect human beings, but rather imper-
fect people, who are relatively at home with their imperfections;
can function at a high level; and can relate to others in a mature
fashion, and with all their emotions at their disposal, including—
and especially—empathy.

However, as I have studied the preceding cases, reconsidered
my own clinical experiences, and recalled other literature on the
subject, it has slowly dawned on me that while there are many
ways of doing analytic therapy, there are nevertheless certain
general givens of analytic therapy. These givens always apply,
whether one is working with an adult or a child, a male or a
female, a mildly phobic individual or an outright catatonic.

1. *Every patient is treatable.* Whenever a patient is dismissed as untreatable it is invariably due to the therapist's countertransference. This
   does not mean that therapists should never let go of patients; it
   means when they do let go they must recognize that it is due to
   their own limitations, not to the patient's untreatability. Every
   patient is treatable, and what is more, every patient is treatable by

means of analytic therapy, although it may take a while before he or she is ready for analysis.

2. *Each patient dictates his or her own therapy approach.* Most of the analysts described here have documented how important it is for a therapist to pay attention to a patient's cues. Therapists who pay close enough attention to their patients' conscious and unconscious messages will never be in doubt as to what approach or technique to use at a particular point in therapy. Patients will always tell them in one way or another.

3. *The therapist must completely accept the patient.* Before a patient will accept a therapist's interventions, a therapist must accept a patient's neurosis, narcissism, or psychosis. This does not mean that a therapist must understand these things in a clinical sense, but that he must actually identify with the patient and recognize that, were he in the patient's shoes, he would act in an identical manner. Therefore the patient's guilt, fear, rage, phobias, paranoia, or delusions are seen as absolutely logical and essential. Moreover, the therapist must also be able to accept that all the patient's responses to the therapist, no matter how neurotic, narcissistic, or psychotic, are also reactions to some real element in the therapist's behavior toward the patient. Only in such an atmosphere will a patient trust the therapist enough to come out of a defensive posture and listen.

4. *Therapists should use whatever intervention works at a particular time with a particular patient.* They should be willing to experiment with varying techniques, not impulsively, but whenever necessary to break an impasse. To stick rigidly to one technical approach or school of therapy is to delimit the range of one's effectiveness.

5. *The core of analytic therapy is analysis.* Sooner or later, whether silently or out loud, therapists analyze patients, helping them obtain both emotional and intellectual insight. In most cases, patients gradually learn to analyze themselves, a process that strengthens their egos, raises their self-esteem, and clarifies their sense of identity.

These five general givens seem to me to be just as important as, and complementary to, the standard techniques.

The Growth of Analytic Therapy

Analytic therapy began with Breuer's cathartic method. Since then, more and more interventions have been developed, including hypnoanalysis, use of the couch, free association, interpretation of transference, interpretation of resistance, using and expressing countertransference feelings, mirroring, and joining the resistance. The range and sequence of interventions has grown in sophistication over the years, as demonstrated by the clinical material contained in this collection. This growth indicates that there are now interventions for just about any kind of patient and every kind of situation that may arise in therapy. Alongside the development of new interventions, there has been an increased understanding of the varieties of emotional disorders, including hysteria, obsessional neurosis, sadomasochism, infantile neuroses, eating disorders, psychopathic personalities, borderline states, childhood psychoses, narcissistic personalities, schizophrenia, and manic-depression.

However, the history of analytic therapy is not just a history of progress, but also a history of human conflict. History itself can be seen as an ongoing progression of territorial wars and revolts against established regimes; the history of psychoanalysis and analytic therapy is no exception. Psychoanalysis began as a revolt against conventional psychiatry, and the attacks on Freud have been well documented and continue even today. Once psychoanalysis became established, there began a series of revolts against it, and against Freud. Ferenczi, Klein, and Reich were among the early revolutionaries; Kohut, Spotnitz, and Kernberg were among the later ones. Such revolts are always considered by the establishment as a deviation or a sickness which must be averted, while the revolutionaries themselves regard their actions as instrumental to rescuing a narrow-minded or sick establishment. In actuality, this process of change is probably natural to all growing things, from amoebas to human beings.

The psychoanalytic establishment—represented by the ego psychology or classical analytic school—initially disparaged all deviations from standard technique, then allowed for "parameters," provided that the analyst returned to standard technique as soon as possible. Even today there is an attitude on the part of classical analysts that those who deviate from standard technique are acting out unresolved neurotic or narcissistic needs. However, the same could be said about classical analysts; their reluctance to adapt to a wide range of patients with new interventions might also be seen as an acting out of neurotic or narcissistic feelings.

As stated in *Ecclesiastes*, "There is nothing new under the sun." Discoverers, whether they be analysts or engineers, do not invent the new, but rather rediscover what is already there to see. Breuer and Freud were accused by the psychiatric establishment of using "housewife's psychology," to cure neurotics. Perhaps there is a certain truth to that. Ferenczi was accused of borrowing early Freudian techniques. Reich was seen as a witch doctor because he used techniques associated with shamans. Klein looked at children's play and saw what others had seen before, but had not recognized. Binswanger stood back and took in the broader picture of human existence. Mahler was willing to see the maternal neglect and abuse that others were afraid to see. Fromm-Reichmann was sometimes viewed as a "Jewish mother," dispensing old-fashioned wisdom and chicken soup, but she knew that these old remedies worked. Winnicott was accused of borrowing other people's terminology and calling it his own, but he knew that what counted most was not whether something was new but whether it worked. Kohut was called to account for employing good classical analytic technique while giving it the name "self psychology." Spotnitz's *toxoid response* was in reality the old folk remedy of "giving somebody a dose of his own medicine." Each saw or used what was already there. In this sense, the history of analytic therapy probably is a reprise of a cycle that has occurred previously in various tribes and cultures throughout the history of humankind.

Like the shamans and witch doctors of primitive societies, therapists serve a dual function. They are both medicine men and moral arbiters. In probing the unconscious, Freud became a social critic and a setter of public standards. He revealed to society its deepest and most hidden ulterior motives, pointing to unhealthy sexual practices, destructive relationships, and errant social values; for doing so, he received society's resentment. Yet individuals as well as society need somebody to keep them from straying into destructive paths, somebody to keep them objective, somebody to help them overcome their individual and social psychopathology.

Looked at from this angle, the protectiveness of classical analysts with regard to retaining certain boundaries serves an important purpose. It is crucial that psychoanalysis and analytic therapy continue to look for and verbalize the basic truths about the motivations of human beings and about human existence, and not be deterred by those who would undermine those truths because of what they reveal about themselves. For example, the rise of homosexuality in Western culture, along with a rise of mass homosexual protest, has intimidated many analysts into retreating from the view that homosexuality is a form of perverse sexuality. A similar rise in narcissistic personalities was a chief cause, I believe, for Kohut and others to offer the concept of "healthy narcissism." Another example of this is the tidal wave of feminist rage, bolstered by complaints of supposed female oppression and victimization, that has caused the psychoanalytic establishment to largely repudiate many, if not most, psychoanalytic theories about female development. Religious leaders have attacked Freud's notions about the neurotic wellsprings and destructiveness of religiosity. These and other forces have eroded psychoanalytic theory and made today's psychoanalysts retreat into a conservative shell. The danger is that psychoanalysts will shirk their roles of social critics and setters of public health standards, that they will no longer speak the truth because that truth may offend certain individuals or groups of individuals, that they will become an elitist, esoteric cult, and that they will then cease to be a viable force in our culture.

About Case Histories

Today, analytic therapy is applied to every form of personality disorder. Yet, there are those outside the field who charge that analytic therapy has become outmoded, primarily because it takes too long. Critics also contend that there is no proof except for the testimonies of analysts and their patients (who may be swayed by their analysts) that analytic therapy works. Moreover, they contend that there is too much reliance on narrative case histories, and a general ignorance of research outside of psychoanalysis.

Eagle (1984), for example, points out that therapy patients tend to experience the kind of insight that corresponds to their therapist's theoretical orientation, so that "we do not know to what extent that which is called insight or self-knowledge is just that or is rather the product of compliance and suggestion" (p. 173). Hence, Freudian patients will tend to have oedipal insights, Kleinian patients will begin seeing their conflicts in terms of good and bad breasts, and Kohutians will view their problems in terms of a need for idealization. Eagle is critical of psychoanalytic researchers who base their theories on psychoanalytic research and cite a "privileged access" rationale for doing so. He states (p. 177), "Part of what underlies the focus on the individual case is the assumption that the patient's acknowledgment is a central, and for some a necessary criterion for evaluating the validity of psychoanalytic interpretations," but he adds that case histories are presented from the point of view of the analyst, and reflect what the analyst conceives of as important and worth reporting. They can be interpreted in many different ways. "The case history exquisitely lends itself, not only to selective interpretation, but to selective culling of evidence" (p. 181). He adds that he is under the impression that recent psychoanalytic writers and theorists pay little attention to the body of knowledge outside of psychoanalysis. "This tendency is partly encouraged by promulgation of the belief that psychoanalysis relies on distinctive methods . . . for acquiring knowledge and hence [need] not concern itself with the question of whether such knowledge is congruent with what is known outside of psychoanalysis" (p. 180).

Holzman (1976) expresses similar sentiments, lamenting the fact that psychoanalysis never developed protocols for research other than the case history. "Large segments of what we teach can neither be confirmed nor proved false. New ideas in psychoanalysis provoke some essays for and against, but these are not sufficient. Unlike . . . literary criticism, we require more than such essays. We need proposals to test the ideas systematically" (p. 269).

There is some truth to these accusations. Psychoanalysis should not rely solely on case histories for the formulation of its theories. A combination of research based on empirical investigations and individual case histories might be best. One does not preclude the other. This would also help psychoanalysis to be accepted by other professions. However, so-called empirical investigations can be just as easily biased as case histories; statistics can be skewed, and an experiment can be contaminated in various ways to produce the result that is unconsciously desired by the investigator. In a way, psychoanalysts are similar to anthropologists and ethologists. The fact that these are not "hard" sciences, based on empirical experiments, but rather are largely erected on participant-observational techniques, does not invalidate them. In either case—whether one is dealing with empirical or participant-observational research—the result depends on the insight and objectivity of the researcher.

Notwithstanding these considerations, I believe this book shows there will never be a substitute for a good case history. While it may be true that a case history does not in fact constitute a validation of a theory, there is no better way to illustrate theory than through a case history. No description or explanation of a theory can adequately convey its meaning as well as a case history, for it is only through its vividness that one can get a visceral sense of what the theory represents.

Through reading Freud's case history of Dora, we understand exactly what he means by dream interpretation. Reich's case about the masochistic character demonstrates firsthand his version of character analysis as no scientific paper could. Klein's description of Erna and her phantasies provides us with an indelible insight into how she formulated her theories. Winnicott's case about the orphan boy gives us a gut understanding of how to hate objectively. Mahler's vignette about Violet made it quite clear how childhood psychosis develops and where her theories of separation-individuation came from. Kohut's analyses of "Mr. Z." provide a moving portrait of self psychology that his more obtuse writings failed to communicate.

Case histories are more than illustrations of theory; they help to remind us that all of our theorizing is nothing more than an attempt to understand human beings. They bring to our attention what lies at the core of analytic research: the patient—a living human being struggling to overcome the faulty conditioning produced by a combination of genes and the environment. Indeed, patients described in good case histories—as in good literature—can be seen as signposts of an era, and as epitomes of the human condition.

The Future of Analytic Therapy

Over the century psychoanalytic research has advanced and analytic therapy has widened its scope. In the beginning only neurotic individuals were considered analyzable, while those with more severe pathologies were not. Through the years analysts began experimenting with new techniques for working with narcissistic, borderline, and psychotic personalities. Some analysts thought that those who used these new techniques should no longer be considered psychoanalysts. Others defended them. Eventually the term "psychoanalytic psychotherapy" was coined to embrace all these new forms of therapy.

Since the advent of analytic therapy, various other kinds of therapy have sprung into existence, each claiming to have made analytic therapy outmoded. There are various short-term therapies, usually based on behavioral principles, which purport to be more effective than analytic therapy in far less time. When one studies these therapies, one usually discovers them to be variations of the active therapy experiments of Ferenczi. They remove symptoms but do not bring about a characterological change. There are various new forms of hypnotherapy, such as those developed by Milton Erickson and his followers. Practitioners of this school of therapy sometimes describe miraculous results and "magical techniques." They appeal to the magical thinking of a narcissistic generation that wants instant gratification. However, long-term follow-ups of the patients of these miracle men are still forthcoming. There are assorted new forms of cathartic therapies, such as primal therapy, psychodrama, and bioenergetics that provide dramatic results (as did Ferenczi and Reich). However, catharsis in and of itself, without the long-term working-through, analysis of resistance and transference, and stabilization of character, can only bring temporary relief. Family systems theories have sprung up, maintaining that the analytic focus on the individual is ineffectual because it deals with only one part of a dysfunctional system. In order to cure an individual, they say, one has to cure the system. However, systems theory may also be a way of avoiding probing too deeply into the unconscious while attempting to manipulate an immediate but illusory change for the better. In my own clinical experience working with couples and families, I have found that there is no substitute for individual analytic work, for until members of a family have gained insight into their own characters, they cannot achieve harmony with others. Then there are psychiatry's answers to emotional problems: drug and shock therapy. It may well be that, because of the growing number of borderlines and psychotics in our society, these methods will become the only viable way to handle many patients, for it is simply not practical for all of them to undergo analytic therapy. However, drug and shock therapy are not cures; they numb a psychotic's rage, but they do not cure it.

Almost every year somebody "invents" a new form of therapy that supposedly supersedes all existing forms of therapy, including analytic therapy. They come and go. Almost every year some person or group discovers a new reason for finding fault with psychoanalysis. But upon closer inspection, it is not a new fault at all but an old one in new clothes. Psychoanalysts say things that people and groups do not want to hear. Every year since psychoanalysis began people have tried to bury Freud and his discovery, but so far nobody has succeeded and probably nobody ever will.

Analytic therapy has changed with the times. While in the early days there was an emphasis on recalling memories of traumatic experiences, more lately there has been more stress on studying and altering destructive defensive behavior (resolving resistances). While in the early days the focus was primarily on transference, more lately the focus has shifted to countertransference. While in the beginning the Oedipus complex and the father's role received more attention, more lately pregenital material and the mother's role have taken the stage. The capacity of analytic therapy to grow and adapt to the times may be the secret of its longivity.

What will the future bring? It seems to me that as long as there are people who want to understand themselves, there will be analytic therapy.

REFERENCES

Balint, M. (1968). *The Basic Fault*. London: Tavistock.

Beland, H. (1988). Alteration of the ego due to defensive processes and the limitations of psychoanalytic technique. *International Journal of Psycho-Analysis* 69:189–203.

Benedek, T. (1949). The Psychosomatic implications of the primary unit: Mother-child. *American Journal of Orthopsychiatry* 19:642–654.

Benjamin, J. D. (1961). The innate and the experiential in child development. In *Childhood Psychopathology*, ed. S. I. Harrison and J. F. McDermott, Jr., pp. 2–19. New York: International Universities Press, 1972.

Blanck, G., and Blanck, R. (1974). *Ego Psychology: Theory and Practice*. New York: Columbia University Press.

Blum, G. (1953). *Psychoanalytic Theories of Personality*. New York: McGraw Hill.

Boesky, D. (1988). Comments on the structural theory of technique. *International Journal of Psycho-Analysis* 69:303–316.

Calef, U., and Weinshel, E. M. (1979). The new psychoanalysis and psychoanalytic revisionism. *Journal of the American Psychoanalytic Association* 48:470–471.

Chessick, R. D. (1989). *The Technique and Practice of Listening in Intensive Psychotherapy.* Northvale, NJ: Jason Aronson.

Dare, C. (1976). Psychoanalytic theories. In *Child Psychiatry: Modern Approaches*, ed M. Rutter and L. Hersov. Oxford, England: Blackwell.

Davis, M., and Wallbridge, D. (1981). *Boundary and Space: An Introduction to the Work of D. W. Winnicott.* London: H. Karnac.

Druck, A. (1989). *Four Therapeutic Approaches to the Borderline Patient.* Northvale, NJ: Jason Aronson.

Eagle, M. N. (1984). *Recent Developments in Psychoanalysis: A Critical Evaluation.* Cambridge, MA: Harvard University Press.

Edelson, M. (1984). *Hypothesis and Evidence in Psychoanalysis.* Chicago: University of Chicago Press.

Eissler, K. (1953). The effects of the structure of the ego on psychoanalytic technique. *Journal of the American Psychoanalytic Association* 1:104–143.

—— (1971). *Discourse on Hamlet and "Hamlet."* New York: International Universities Press.

Epstein, L., and Feiner, A. H. (1979). *Countertransference.* Northvale, NJ: Jason Aronson.

Erikson, Erik H. (1950). *Childhood and Society*, 2nd ed. New York: W. W. Norton.

—— (1958). *Young Man Luther: A Study in Psychoanalysis and History.* New York: W. W. Norton.

—— (1959). *Identity and the Life Cycle.* New York: International Universities Press.

—— (1969). *Gandhi's Truth.* New York: W. W. Norton.

—— (1975). *Life History and the Historical Moment:* New York, W. W. Norton.

Ethan, S. (1989). From a private discussion with author, in October 1988.

Fairbairn, W. R. D. (1952). *Psychoanalytic Studies of the Personality.* London: Tavistock Publications.

—— (1958). On the nature and aims of psychoanalytic treatment. *International Journal of Psycho-Analysis* 39:374–385.

Ferenczi, S. (1919). Technical difficulties in the analyses of a case of hysteria. In *Further Contributions to the Theory and Technique of Psycho-Analysis*, pp. 189–197. New York: Brunner/Mazel.

——— (1933). Confusion of tongues between adults and the child. In *Final Contributions to the Theory and Technique of Psycho-Analysis*, pp. 156–167. New York: Brunner/Mazel.

Freud, S. (1900) The interpretation of dreams. *Standard Edition* 4.

——— (1905a). Three essays on the theory of sexuality. *Standard Edition* 7:125–248.

——— (1905b). Fragment of an analysis of a case of hysteria. In *Collected Papers of Sigmund Freud* 3:13–148. New York: Basic Books.

——— (1911). Foundations on two principles of mental functioning. *Standard Edition* 12:218–226.

——— (1912). Recommendations to physicians practicing psychoanalysis. *Standard Edition* 12:109–120.

——— (1920). Beyond the pleasure principle. *Standard Edition* 17:3–122.

——— (1921). Group psychology and the analysis of the ego. *Standard Edition* 18:65–143.

Fromm-Reichmann, F. (1950). *The Principles of Intensive Psychotherapy*. Chicago: Phoenix Books.

——— (1959). *Psychoanalysis and Psychotherapy*. Chicago: University of Chicago Press.

Frosch, J. (1983). *The Psychotic Process*. New York: International Universities Press.

Gero, G. (1981). Edith Jacobson's work on depression in historical perspective. In *Object and Self: A Developmental Approach*, ed. S. Tuttman, C. Kaye, and M. Zimmerman. New York: International Universities Press.

Greenberg, J. (1964). *I Never Promised You a Rose Garden*. New York: Signet Books.

Greenberg, J. R., and Mitchell, S. A. (1983). *Object Relations in Psychoanalytic Theory*. Cambridge, MA: Harvard University Press.

Greenwald, H. (1959). *Great Cases in Psychoanalysis*. New York: Ballantine Books.

Grosskurth, P. (1986). *Melanie Klein: Her World and Her Work*. Harmondsworth, England: Penguin Books.

Guntrip, H. (1961). *Personality Structure and Human Interaction.* London: Hogarth Press.

—— (1969). *Schizoid Phenomena, Object Relations and the Self.* New York: International Universities Press.

—— (1971). *Psychoanalytic Theory, Therapy, and the Self.* New York: Basic Books.

—— (1975). My experience of analysis with Fairbairn and Winnicott. *International Review of Psycho-Analysis* 2:145–156.

Haley, J (1973). *Uncommon Therapy.* New York: Norton.

Harlow, H. F. (1958). The nature of love. *American Psychologist* 13:673–685.

Harrison, S. I., and McDermott, J. F., eds. (1980). *New Directions in Childhood Psychopathology.* Vol. 1. New York: International Universities Press.

Hartmann, H. (1958). *Ego Psychology and the Problem of Adaptation.* New York: International Universities Press.

Holzman, P. S. (1976). The future of psychoanalysis and its institutes. *Psychoanalytic Quarterly* 65:250–273.

Jacobson, E. (1943). Depression: the oedipus conflict in the development of depressive mechanisms. *Psychoanalytic Quarterly* 12:541–560.

—— (1946). The effect of disappointment on ego and superego formation in normal and depressive development. *Psychoanalytic Review* 33:129–147.

—— (1964). *The Self and the Object World.* New York: International Universities Press.

—— (1967). *Psychotic Conflict and Reality.* New York: International Universities Press.

—— (1971). *Depression: Comparative Studies of Normal, Neurotic and Psychotic Conditions.* New York: International Universities Press.

Kennell, J., Trause, M., and Klaus, M. (1974). Maternal behavior one year after early and extended postpartum contact. *Developmental and Medical Child Neurology* 16:172–179.

Kernberg, O. (1975). *Borderline Conditions and Pathological Narcissism.* Northvale, NJ: Jason Aronson.

—— (1976). *Object Relations Theory and Clinical Psychoanalysis.* Northvale, NJ: Jason Aronson.

—— (1980). *Internal World and External Reality.* Northvale, NJ: Jason Aronson.

—— (1984). *Severe Personality Disorders: Psychotherapeutic Strategies.* New Haven, CT: Yale University Press.

Kernberg, O. F., Selzer, M. A., and Koenigsberg, H. W., et al. (1989). *Psychodynamic Psychotherapy of Borderline Patients.* New York: Basic Books.

Khan, M.M.R. (1975). Introduction. In *Through Paediatrics to Psychoanalysis*, pp. xi–xviii. New York: Basic Books.

Klein, M. (1932). *The Psychoanalysis of Children.* Trans. Alix Strachey. New York: Delacorte Press, 1975.

Kligerman, C. (1989). From a telephone interview with the author in September 1989.

Kohut, H. (1971). *The Analysis of the Self.* New York: International Universities Press.

—— (1977). *Restoration of Self.* New York: International Universities Press.

—— (1979). The two analyses of Mr. Z. *International Journal of Psycho-Analysis* 60:3–27.

—— (1984). *How Does Analysis Cure?* Chicago: University of Chicago Press.

Kolb, L. C. (1977). *Modern Clinical Psychiatry.* Philadelphia: W. B. Saunders.

Langs, R., and Searles, H. F. (1979). *Intrapsychic and Interpersonal Dimensions of Treatment: A Dialogue.* Northvale, NJ: Jason Aronson.

Lindner, R. M. (1944). Rebel without a Cause. New York: Grune and Stratton.

—— (1946). *Stone Walls and Men.* New York: Odyssey Press.

—— (1952). *Prescription for a Rebellion.* New York: Rinehart.

—— (1955). *The Fifty-Minute Hour.* New York: Holt, Rinehart and Winston.

Mahler, M. S. (1968). *On Human Symbiosis and the Vicissitudes of Individuation.* New York: International Universities Press.

—— (1989). *The Memoirs of Margaret Mahler.* Ed. Paul Stepansky. New York: Free Press.

Mahler, M. S., Pine, F., and Bergman, A. (1975). *The Psychological Birth of the Infant*. London: Maresfield Library.

Malcolm, J. (1981). *Psychoanalysis: The Impossible Profession*. New York: Vintage Books.

Margolis, B. D. (1986). Joining, mirroring, psychological reflection: terminology, definitions, theoretical considerations. *Modern Psychoanalysis* 11:19–35.

———— (1987). Treatment and transition: observation on modern psychoanalysis. *Modern Psychoanalysis* 12:163–178.

Marshall, R. J. (1979).Countertransference with children and adolescents. In *Countertransference: The Therapist's Contribution to the Therapeutic Situation*, ed. L. Epstein and A. H. Feiner. Northvale, NJ: Jason Aronson.

McGlashan, T. H., and Keats, C. J. (1989). *Schizophrenia: Treatment Process and Outcome*. Washington: American Psychiatric Press.

Meadow, P. (1987). The myth of the impersonal analyst. *Modern Psychoanalysis* 12:131–150.

Meyerson, P. (1981). The nature of the transactions that occur in other than classical analysis. *International Review of Psycho-Analysis* 8:173–189.

Monte, C. F. (1977). *Beneath the Mask: An Introduction to Personality Theories*. New York: Praeger.

Ornstein, P. (1981). The bipolar self and the psychoanalytic treatment process: clinical–theoretical considerations. *Journal of the American Psychoanalytic Association* 29:353–376.

Ostow, M. (1979). Letter to the editor. *International Journal of Psycho-Analysis* 60:531–532.

Pao, P. (1979). *Schizophrenic Disorders: Theory and Treatment from a Psychodynamic Point of View*. New York: International Universities Press.

Reich, W. (1933). *Character Analysis*. 3rd ed. Trans. U. R. Carfagno. New York: Pocket Books, 1973.

Roazen, P. (1984). *Freud and His Followers*. New York: New York University Press.

Sandler, J., Dare, C., and Holder, A. (1979). *The Patient and the Analyst*. London: Maresfield Reprints.

Schoenewolf, G. (1989). *Sexual Animosity between Men and Women.* Northvale, NJ: Jason Aronson.

———— (1990). *Turning Points in Analytic Therapy: The Classic Cases.* Northvale, NJ: Jason Aronson.

Searles, H. (1955). Dependency process in the psychotherapy of schizophrenia. *Journal of the American Psychoanalytic Association* 3:19–66.

———— (1959). The effort to drive the other person crazy—an element in the aetiology and psychotherapy of schizophrenia. *British Journal of Medical Psychology* 32:1–18.

———— (1965). *Collected Papers on Schizophrenia and Related Subjects.* New York: International Universities Press.

———— (1972a). The function of the patient's realistic perceptions of the analyst in delusional transference. In *Countertransference and Related Subjects,* pp. 197–223. New York: International Universities Press.

———— (1972b). Unconscious processes in relation to the environmental crisis. *Psychoanalytic Review* 59:361–374.

———— (1975). The patient as therapist to his analyst. In *Countertransference and Related Subjects,* pp. 402–426. New York: International Universities Press.

———— (1976). Transitional phenomena and therapeutic symbiosis. In *Countertransference and Related Subjects,* pp. 552–557. New York: International Universities Press.

———— (1979). *Countertransference and Related Subjects.* New York: International Universities Press.

———— (1986). *My Work with Borderline Patients.* Northvale, NJ: Jason Aronson.

———— (1989). From a letter to Gerald Schoenewolf.

Spitz, R. (1965). *The First Year of Life.* New York: International Universities Press.

Spotnitz, H. (1961). *The Couch and the Circle: A Story of Group Therapy.* New York: Alfred A. Knopf.

———— (1976). *Psychotherapy of Preoedipal Conditions.* Northvale, NJ: Jason Aronson.

———— (1985). *Modern Psychoanalysis of the Schizophrenic Patient.* 2nd ed. New York: Human Sciences Press.

—— (1988). Treatment of a pre-schizophrenic adolescent: a case presentation on the reconstruction of a psychotic ego. *Modern Analysis* 13:5–204.

Spotnitz, H., and Meadow, P. (1976). *Treatment of the Narcissistic Neuroses*. New York: Manhattan Center for Advanced Psychoanalytic Studies.

Stern, D. (1977). *The First Relationship: Mother and Infant*. Cambridge, MA: Harvard University Press.

Stolorow, R. D., and Lachmann, F. M. (1980). *Psychoanalysis of Developmental Arrests*. New York: International Universities Press.

Szasz, T. (1970). *The Manufacture of Mental Illness*. New York: Harper and Row.

Tanguay, P. (1977). Book review of *The Psychological Birth of the Human Infant*, by M. Mahler. *Journal of the American Academy of Child Psychiatry* 16:540–544.

Tauber, E. S. (1983). Countertransference reexamined. In *Countertransference: The Therapist's Contribution to the Therapeutic Situation*, ed. L. Epstein and A. H. Feiner, pp. 59–71. Northvale, NJ: Jason Aronson.

Volkan, V. D. (1981). *Linking Objects and Linking Phenomena*. New York: International Universities Press.

Weigert, E. (1959). Foreword. In *Psychoanalysis and Psychotherapy* by F. Fromm-Reichmann. Chicago: University of Chicago Press.

Winnicott, D. W. (1947). Hate in the countertransference. In *Through Paediatrics to Psycho-Analysis*, pp. 194–203. New York: Basic Books, 1975.

—— (1953). Symptom tolerance in paediatrics. In *Through Paediatrics to Psycho-Analysis*, pp. 101–117. New York: Basic Books, 1975.

—— (1986). *Holding and Interpretation: Fragment of an Analysis*. New York: Grove Press.

Yankelovich, D., and Barrett, W. (1970). *Ego and Instinct*. New York: Random House.

INDEX

237